Our American Theatre

THE WHARF THEATRE, PROVINCETOWN, MASSACHUSETTS
Here on an Old Fishing Dock, Recently Destroyed by Fire, the Provincetown Players Were Formally Born in the Summer of 1915

Our American Theatre

By
OLIVER M. SAYLER

WITH TWENTY-FIVE ILLUSTRATIONS
FROM DRAWINGS
BY
LUCIE R. SAYLER

BENJAMIN BLOM, INC.

First Published 1923
Reissued 1971
Benjamin Blom, Inc., New York 10025

Library of Congress Catalog Card Number 70-89600

Printed in the United States of America
at Westbrook Lithographers
Westbury, N.Y.

PREFACE

PREFACES — that is, the kind that deserve to show their faces at all — are probably written by careless folk who use them as carpet-sweepers in the trail of their labors to collect neglected ideas. Or else they are composed in advance of the work itself, in which case the author probably wishes again and again that he hadn't used up that particular phrase.

This preface, to be frank, is written after the manuscript is complete, thus brazenly belying its title. And if there are any serious omissions of significant men and movements within the fifteen-year period of this survey, I do not propose to bestow the faint praise of rescuing them here. My motive, as I have indicated more than once in the succeeding chapters, has been to sketch in the highlights of this period and, in so far as possible, as I aimed to do in " The Russian Theatre," to make our American Theatre live through intimate studies of the men and women who have been responsible for its record. Samples, representatives, whipping-boys.

My thanks are due to a greater number of the theatre's workers than I can mention for assistance in collecting data concerning the period under scrutiny. I am indebted particularly to Kenneth Macgowan, author of "The Theatre of Tomorrow," " Continental Stagecraft " and " Masks and Demons," who has read my manuscript for errors of fact on condition that I absolve him from responsibility for my opinions. For the right to reprint expressions of many of the ensuing opinions in the same or other words, my thanks are due to *The Century Magazine, The New Republic, The Freeman, The North American Review,* the *Boston Evening Transcript, Shadowland, Theatre Arts Magazine* and *Drawing and Design* (London).

OLIVER M. SAYLER

NEW YORK CITY,
October, 1923.

CONTENTS

CHAPTER		PAGE
I.	The Period and Process of Awakening	1
II.	Our Playwrights	11
III.	Eugene O'Neill, the American Playwright	27
IV.	Our Producers	44
V.	Our Institutional Theatres	67
VI.	The Washington Square Players and Their Inheritors, the Theatre Guild	75
VII.	The Provincetown Players	89
VIII.	The Neighborhood Playhouse	102
IX.	The Little Theatres	113
X.	The Theatre in the College	123
XI.	Our Actors	136
XII.	Our Designers for the Stage	149
XIII.	Our American Playhouse	169
XIV.	Our Critics of the Theatre	177
XV.	Our Theatre Audience	187
XVI.	Realism on our Stage	194
XVII.	The Revolt Against Realism	205
XVIII.	The Theatre of "Let's Pretend!"	220
XIX.	Our Civic Theatre	233
XX.	Revue, Variety and the Dance	246
XXI.	America as Host to Foreign Drama	259
XXII.	The Economic Problems of our Theatre	275

APPENDICES

| I. | Important Productions on the American Stage, 1908–1923 | 287 |

CONTENTS

APPENDICES	PAGE
II. The Pulitzer Drama Prize Awards	316
III. The Harvard Prize Play Awards	318
IV. A Complete List of the Plays of Eugene O'Neill	320
V. The Record of the Washington Square Players	323
VI. The Record of the Theatre Guild	329
VII. The Record of the Provincetown Players	332
VIII. The Record of the Neighborhood Playhouse	340
IX. List of Little, Experimental and Community Theatres in the United States	344
X. The Leading Commissions of Robert Edmond Jones	365
XI. The Leading Commissions of Lee Simonson	367
XII. The Leading Commissions of Norman-Bel Geddes	369
Index	371

LIST OF ILLUSTRATIONS

The Wharf Theatre, Provincetown, Massachusetts, Birthplace of the Provincetown Players *Frontispiece*

	PAGE
Forest Scene in Maude Adams' Production of Rostand's "Chantecler"	7
The Love Boat in "The Yellow Jacket," by Benrimo and Hazelton	17
On Blackwell's Island in O'Neill's "The Hairy Ape"	39
The Ants Tread the War Mill in "The World We Live In"	51
Scene from "The Poor Little Rich Girl," Produced by Arthur Hopkins	57
Ibsen's "Peer Gynt," at the Theatre Guild	69
Bernard Shaw's "Back to Methuselah," at the Theatre Guild	85
On Congo's Banks in O'Neill's "The Emperor Jones"	93
Festival of the Tabernacles at the Neighborhood Playhouse	107
Walt Whitman's "*Salut au Monde,*" at the Neighborhood Playhouse	111
Andreieff's "The Life of Man," Produced by the Washington Square Players	119
Maeterlinck's "The Death of Tintagiles," at the Carnegie Institute, Pittsburgh	133
Jane Cowl and Rollo Peters in "Romeo and Juliet"	143
"Hamlet" on the Stairs	155
Liliom on the Bridge, Produced by the Theatre Guild	161
"Will Shakespeare," Produced by Winthrop Ames	165
The Century Theatre from the Park	171
"The Return of Peter Grim," Produced by David Belasco	199

ILLUSTRATIONS

	PAGE
The Apparition Scene in the Hopkins-Jones Production of "Macbeth"	213
Russian Babi in Balieff's Chauve-Souris	225
"The Pilgrim Spirit," at Plymouth, Massachusetts	243
Urban Brings Design into the Ziegfeld "Follies"	253
The Perfume Ballet, from "The Greenwich Village Follies of 1920"	257
The Robots Rise in Capek's "R. U. R.," at the Theatre Guild	263

OUR AMERICAN THEATRE

Chapter I

THE PERIOD AND PROCESS OF AWAKENING

SOMETHING has happened to our American theatre. Not so long ago, it was a luxury, a pastime, an industry. A harmless adjunct to life, a game played according to traditional rules, a little world set off to itself whose personalities and scandals were discussed with a sentimental flutter. Today, it is the most provocative of the arts. The art of the theatre in the midst of life, drawing new life therefrom. The theatre not only in the theatre, but in halls, on hillsides, on the campus; in newspapers, in magazines, on the book stalls. The theatre in exhibition galleries, under chautauqua tents; on the lecture platform, in women's clubs, on Pullman smokers, on the radio.

Something has happened. Not only to the theatre itself, but to the whole public attitude toward the theatre. Many things have happened. Some of them good, some bad. Encouraging, discouraging. Working together, they have given the theatre a vitality, an importance, a significance, it has never known before on our continent. Men and women quarrel about the theatre. In print; face to face.

The things that have happened have not happened all at once. Nor obviously. The cause has often vanished — a failure, forgotten — before the results appeared. Roughly, the period of awakening has been the last fifteen years. The year 1908 is an arbitrary starting point, but it will serve for purposes of contrast. The process of awakening has been evolutionary, although if we range the poles of the period side by side, it will look like revolution. Suppose we try.

Fifteen years ago Eugene Walter had written " Paid in Full," hesitant omen of " The Easiest Way." Eugene O'Neill was running afoul of the authorities at Princeton, recking not of sea-roving or of subsequent playmaking. Zoë Akins was still treasuring ardent lyric verse written at Humansville, Missouri. Owen Davis was known for such as " Nellie the Beautiful Cloak Model." Edward Sheldon had won startled attention with " Salvation Nell." Percy MacKaye had timidly tried the deep waters of the civic pageant with his Saint-Gaudens Mask-Prolog.

Arthur Hopkins was contentedly producing and booking vaudeville acts. Winthrop Ames was dabbling in the affairs of a Boston stock company. George M. Cohan was still dependent on his legs rather than his pen. Morris Gest was scouring Europe for Makhno the Giant and other monstrosities for Hammerstein's Victoria. Only Belasco was serenely practising his matured craft.

A decade and a half ago, the project of the New Theatre was vaguely in the air. The Institutional Theatre was yet unborn, the Little Theatre not even a dream. In the colleges, the class play was the peak of academic dramatic ambition.

The profession of player presents less abrupt contrast: Maude Adams as Rostand's cock, Mrs. Fiske as Sheldon's bonneted heroine of the tambourine, Arliss as Arliss — incidentally Molnar's Devil, Ethel Barrymore as the grand and laughing Lady Frederick. True, John Barrymore was just Jack and Lord Meadows in "Toddles," and a host of today's most promising youngsters were still in grade and boarding school.

To make up for the player, however, consider the designer. In 1908, scenery was still daubed by the yard according to traditional rote. Robert Edmond Jones was a Harvard sophomore, Lee Simonson of like stature and scholastic allegiance, Norman Geddes fretting in a Detroit high school. Theatre buildings, too, had just begun to emerge from horseshoe bondage. Critical horizons, with the exception of Huneker's and Mencken's, terminated with the Statue of Liberty. Bitterly rival theories of the theatre, the whole conception of the theatre as a separate and distinct art in its own right, were sleeping dogs. The American revue was cautiously creeping out of its "Black Crook" chrysalis with the first Ziegfeld "Follies." Published plays were curiosities; Brander Matthews monopolized the shelves of books about the theatre. A smug insularity disdained such dramatic emissaries from abroad as the Russian Vera Kommissarzhevskaya and Fyodor Chaliapin, just as it had Réjane and Duse a few years before.

Consider now contemporary cases. O'Neill is a name to match with any living playright. His "Anna

Christie" conquers Britain. "The Hairy Ape" is accepted for production all over the world. Owen Davis, living down the ten-twenty-thirty thriller, wins the Pulitzer prize with "Icebound." MacKaye's pageant dramas, "Saint Louis" and "Caliban," have opened up new vista for the Civic Theatre. Sheldon's "Romance," Benrimo and Hazelton's "The Yellow Jacket," have long been in international repertories.

Hopkins visits Central Europe, loses his complacency, becomes the clearing house of the younger artists, actors, playwrights. Ames weathers the New Theatre catastrophe to grow into one of our most suave producers. Gest aspires to gorgeous spectacles such as the world has never seen, loses a fortune, and recoups by moving on to sponsorship for the cherished treasures of foreign stages. Cohan captures the characteristic American comic sense by writing "Seven Keys to Baldpate" and "Broadway Jones," and producing "Two Fellows and a Girl," while keeping his guiding hand if not his own nimble toes in the game of song and dance. F. Ziegfeld, Jr., John Murray Anderson, Hassard Short, Irving Berlin, J. J. Shubert and Charles Dillingham carry the revue to typically American heights of lavishness and extravagance which challenge the admiration even of a Reinhardt, and inspire, in those who go abroad with a captious spirit, the zeal to open alien eyes by exhibiting to them our achievements in this field. Fresh leadership appears from here, there, nowhere — Brock Pemberton, Sam H. Harris, William Harris, Jr., the Selwyns, George Tyler, Richard Herndon, many others. Intelligent, sensitive

THE PERIOD OF AWAKENING

direction stands at various beck and call, preferring to remain unhampered by managerial responsibility — Robert Milton, Frank Reicher, Augustin Duncan. The Shuberts build rows of theatres to house their productions, then relax their interest in production, preferring to organize, dominate, the financial side of the theatre, to stand as the power behind many thrones. And Belasco goes still serenely on his way.

Profiting by the fiasco of the New Theatre, the makers of institutional theatres begin modestly, build from the ground up. All except the National Theatre and Equity. The Provincetown Players, whether reborn or not after interval of disintegration, stand as object lesson for any similar venture in future. The Neighborhood Playhouse persists for fresh and expanding function. After nine years of the Washington Square Players and their inheritors, the Theatre Guild, the time is deemed ripe at last for raising a loan to erect their own home. Heeding, too, the same precept of the seed before the threshing bee, scores and hundreds of Little Theatres spring up over the land, some of them, born of idle pastime and social ambition, to wither as swiftly as they sprouted, while others retain their hold, even grow, as potential foci for ambitious institutional playhouses to take the place of the vanishing road company.

In the universities, the theatre is coming into its own, grudged by Puritan disdain in spots but stoically advancing nevertheless. With adequate equipment niggardly denied, Professor George Pierce Baker at Harvard has passed on to Broadway a score of practicing playwrights and has made English 47 the most widely known course in any American curriculum. At Carnegie Institute of Technology, with the plant Baker lacks, Thomas Wood Stevens is training modestly but efficiently craftsmen in all the theatre's component avenues, while first steps in a like direction are being taken by numerous other seats of learning.

The player lags. John Barrymore has reached an irregularly inspired Hamlet in his ascent; Jane Cowl, a rare and glowing Juliet. Ben-Ami and young Schildkraut are recruits but neither has fulfilled first promise. Ethel Barrymore returns periodically to her great ladies; Miss Adams toys with lights, begrudging the light of her own spirit; Mrs. Fiske picks the season's worst plays but reaches currently and successfully for succor through Belasco. Youngsters forge forward, actresses rather than actors, despite lack of opportunity for rounded training. The clowns flourish — notably Jolson and Rogers. And all, young and old, caught in the vicious circle of the Equity struggle with the producing managers.

It is otherwise, as I have said, with the designer. Taking the bit in his teeth, he has run away from the procession, often unwittingly and unintentionally monopolizing attention to his resurgent craft. With Jones, Geddes and Simonson from native ranks, Urban and Rosse from overseas, and a swarm of straining novices, it is no wonder that the scenic artist is envied or that Reinhardt is stirred by the thought of coöperation here with them. The scenic artist, too, as theatre designer, architect, a logical development which

THE COCK HAILS THE DAWN

Forest Scene in Rostand's "Chantecler," in Which John W. Alexander Devised for Maude Adams Fresh and Shimmering Beauty by Pioneer Lighting Methods

augurs unique and specialized auditoriums to add to our already excellently workaday playhouses such as the Selwyn, the Apollo, the Music Box, the Little, in New York and the Apollo in Chicago.

Critics, too, with an increasing world horizon, gained by actual contact. Youthful, pugnacious, biased, extravagant, at times. In love with their own phrases, hobbies. But insular no more, nor smugly complacent. Richly diverse theories of the theatre are edged tools which they and the large body of the theatre's patrons handle with respect if not yet with poise and skill. There is hardly a publisher who does not contribute annually at least one volume to the discussion of these contending theories and their practice, while that egregious mongrel, the novelized play, has all but departed with its vanishing partner, the dramatized novel, making way for the prompt publication of plays as plays simultaneously with their production on the stage. No longer, either, is the professional critic the lonely lord of dramatic discussion. Dozens of lecturers make their living thereby; free lance and connoisseur swarm the periodicals; the radio broadcasts criticisms as well as the plays themselves. The theatre is in everyone's eye, at everyone's ear, on everyone's tongue — the most ubiquitous and provocative of the arts.

And not the least manifestation of its vitality today is the cosmopolitan hospitality and intelligence with which major plays and players from abroad, even those speaking their own language, are received and welcomed. For our neglect of Kommissarzhevskaya in 1908, we atone in 1923 by acclaiming the Moscow

Art Theatre and paying near three quarters of a million to see it. America emerges more and more surely as the refuge, clearing-house, testing ground, for the theatre of the world.

Whence has come this evolution that looks so like revolution? What stimulating forces have impinged on our stage — from abroad, from within? Their full force, identity, manner of attack, can be made evident only in the course of the succeeding chapters. Sufficient here to hint at the impact of Gordon Craig's *The Mask,* his " On the Art of the Theatre," his " Towards a New Theatre "; Pavlova, Mordkin, the Russian Ballet; fleeting glimpses of Reinhardt's " Sumurûn "; the early vision of Eugene Walter; the report, precept and practice of observant travellers returning from Europe, such as Robert Edmond Jones, Arthur Hopkins, Sam Hume, Kenneth Macgowan, Samuel A. Eliot, Jr., and Hiram K. Moderwell; Sheldon Cheney's illuminating interpretation of new men and methods from afar; the chronicles of the *Boston Evening Transcript* under H. T. Parker, of *The Drama* and of the *Theatre Arts Magazine,* soon to become a monthly under the driving vision of Edith J. R. Isaacs; the advent of Joseph Urban, Granville Barker, Maurice Browne, to work among us; the patient and intuitive search after light in lighting by Belasco.

A movement largely foreign in its sources and its inspiration is in process of becoming thoroughly and honestly American. Its imitative period is passing with the development of original native ideas, with the increasing assurance of hands apprenticed abroad, with the growing freedom and expanding numbers of independent groups and individual artists, and with the tolerance and even welcome which the established theatre extends to new ideas.

Chaos here still, confusion, contradictory currents. Cross-currents, cross-purposes, a patchwork of perversity. Our actors stagnate, absorbed with their rights in Equity rather than with their privileges and responsibilities in their art. Our playwrights lag behind, heedless of the challenge of new forms, new themes, the suddenly attained dignity and moment of their profession. Our producers timidly shy at the supposed bogey of the repertory system, the permanent company with its attendant economy and boon of thorough rehearsal. The theatre in New York stands in awe of its master, ground rent; on the road — of its master, neglect, need, play-hunger.

The American theatre, like every other phase of our life, is a here-and-now, opportune institution. We cut and sew our political and intellectual and artistic linen in the streets, and we wash and mend it with equal shamelessness. And yet we are stumbling, with all our awkwardness, into an appreciation of the need for a more vivid theatre. We shall discover the ways to achieve it, just as we blundered into the expedients which make for social welfare. We are willing to try anything once, and our theatre will be the gainer for that spirit of gameness.

Chapter II

OUR PLAYWRIGHTS

At the heart of the theatre, the play — and the playwright. Actors, producers, designers, great and small, live and die, but the play — the supreme play — lives on forever. Without the play, the theatre is impossible. Even the ceremonial dances of the Greeks and the rough outlines of the impromptu *commedia dell'arte,* which Craig and others would revive today, were plays in essence, germs of plays. With the play, any man can make his own theatre, although, of course, the play reaches its full stature only on the stage in the presence of an audience.

From this key position of the play and the playwright, it might be supposed that leadership would repose here, that the playwright would be pioneer in any forward movement. He was in Ireland. Yeats, Lady Gregory and Synge were playwrights, or became playwrights. He was in Scandinavia, with Ibsen in the van. He was in Russia, and still is. Tchehoff preceded, to a large extent inspired, the Moscow Art Theatre. Blok at least coincided with Meyerhold. Yevreynoff undoubtedly spurs the Kamerny, although he has never coöperated with Tairoff. The playwright was pioneer in Germany — Hauptmann, Sudermann, Kaiser, Hasenclever. He was in England — Bernard

Shaw, Barker, Houghton, Galsworthy. In France? But rebirth has scarcely begun in France.

Why, then, does the American playwright lag, permit command to go by default to other craftsmen? The reasons for the scenic artist's usurpation of his rightful place may be better considered in the chapter on our stage designers. Viewed directly, however, the playwright's lapse is closely bound up with the fact that we commandeered our dramatic renaissance bodily from abroad. We are making it our own, but with different speed in the various crafts of the theatre. The playwright is an oak. He grows slowly, surely; and he has not yet caught up.

Still, though the playwright loiters, there is more vitality in him today than ever before. We have O'Neill, of whom we need be ashamed before no man and who demands a chapter to himself. We have others who may in time become O'Neills — or better yet, their own selves, equal to or superior to O'Neill. And besides, we have many more who address themselves to an adult intelligence. I could name thirty whose premieres can be attended by the reasonably exacting playgoer with at least an even chance of finding something to hold his attention. Never before have we had so many practicing dramatists. In sheer numbers, I doubt whether any European capital can surpass us. And out of these numbers, by competition, contagious rivalry and mutual stimulus, something is bound to happen.

The trouble with the American playwright today is that he doesn't take his profession seriously, earnestly, passionately enough. Still intimidated by the fallacious and obsolete warning to play down to his audience, he fails too often to give the best that is in him. The best is none too good. Plays that reach beyond intelligent pastime afford scant cause for concern to the annual judges of the Pulitzer Prize Award. Opportunity — undreamed, kaleidoscopic opportunity — stands impatient for the playwright to seize his ignored heritage.

The patterns of the kaleidoscope are richly varied. Some of the simpler ones we have known and practiced more or less intuitively. Many new ones are now within our reach, ready to be adopted, adapted to our peculiar needs and filled in according to our own fancy. If we are wise, we shall profit by the experience of others and save ourselves futile dalliance with false and deceptive viands. The broad range of thirty years of European experiment is arrayed on the table as we begin our first course. A glance at the diverse products of this busy kitchen-laboratory will help us to avoid many a false choice.

Consideration of the various kinds of play open to our practice and their particular commendations may be left to the chapter on our theories of the theatre. It is sufficient here to admit that we have traditional modes of our own which we can and should respect and retain; to insist that we reconceive and recreate alien modes rather than merely imitate them, and that we keep our imagination open for the invention of modes and forms intrinsically our own. Yet never the new just because it is new. Childish inconstancy.

Freedom as a fetish. The slavery of freedom. Nor yet disrespect for the old just because it is old. Is it faithful to beauty, to truth, to the manifold and insistent call of the human spirit? That is the only authentic test.

Who, then, are our playwrights? And how far do they honor in practice this creed of an open but respectful mind?

Out of the age of isolation which produced Bronson Howard and Fitch, Herne, Hoyt and Ade, there are few survivors. America's active dramatists are young, averaging less than forty years. Chief links to the past are Augustus Thomas, David Belasco and Owen Davis. Belasco seldom writes any more, contenting himself with revision and rewriting of others' manuscripts. Thomas's pen likewise languishes, yielding to an ascending interest in the executive side of the theatre. When he does write, however, he lets a solemn pedantry dominate his old time narrative skill as in " As a Man Thinks " and " Nemesis." Davis, on the contrary, is fecund, grows, expiates the egregious thrillers of his youth with " The Detour " and " Icebound," realistic glimpses of middle-class character which take their cue consciously or unconsciously from O'Neill.

Next in sequence from the past are those frankly popular playwrights whose major aim is to tell a story in the theatre that will appeal to the multitude. Of all generations, all theatres. Avery Hopwood, Mary Roberts Rinehart, Winchell Smith, Roi Cooper Megrue, Edgar Selwyn, Channing Pollock, Samuel and

Louis Evan Shipman, Jules Eckert Goodman, Aaron Hoffman, Cleves Kinkead, William C. Hurlbut and a score less notable even at this plebeian vocation. Counterparts, these, to the Harold Bell Wrights, the Gene Stratton Porters, the George Barr McCutcheons, the Howard Chandler Christys, the Edgar Guests. Periodically, one of them like Pollock in "The Fool" conceives himself to be a Man with a Mission. Few of them would resent being taken more seriously. Watch Samuel Shipman, college-trained, at the premiere of a play by O'Neill, the roustabout, the self-educated. Wandering from one knot of discussion to another during the intermissions, he is all ears to discover the secret of the regard in which O'Neill is held.

On the way, next, to substance and sound prospects are those strange accidents of the theatre, authors of one play or more which arrested attention, won merited praise, whetted the appetite for more. Then silence — or worse than silence. Eugene Walter writes "The Easiest Way," one of the immediately unmistakable heralds of our awakening theatre at its first performance in January, 1909. Fourteen years pass in ingrowing indignation and he has not composed another of half or a quarter the strength, the conviction, the power of observation. Langdon Mitchell propounds brilliantly "The New York Idea" and then languishes in Philadelphia. Likewise, Benrimo and Hazelton distill world-conquering charm from the exotic and archaic Chinese theatre in "The Yellow Jacket" in 1913, only to sunder their partnership and live a sea apart. Now Hazelton is dead and Benrimo alone and mute in Britain.

With lesser lapses, the chronicle is rife. Avery Hopwood arrests the attention of the few with " Clothes " and " Nobody's Widow "; thereafter slacks and is satisfied with that of the many. Charles Kenyon writes " Kindling," penetrating and poignant, and quits. Edward Knoblock plumbs fantasy in " The Faun," " Kismet " and " Marie-Odile," collaborates with Arnold Bennett in the shrewd realism of " Milestones " and then wanders helplessly between the two doors. Edward Locke tells a simple tale exquisitely and reticently in " The Climax." A title only too prophetic. A. E. Thomas works skilfully in comedy and sentiment in " Her Husband's Wife," forthwith losing the whimsical note in the former and permitting the latter to dissolve into sentimentality. Louis K. Anspacher has a viewpoint and a style in " The Unchastened Woman." Both vanish by the time his calendar arrives at " That Day." George Ade ceased poking his disturbingly pointed finger at our national foibles years ago. Booth Tarkington has everything his own way for the first time with " Clarence," likes himself and his independence almost as much as the public does the result, but years pass before he masters the temerity to try again in " Tweedles." Alice Brown ventures into the theatre to win the Winthrop Ames prize with " Children of Earth " and then beats a retreat back to the fasthold of fiction. Frederick Ballard, Florence Lincoln — the Harvard prize plays, " Believe Me, Xanthippe," and " The End of

THE LOVE BOAT IN "THE YELLOW JACKET"
In Which Benrimo and Hazelton Distilled World-Conquering Charm from the Exotic and Archaic Chinese Theatre

the Bridge " — without successors. Thompson Buchanan, pungent in "A Woman's Way," crude and blundering thereafter. William De Mille, intense and gripping in "The Woman," weak and flabby ever since. C. M. S. McClellan forgets frivolity long enough to write "Leah Kleschna" but only long enough. Bayard Veiller proves with bravado how arresting and moving a mere " thriller " can be in " Within the Law," and then sulks in the motion pictures. Margaret Mayo, shrewd mistress of farce's edged tools, lets them rust with disuse. Gilda Varesi, "Enter Madame." Exit. George Cram Cook, genial satirist of "Suppressed Desires," gets hopelessly tangled in overserious contemplation of his own targets. Stuart Walker leaves the elfin whimsies of "Six Who Pass" to struggle with summer stock companies in Indianapolis and Cincinnati. Richard Walton Tully gives to the old-fashioned melodrama, "The Bird of Paradise," the strange lure of the tropics, and then counts royalties for a decade. Rita Wellman gets no farther than " The Gentile Wife." Clare Kummer contrives a rare blend of fantasy and fun in her provocative trio, "Good Gracious, Annabelle," "A Successful Calamity" and " Be Calm, Camilla," and then loses the recipe. Philip Moeller scorns the saucy pen that scribbled the provocative "Madame Sand" to rule and ruin more than one of the Theatre Guild's productions. Porter Emerson Browne partly atones for "A Fool There Was" with "The Bad Man" and then lets payments lapse. Theodore Dreiser writes the first expressionist plays in America in " Plays of the Natural and the

Supernatural " and then leaves the field he has ploughed and sown for others to reap.

Waste, impotence, perversion. Talent thrown to the winds. Children seeking new toys. Bonds left with coupons uncut. The prodigal goes on a long journey to a far country. Will he ever return?

Meanwhile, new names, fresh talents, press forward. Alongside a few of the older ones who persist and grow. Realistic reflection of the contemporary scene, the mirror held up to nature. Realism modified, sometimes heightened, by romance; the playwright as interpreter rather than reporter, scanning the world through colored glass and thereby seeing it often more truthfully. Comedy — realism on stilts, on hands and knees, from behind street lamps; smiling amiably, grinning sardonically, at passers-by, nipping their ankles, jumping at them out of the dark. Particularly the latter pastimes — the forte and function of satire. And finally the newer forms — postures, angles of vision, unique, extreme, exaggerated, suggestive of mood, of emotional and spiritual reality rather than material actuality.

These rival schools, their esthetic means, motives, methods, will receive more explicit treatment in Chapters XVI through XX. Here, they will serve as compartments in a Pullman for the readier review of our operative dramatists.

Realism, relentless, unmixed, impersonal as a Father Confessor, intimate as a diary, has had few devotees in America. Rachel Crothers has worked close to this field with her tales of today's troubled society, closer, perhaps, in her earlier plays, " The Three of Us " and " A Man's World," than in " Nice People " and " Mary the Third," but she has maintained a safe foothold in sentiment and the other expedients of the popular theatre. Aside from O'Neill and the reformed and penitent Owen Davis, there are only two or three others who fall into the realistic category. Arthur Richman probably belongs here for the sake of " Ambush," an honest, painstaking but heavily-shod chronicle of white-collar impotence and unhappiness. The same stratum of middle class misery and mis-direction of effort served Lewis Beach in " A Square Peg," Gilbert Emery in " The Hero." In Richman and Beach and Emery, though, is the taint of Lewis, " Main Street," " Babbit " — the taint of preconception, prejudice, dogmatic limitation of tone, color, topic. Not quite downright propaganda, but —. Why is it our novelists, poets, playwrights seldom see our small communities whole — their sound contentment and modest ambitions as well as their petty scandals and hypocrisies?

Pierrot in " civvies " is almost as rare — the romantic realist who sees life in terms of its overtones, its potentialities. Still, there is here a mixed, a very mixed, sextet — Zoë Akins, Edward Sheldon, Edna St. Vincent Millay, Philip Barry, Sidney Howard, Percy MacKaye. MacKaye, the eldest of the six, staked out his claim with " The Scarecrow," then abandoned it for the grandiose acres of the pageant, and only recently with his tools of fantasy has broken fresh and fertile soil in the Kentucky mountains.

Sheldon started as a realist, the realist as social exhorter, in "Salvation Nell" and "The Boss," but found his true metier in the aptly named "Romance," produced round the world. Illness, however, has slowed his pen, and the Cavallini awaits her true successor. Miss Millay, of Maine, Greenwich Village and the Quartier Latin, has made timid but encouraging trial of her lyric talents as servants to drama in "Aria da Capo." Barry, of Yale and Harvard's English 47, is known only by the wistful "You and I," but if he lives up to its promise, a near namesake need not be ashamed of him. Howard, too, is really still to be heard from, for he gritted his teeth too hard in his first effort, "Swords."

And yet, despite her poverty of ideas, Zoë Akins is still the chief romancer of our stage. Voluptuous in taste, sensuous after the unequivocal but reticent manner of the Orient, mistress of sentiment held in leash by sophistication, instinctive warder of words and word sounds, she lavishes her gifts on attenuated tales and on minor tragedies of life's supernumeraries. Two roads awaited her as she emerged from Humansville to St. Louis — satire and sentiment. The bold and provocative "Papa" gave hint of the former; the many-hued passions of "The Magical City" foretold the latter. She chose sentiment on proceeding to New York — perhaps wisely for New York, though not for her art. Sentiment thrives on repose; satire requires mental powers on edge. Possibly "Papa" was an accident; sentiment, Miss Akins' home. She has admitted herself that from earliest youth her dream of the theatre has been to create in it "grand" drama, akin to grand opera. Her succeeding works, "Déclassée," "Daddy's Gone a-Hunting," "The Varying Shore" and "The Texas Nightingale," disclose in uneven degree the grand manners, gestures, verbal music, of opera. And yet, what is it she has said so well? Miss Akins needs ideas on which to hang her resplendent wardrobe.

Comedy, satire. Here is the smoking room of our Pullman. Crowded, good-natured, cosmopolitan. Everyone talking at once, and not so much to be heard as to be talking. Kaufman and Connelly, travelling salesmen from Pittsburgh, chin with Cohan, promoter from Providence, and with Craven, farmer from Vermont. Nothing, nobody, is safe in this democratic star chamber. Neither President nor pugilist, railroad rates nor women's styles, world court nor local sewer tax.

Cohan's refreshing impudence dominates them all — George M., once the nimbletoes of the Four Cohans, now The Cohan, author with Earl Derr Biggers of our most brilliant satiric comedy, "Seven Keys to Baldpate," adapter, composer, producer, actor on occasion for variety's sake to spice his other professions. As American as a comic supplement, a jazz band, the memory of a cocktail. If Cohan should spend all his time contriving seven times "Seven Keys," our stage would be the richer. Here is sheer, arresting, rapid-fire entertainment, set between prolog and epilog in such a way as to provide for desiring eyes the most devastatingly ironic commentary on the whole of American life.

But Cohan won't spend his time thus. He wouldn't be American if he did. He has done it once. Why cover the same ground a second time? Life is too short. Time is money. Money. "It's a grand old flag." Money. Besides, who knows what's "over there"? "Her father was a swell — and then he fell — and then he fell — well, who'd he fall for?"

Others beside Cohan have upheld the American tradition in satiric comedy, a tradition without bitterness, without great depth or philosophic significance, concerned chiefly with the foibles and absurdities of humankind and treating them with grin and guffaw rather than with wink and smile. Hoyt established this tradition. Frank Craven and James Forbes have aided Cohan in maintaining it — Craven most ably in "The First Year," and Forbes in "The Show Shop," for although "The Famous Mrs. Fair" may be a better play, it is inferior in originality and spontaneity.

Cohan, Craven, Forbes & Co. have junior partners whose names will be included in the firm in time. The glib-tongued George Kaufman and the suave Marc Connelly are inseparable partners in penning up in play form the peculiarly American gaucheries of a dumb Dulcy, a blundering Leonard Beebe, a naïvely conceited Merton. George Middleton and Guy Bolton both underrate their public and their own powers but, in collaboration or separately, risk something occasionally as fresh and original as "Polly with a Past" or the first act of "Polly Preferred." Martin Brown, author of "A Very Good Young Man" and several better plays still unproduced, is another whose besetting fault is timidity. Don Marquis, too, who required the persuasions demanded by a coquette to risk his nimble pen on "The Old Soak." A satirist, a comedian, timid? There was Goldsmith, you know. Freedom from this fault is likely to carry George Kelly, youthful author and producer of "The Torchbearers," at least as far as he deserves. And the Nugents, father and son, of "Kempy."

All these, of course, are so American that London in the presence of "Merton" knows not when to laugh or whether. That satire, that comedy, which is of the intellect and therefore international, is rarer with us though not wholly absent. Jesse Lynch Williams has proved twice that he knows the formula — in "Why Marry?" and "Why Not?" Harry Wagstaff Gribble is an even more dexterous juggler of verbal wit, but the steel-cold brilliance of "March Hares" set too fast a pace for the average American intellect. Ben Hecht, too, playboy of Chicago's artist colony, gave hint in "The Egoist" of ultimate right to membership among American Shavians.

There remain the experimentalists in the newer forms, the seekers after uncharted truth and beauty. Two of them seem to have found a spring. Others persist on trails that may lead somewhere, nowhere. Zona Gale made not quite so good a play out of her novel, "Miss Lulu Bett." She may make a better out of her "Faint Perfume," or, still better, a better play independently conceived. New form to her is simply the evolution of realism to the point where suggested detail tacitly and with startling power tells the entire story. Susan Glaspell seemed to have discovered a similar knack in her one-act masterpiece, "Trifles," and her longer play, "Bernice," in which the dominant character lies dead in an adjoining room. Propaganda and the perverse wish to be obviously rebellious mar her later works, "Inheritors" and "The Verge."

For the rest, less springs than mirages. Alfred Kreymborg plays with words as sounds rather than with, or at least supplemental to, their function as channels for ideas. John Howard Lawson with "Roger Bloomer"; Henry Myers with "The First Fifty Years" and numerous unproduced manuscripts; Elmer Rice with "The Adding Machine," metamorphosed from the cognomen Reizenstein and trick melodramas like "On Trial" — all seek freedom in expressionism, but thus far find in it only prison bars to public comprehension and to the articulate release of their own spirits. These and many more: all dressed up; plenty of places to go. Whither? They know not. But like good Americans, they're on their way.

The American playwright lags. But he doesn't stand still. His pace is challenged. Will he heed the spur? Wouldn't it stimulate his vitality if talents now devoted to other arts were diverted to the theatre? Let Vachel Lindsay apply to drama his dream of modern hieroglyphics — a hotly exciting ritual, concrete, contemporary and evocative as a billboard. Let Robert Frost advance from the strictures of the printed page into the ampler confines of the proscenium to release therein the repressed soul of New England — and of America. Let Sherwood Anderson see whether the drama will ease his tortured struggle for self-expression. Let Ring Lardner and John V. A. Weaver make serio-comic and earnest effort to dramatize their conception of the American tongue and character. Let Alexander Woollcott weave a unique pattern of sentiment and humor so that the spectator will never quite know which is which. Let Robert Benchley have the courage really to be as actual playwright what he potentially is — our chief satirist.

Boot, saddle, to horse, and away!

Chapter III

EUGENE O'NEILL, THE AMERICAN PLAYWRIGHT

Not long ago when an American critic and an American stage designer racked their minds for appropriate dedication for their joint work on the European theatre, wishing to suggest both spur and compliment and hesitating to name Eugene O'Neill in so many letters, they compromised on "To the Playwrights of America." Too late they realized that by slight variation they could have been as aloof as a judge and, by implication, as specific as a want ad. — "To the American Playwright."

Eugene O'Neill, the American playwright. The point needs argument, proof, as much as that the skyscraper is our contribution to architecture. But the reasons are interesting, suggestive. First, there is our innate national desire to personify ideas and movements in human guise — Edison, our native ingenuity; Ford, business efficiency; Rockefeller, enormous wealth; Roosevelt, the strenuous life. Therefore, O'Neill, the personal symbol of our awakening American drama.

But the reasons for electing a single individual for detailed study in a separate chapter, the reasons why O'Neill is the American playwright, the personal symbol of our awakening drama, lie deeper than this. O'Neill is the sole engrossing talent thus far given to and accepted by the theatre of the world. His plays even before translation are read as fast as they are published in France, Central Europe and Scandinavia, more eagerly than the new work of native dramatists. "Anna Christie" was a triumph in London. "The Emperor Jones," "The Hairy Ape," are accepted for production in a dozen capitals. Managers fight for the rights. Friends bcome enemies over them.

At home, next, consider the half dozen best American plays to date: "The Easiest Way," "The Yellow Jacket," "The Great Divide," "Seven Keys to Baldpate." That leaves two places for O'Neill. "Anna Christie," "The Emperor Jones," "The Hairy Ape," "Beyond the Horizon," "Diff'rent"? "The Fountain," "Welded," unproduced, unpublished? O'Neill alone could supply the entire half dozen.

Best of all, his period of trial is over. He has faults, some of which he may never overcome. He has not yet reached his full stature. But he is no longer an accident, an apprentice. The variety of his work thus far, the vigor of his imagination, the originality of his technique, the evident growth of both from play to play — all proclaim him the American playwright.

O'Neill's life has been composed of just those struggles, he has overridden just those obstacles in just those ways we like to think characteristic of our continent. Born in the old Barrett House, Forty-third and Broadway, in 1889, he was carried to the four winds of the country by his father, the late James O'Neill, then at the height of his fame in "Monte

Cristo." Private schooling prepared him for Princeton, but his first year there ended in expulsion and merged into a vagabond career that led far beyond the horizon. Secretary to a mail-order firm in lower Broadway and boon comrade of Benjamin Tucker and other radicals; gold prospector in Honduras and victim of fever there; assistant manager for Viola Allen in " The White Sister " in the Middle West — these, the early chapters.

Lured then by Conrad's " The Nigger of the *Narcissus*," he shipped on a Norwegian bark for Buenos Aires, remaining there a year and a half in successive service to the far-flung American commercial vanguard, Westinghouse, Swift, and Singer. A voyage to Durban, South Africa, and back was holiday, and finally he returned in a British tramp to New York, whence he shipped several times as able seaman in the American Line. Further adventures on land as denizen of the docks, friend of gamblers and Tammany ward-heelers, actor and newspaper reporter, culminated in an attack of tuberculosis and, incidentally, in leisure to set to paper his first crude dramatic experiments, " Thirst and Other Plays," published at his father's expense in 1914. The following winter he devoted to Professor Baker's English 47 at Harvard. Thenceforth, the scenes of his labors as growing playwright have been those two aspects of the same mood — Greenwich Village, Manhattan; and Provincetown, Massachusetts — together with a recently acquired winter home in Connecticut, safely distant from New York's confusion but within range of Broadway rehearsals.

It is Peaked Hill Bar, though, that most surely expresses O'Neill, most richly stimulates him to creation. Here in the old coast guard station on the ocean across the shifting sand-dunes from Provincetown, while his young son Shane plays on the beach and his wife, Agnes Boulton, writes short stories in the room where they used to lay out the corpses after a wreck, he sits listening to the eternal tale of the surf he loves and molding in form of plays the struggles of men and women he has known and of those from other times and lands whom his experience has taught him to understand. After a month in the city, which he neither loves nor hates but always fights, he finds release on the sand under the sun, like primitive and pagan man; in his kayak out of sight of land, like the pioneers; or propped in bed scribbling in microscopically minute hand upon a huge drawing board — the ironic and mysterious spectacle of civilized man in sensitive union with the untamed sea.

O'Neill's lifetime of adventure, crammed into a few aimless, wild, carousing, feverish years, has left its record stamped relentlessly on his face, manner, mind. A record, though, revealing a personality immune to the usual results of such adventure. No slackening of the inner fire, no flabbiness of muscle or of mental fibre. Tall, lithe, dark; intense, but reticent; with a poet's eyes and a mouth that takes nothing in life for granted. Experience has given him poise and severe judgment and a corresponding deliberateness of mental process and of speech. Nothing ruffles him or excites him. He is neither ashamed nor proud of his devil-may-care past. There it is, in the past; and here he is now. And what else matters? Alongside disillusionment and a fatalism that is almost cynical at times, there are a kindliness in little things, a naïve simplicity, a sense of quiet humor — traits that are beginning to emerge in his work to the confutation of those who had him securely pigeon-holed among the perpetual pessimists.

O'Neill the artist through the medium of O'Neill the man is likewise product and expression of this harsh career. The impact of life upon him opens his eyes to things as they are: to the sombre, ironic and pitiable intimacies of the common sailors in the short plays published as " The Moon of the Caribbees "; to the tragic consequences of misplaced vocations in " Beyond the Horizon "; to the appalling denouement of sex repression in " Diff'rent "; to the insidious course of stalking disease and the heartrending realization of love after it is too late in " The Straw "; to the hole in the armor, both physical and spiritual, which prevents the escape of the Black Emperor, Brutus Jones; to the frank moral adjustments of " Anna Christie "; to " Yank " Smith's living challenge not only to civilization but to the human race in " The Hairy Ape "; to the sad beauty of Ponce de Leon's hopeless quest in " The Fountain "; and to the invisible but potent bonds which unite man and wife in " Welded." All these plays are the logical outcome of a mind that has known life bitterly face to face, but not long enough to become cowed by it or sentimental over it. Call this cynicism if you like, but there is here neither the wounded pride nor the sly striving for effect which we usually associate with cynicism. Neither is it mere sophomoric impatience with a disillusioning world. O'Neill is too terribly in earnest and too firmly grounded in experience to make either of those mistakes. Increasing maturity is tempering his harshness without relaxing his honesty and conviction, just as it did that of Ibsen.

The side door of the one-act play was O'Neill's entry into the theatre. "Thirst" and others in that early groping volume were incredibly bad, but he soon struck his pace in association with the Washington Square Players and particularly the Provincetown Players. The seven resultant sketches of life on or near the sea, published under title of the first, "The Moon of the Caribbees," are sufficient to themselves, foreshadowing at the same time the longer, more sustained work that has followed. Water-wings, these — rehearsals, galley-proofs, pencil sketches an artist makes before he sets to work with oil and canvas. To be preserved, respected, cherished, like the preliminary drawings of Leonardo, Turner, Whistler, not alone for sentimental associations but for intrinsic worth.

The heart of this early work is a series of four episodes in the life on sea and land of the motley crew of the British tramp steamer, *Glencairn*. Scotch and Irish, Swede and Russian, Yank and Briton, rubbing shoulders, matching wit and profanity on deck, in forecastle, in seaport dive — the men the playwright knew in his own years before the mast, drawn with swift, sure strokes. "The Moon of the Caribbees" —

the hot passions of West Indian harborage *vs.* memories of home steeled by rum; " Bound East for Cardiff " — the incomprehensibility of death; " The Long Voyage Home " — the fatal recurrence of accident in keeping a homesick sailor tied to the sea; " In the Zone " — the mutual humiliation which abashes both victim and tormentors when a suspected bomb turns into a bunch of old love-letters. In addition, there is " Where the Cross Is Made," a tragedy of treasure-mania from which " Gold " was later and most unhappily expanded; " The Rope," a study in the sour and sardonic consequences of greed; and " 'Ile," wherein madness seizes the wife of a whaling captain in the loneliness of the polar sea. Unknown for the most part, produced piecemeal in Macdougal Street and other byways while O'Neill was still caviar, they await revival for his wider audience of today. The *Glencairn* group, at least, should make a compact evening's bill, with two characters present in all four plays and five others in three of them.

" Beyond the Horizon," O'Neill's first full-length play preserved, was also the first of any length to reach the professional stage in the Williams-Bennett production, February, 1920. Immature, too long by a fourth or a fifth, broken up into too many scenes, needlessly heedless of the practical limitations of the theatre, it is still sound and convincing drama, cutting clean home to the primal facts of life. Love, ambition, jealousy, hatred. Two brothers — farmer who should have been sea-rover; sea-rover, farmer. And the wife of one who belonged by right to the other.

Few plays in the modern theatre plunge so inexorably downward in tragic disintegration of human hopes. Its austerity is almost Greek; its catastrophe, classic, proceeding not so much from conscious or avoidable mistakes as from the grim fatality of a choice whose innate consequences its victims were unprepared to see. O'Neill's achievement consists not only in following this catastrophe with stern veracity to its inevitable conclusion but also in conveying by subtle and unobtrusive touches the impression of unremitting dissolution, of the appalling gloom of the years that intervene between the crucial episodes of his narrative.

Disregarding "The Emperor Jones," which reached the stage next, and pursuing O'Neill's realistic vein, we come to another New England tragedy, "Diff'rent." Different. Missing the favor its articulated, economic and fluent workmanship deserves — in America, because it bares disturbingly the intimacies of thwarted sex; abroad, because those intimacies seem like a tempest in a tea-pot. Too short, also, and too long for the theatre's conventional clock. And yet, with its precision of workmanship in miniature, its mastery of the nuances of life, it brings us appreciably nearer an American counterpart of "The Father," "The Sea-Gull," "The Awakening of Spring."

"The Straw," in turn, and "Anna Christie" — almost simultaneously. "Anna Christie," a play of passion and perversity, purged white by sea-fog and the will to wish. A superb play, a play without an ending, reaching an ironic finger into the future, like life. To this the critics are blind. They know the theatre — or do they? Certainly not life. And the theatre has endings — happy endings, tragic endings. O'Neill's theatre has been pigeon-holed as tragic. But here at the conclusion, is hint of wedding-bells. Happy, at least for a while. The critics resent that. Not the happy ending, but the need for new appraisal of O'Neill. Besides, under cover of attacks upon O'Neill, they can do penance for their suppressed preference for the happy ending.

Not so strange, then, that they rejoice over "The Straw." O'Neill runs true to form in this heart-breaking tragedy of passion kindled on the edge of the grave. Its beauty is tenuous, though a bit awkward, embarrassing, intimate. It goes; "Christie" stays.

Then in the heat of controversy over "Anna Christie" came the determination to write "the last word in realism" and bid it farewell. To confute those who over-praised "Anna Christie" and show them what lay beyond, that nothing lay beyond a certain point in the path of realism except absurdity.

Thus, "Welded," still in manuscript. A study of husband and wife who can not live with each other — or without each other. The uttered word, stenographic, evocative. Silence, gesture, expression, intonation, telling more than words. The things one does not say, does not do, more eloquent than those one does. Stupendous challenge to the actors, intense strain upon the spectators' attention, emotions. Verily, the last word in realism. A step farther — no words — realism denying itself! And yet, it would not be surprising if O'Neill found this dance of death on esthetic precipice sufficiently fascinating to weave still other tales in perilous posture.

So much for the playwright on his way to realism's rainbow tip. There is another side to O'Neill, probably in time the ruling side if not so already — the aspect first feebly discernible in "Fog," published with "Thirst"; more surely evident in "Where the Cross Is Made" and "Gold"; but finally dominant for the first time in "The Emperor Jones," and proved in "The Hairy Ape" and "The Fountain" to be something more than accident. The imagination unchained, released not to an orgy of disorder but to freedom to makes its own laws, mold its own forms. A new and virile kind of romance — unafraid of, rather stimulated by, such strangers to the elder romance as psychology, economics, sociology, tamed to esthetic instead of didactic ends. Here is the O'Neill whose eyes have got the better of his mouth, whose own vital force found anchorage in time, but not before he had seen the essential tragedy of life face to face on stormy seas, in unkempt lodging-houses, in notorious bar-rooms.

Delving into the newly-charted realms of the subconscious, "The Emperor Jones" provides a startling panorama of the human mind counter-marching on its hidden memories. In flight from his rebellious subjects, the black monarch of the Caribbees, once a Pullman porter, succumbs first to personal and then to racial terrors — the images of trainman and prison guard whom he had murdered, and after them, as he plunges deeper into the jungle, the visible hallucinations of his inherited fears: the auction block, the slave-ship, the priest of voodoo on Congo's banks. Here, as in all O'Neill's work, there is evidence of his dual gift of depicting character in swift, vivid strokes and scenes, and of expressing himself in a language that is lyric in its insistence on utterance by the human voice.

If "The Emperor Jones" is expressionism — eight tense staccato scenes, each concerned with the sublimation of a mood, a mental state, rather than with the narration of an episode — how much more truly may "The Hairy Ape" be so classified! In eight scenes, "Yank" Smith, stoker on an ocean liner, and the muscle in steel, loses the faith that he "belongs" and finds none other.

In the sweat and grime of the forecastle, he shouts his creed: "Every ting else dat makes de woild move, somep'n makes it move. It can't move witout somep'n else, see? Den yuh get down to me. I'm at de bottom, get me! Dere ain't nothin' foither. I'm de end! I'm de start! I start somep'n and de woild moves! . . . Steel, dat stands for de whole ting! And I'm steel — steel — steel!"

To him in the stoke-hole comes a pampered darling of the class that doesn't "belong." She stands aghast at "the hairy ape." His faith crumbles. He seeks revenge. He hurls himself against the automatons of the church parade on the avenue, and earns Blackwell's Island for his pains. In his cell he hears of the I. W. W., hunts them out, and gets pitched into the gutter as an agent provocator.

"I'm a busted Ingersoll, dat's what," he muses. "Steel was me, and I owned de woild. Now I ain't steel, and de woild owns me."

Only for a day more, though. At twilight next evening he confronts the gorilla in its cage at the zoo, chums with his "kin" in his groping effort to think out his place in the scheme of things, releases the beast, and is crushed to death for thanks. "And, perhaps," in O'Neill's words, "the Hairy Ape at last belongs."

Here is stark, grim challenge not merely to tradition, government, the social order, civilization, but to all humankind. Are we worth the fuss and circumstance of existence if we breed such as "Yank"? Must we return to the animal and begin again? Rather a warning that the animal will reclaim us if we do not order life more humanely.

Why the tolerance of such a menace to things as they are? Well, the police do try to stop it — on specious grounds of language. But reaction is weak-kneed in a pinch. Besides, editorial opinion, from *The New York Tribune* to *Solidarity*, finds canny support for itself in judicious quotations and superficially logical interpretations. O'Neill's real meaning is harmless as long as the "opinions" last.

"The Fountain," latest on this path as "Welded" is in O'Neill's realism, likewise awaits print and premiere. Neither prosaic realism, nor traditional romance, nor feverish modern peep-shows like "The

O'Neill is vulnerable. He is no god who can do no wrong. But, with all his American critics, he has had to await the analytical pen of an Austrian, Hugo von Hofmannsthal, who, withal, admires him intensely, to have the weak points in his armor designated.

"Masterly dialog," writes von Hofmannsthal, "resembles the movements of a high-spirited horse: there is not a single unnecessary movement, everything tends toward a predetermined goal; but at the same time each movement unconsciously betrays a richness and variety of vital energy that seems directed to no special end; it appears rather like the prodigality of an inexhaustible abundance. . . . Measured by this high ideal, the characters in Mr. O'Neill's plays seem to me a little too direct; they utter the precise words demanded of them by the logic of the situation; they seem to stand rooted in the situation where for the time being they happen to be placed; they are not sufficiently drenched in the atmosphere of their own individual past. Paradoxically, Mr. O'Neill's characters are not sufficiently fixed in the present because they are not sufficiently fixed in the past. . . . His first acts impress me as being the strongest; while the last, I shall not say go to pieces but, undoubtedly, are very much weaker than the others. The close of 'The Hairy Ape' as well as that of 'The Emperor Jones' seems to me to be too direct, too simple, too expected; it is a little disappointing to a European with his complex background, to see the arrow strike the target toward which he has watched it speeding all the while."

As for von Hofmannsthal's first stricture, O'Neill, I

believe, has already grown as if in answer in the enriching detail of essential non-essentials in " Welded." As for his second — well, in America, we still dote on that game of arrow and target, even though we permit Cohan to fool us in " Seven Keys."

O'Neill's future, though, is independent of criticism, of influence. Out of himself will come whatever he is to be. What that self is, may be discerned in the large, apart from glimpses for the observant in his plays, in this his credo:

" Life is struggle, often, if not usually, unsuccessful struggle; for most of us have something within us which prevents us from accomplishing what we dream and desire. And then, as we progress, we are always seeing farther than we can reach. I suppose that is one reason why I have come to feel so indifferent toward political and social movements of all kinds. Time was when I was an active socialist, and after that, a philosophical anarchist. But today I can't feel that anything like that really matters. It is rather amusing to me to see how seriously people take politics and social questions and how much they expect of them. Life as a whole is changed very little, if at all, as a result of their course. It seems to me that, as far as we can judge, man is much the same creature, with the same primal emotions and ambitions and motives, the same powers and the same weaknesses, as in the time when the Aryan race started toward Europe from the slopes of the Himalayas. He has become better acquainted with those powers and those weaknesses, and he is learning ever so slowly how to control them. The

dreamed and who still seems discouragingly remote in every land.

Practically and actually, however, Europe — especially Central Europe, Scandinavia and Russia — know, grow and cherish the producer as artist. Copeau, Gémier, Reinhardt, Jessner, Stanislavsky, Meyerhold, Tairoff — these, whose names are known in America, are only a few from a long and distinguished list. Under economic desperation, it is true, times are changing. Owners of chains of theatres emerge. The *regisseur* as wholesaler. As gambler. As manipulator of real estate. In Russia, to earn bare bread, the actor and the *regisseur*, as well, accept numerous simultaneous commissions. *Haltoora*. The custom, with motion picture complications, has its counterpart farther west. And yet, Reinhardt, driven thereby from Berlin, purchases the Josephstadt Theater in Vienna and transfers his permanent activities to the Austrian capital, his temporary ones to America; Copeau finds ever-new, though frugal, subsidies; Stanislavsky keeps his company intact in overseas haven. The tradition of the producer as artist survives precariously, but it survives.

If we ever had that tradition in America — and we probably did a generation ago in a rudimentary and spontaneous form — we all but lost it until, about a decade and a half ago, we began to rediscover it. The American producer is the logical outgrowth of our own peculiar conditions. At his worst, he is without parallel for ignorance, incompetence. At his average, he is an excellent showman. At his best, he has never let the old tradition completely vanish and he is now assiduously at work to revive it.

Against the ideal, against Europe's mature record, the American producer makes heterogeneous showing. He is by turns awkward as seventeen; trim as a stallion; proud; patronizing; exciting in his native eagerness, virility; dull as a day in the doldrums; hesitant; bold; startlingly original, either with unconscious or sophisticated intent; weakly, blindly imitative; flatteringly, constructively imitative, borrowing frankly but proceeding therefrom to new goals.

This aspect of paradox, contradiction, perverse patchwork, proceeds directly from the fact that our producers, for the most part, have been self-made. Like Topsy and our once-lauded but now forgotten captains of industry, they "jest growed." As the most energetic builder in a pioneer community becomes by sufferance its architect, so the American showman has become the American producer. Common sense has been his only esthetic theory; experience, his only school. The theatre was one of the community's gainful occupations. Human nature saw to that. Hardly a business. Hardly a profession. Beset by blind chance, and therefore alluring to the gambler's instinct. The directing mind which took the lead in this impromptu, upstart, mushroom theatre, had to be shrewd, alert, wise in the ways of the world; tricky, to avoid being tricked; a personality, instinctively acquainted with public taste, willing to accept its dicta, to assume extravagant poses for its edification. As time passed, he became wise, too, in judging the worth of the personality of others as well as that of real estate. In short, he became the showman our fathers knew. The showman as super-charlatan: P. T. Barnum. The showman as suave, industrious, ambitious, middleman of the drama: Augustin Daly, A. M. Palmer, the Wallacks, the Frohmans. Undoubted talents, the greater of these, responsible for keeping alive the native vigor and vitality of our stage against the day when, thus equipped, that youthful stage could plunge forward to intelligent maturity.

For that service, these pioneers received scant credit in their time; just as our producing managers today are blamed for all the theatre's growing-pains. A thankless rôle, that of producing. At his post as intermediary between playwright and audience, he is the butt of the impatience, the restlessness, the whims, of both. The playwright blames him for not producing his plays which he is sure the public is eager to see. The public blames him for not extracting from dramatists' desks wished-for manuscripts not yet written. He is mocked for taking foolish risks. He is chaffed for taking none. In a theatre which is still commercially competitive, unlike the financially sheltered stages of Europe, it is his funds in the jack-pot, but few remember that. It is small wonder, therefore, when he finds a play that the public desires, if he takes a saturnine kind of pleasure in making it pay for its rejected fellows. If the American producer is less artist than showman, the conditions under which he has developed are largely at fault.

The Elder Showman! What glimpse of pioneer

days, of early Manhattan, of barnstorming into the West, is summoned by that phrase! Of Fourteenth, the former Forty-Second Street. Of Union Square, then Madison, grandparents of Times. Of "Uncle Tom's Cabin" in tent, town-hall and "op'ry" house. Of bill posters' battles in Bar Harbor and Brownsville. Of plays presented on tour with the stock wing sets of the local theatres. Of "Hazel Kirke," "Under the Gas Light," "The Colleen Bawn," "The Black Crook."

Only a single dominant figure out of these early days survives — David Belasco, master of traditional finesse, inheritor, practitioner and interpreter of that past as well as occasionally willing student of the new, living link between two distant and unacquainted generations. Others there are, apprenticed to the pioneer traditions — call-boys, program boys, chips of the old block, youngsters trained under the Elder Showmen and absorbing some of their manners, methods, secrets. That lore they still apply today by rote, by shrewd adaptation to new conditions, with even an occasional recognition of the theatre's wider vista.

George C. Tyler, for instance, hired out to James O'Neill and the Hanlon Brothers; formed Liebler and Company with an old-time lithographer partner; made the firm's first strike with Charles Coghlan in "The Royal Box"; won fortunes with "The Christian," "Mrs. Wiggs," "The Man from Home," "The Garden of Allah"; lost them with "Children of the Ghetto," Réjane, "The Garden of Paradise" — one of the theatre's most daring gamblers in the best

birth-cry of the higher men is almost audible, but they will not come by tinkering with externals or by legislative or social fiat. They will come at the command of the imagination and the will."

Chapter IV

OUR PRODUCERS

On the one side, the playwright and his play. On the other, the audience. In between, the producer, interpreter of the one to the other, and his collaborators: the actors and designers, the architects and mechanics. The producer may be an individual, a group, an institution. He may be an artist, a showman, a business man, a real estate broker, a gambler. All these genres rub elbows in our Producing Managers' Association.

From the nature of his contacts, his relationships, the producer has the post of greatest trust in the theatre. His responsibility, his opportunity, are limited only by the ultimate range of the human spirit with which he has to deal. He is the master electrician who lays the wires along which passes the emotional shock which is the soul of the art of the theatre. To the extent that he stimulates, inspires, the creator; kindles, illuminates, the creator's work with fresh vision; rouses the connoisseur out of his natural lethargy and organizes him into a faithful clientele for the effectual support of his projects — to this extent he is creator, artist, himself. And if, in addition, he should assume successfully the rôle of playwright and that of chief or leading actor, then, indeed, he would be that superartist of the theatre of whom Craig and others have

ON BLACKWELL'S ISLAND IN O'NEILL'S "THE HAIRY APE"
Way Station for "Yank" Smith En Route from Stokehole to the Gorilla's Clutch in the Zoo. From a Setting Designed by Robert Edmond Jones and Cleon Throckmorton

Emperor Jones " and " The Hairy Ape," this rich and majestic tapestry of Ponce de Leon's legend weaves many threads into its eleven scenes — how effectively, it will be difficult to tell until production, for O'Neill depends here more on atmosphere and illusion and less on idea and characterization than usual.

Next comes " Marco Polo." And after —. But O'Neill is too fecund, too much the servant of what he calls " creative *élan* " to predict his path. As he describes it, " either you have the rhythm or you haven't, and if you have you can ride it, and if not, you're dead." At the age of thirty-four, he has — well, he has just begun his career. But he has begun it at a point beyond where most others leave off.

Such a figure, of course, stirs envy, and if not envy, at least doubt, incredulity, disparagement. " Mama's boy! " " Teacher's pet! " " Wait and see! " No one is readier for intelligent, relentless criticism than O'Neill. Few artists have received so little. The petty, puppy-dog attacks upon him send him back to Provincetown to trudge the dunes and forget the stupidity of man under the solemn spell of nature.

What are the odds if he sees tragedy at the end of the trail? Is tragedy necessarily depressing, anathema? If he writes a play without an ending like " Anna Christie," why must he defend himself from those who have clamored for a happy ending and are unhappy when they think they have it, unable to see that the ending, such as it is, is far from happy? Must he abjure the sea to avoid charge of copying Conrad? Irishmen, to escape the slur of stealing Synge?

sense of that term, willing to stake everything, whether he has it or not, on the new, the untried, the unlikely, the impossible; on Joseph Urban as recruit from opera to drama, on O'Neill, on Geddes.

Cohan, son of Père Jere, born barnstorming, brought up barnstorming, barnstorming still on a scale commensurate with contemporary Manhattan, playwright by the grace of God, showman by force of training and habit. And as producer, he has uncanny instinct to know what goes, from comedy and melodrama to farce and revue, building his effort, whether " Seven Keys " or " Little Nellie Kelly," not only of the theatre, by the theatre, for the theatre, but also in the theatre in course of rehearsal. His partner for sixteen years, Sam H. Harris, shares many of Cohan's qualities as showman, surprising many by his ability to go it alone when the firm was dissolved. Unlike Cohan, however, from Bowery to Broadway via Grand Street and Eighth Avenue, Miner's Theatre and management of Terry McGovern, Harris has preferred neither to be seen nor heard, except through the unobtrusive medium of an ever more ambitious program.

Selwyn, too, Edgar of Selwyn and Co., adapts to current necessity the axioms of the Elder Showmen, learned in early association with the Herald Square Theatre, Mansfield and Gillette. As actor in support of Ethel Barrymore in " Sunday " and of Maude Adams in " That Pretty Sister of José " and on his own account as star of De Mille's " Strongheart " and his own " Pierre of the Plains "; as popular playwright of "The Country Boy," "Rolling Stones" and many more; as playbroker; and finally as sponsor, if not in every case producer, of "Within the Law," "Twin Beds," "Fair and Warmer," "Romeo and Juliet" and "The Fool," he has run the gauntlet the Elder Showmen loved, with only occasional lapses in the attempt to become something more as with "Johannes Kreisler."

One of the Elder Showmen with less concern to disguise the fact is William A. Brady, bluff, bullheaded, ready for argument or altercation on slight provocation; adopted little brother of the California pioneers and forthwith their bitter rival; independent in the theatre and on occasion independent of it as manager of prize pugilists; displaying paradoxical Irish whims in spending a half million to train his wife, Grace George, as a comedienne, or a lesser but snug fortune to mount a serious work like the Capeks' "The World We Live In," without knowing in the least how to go about finding its large potential public. Another of Brady's era, but without other parallel, is Harrison Grey Fiske, practically retired for several seasons. And another who is younger but close kin to Brady in uncouthness, confidence, and strange ambitions now and then for intellectual repute, is Al H. Woods, sponsor of Theodore Kremer, Owen Davis and the "ten-twent-thirt" melodrama, and latterly of Avery Hopwood and the bedroom farce. From these, the record of pupils of the Elder Showmen trails off gradually through such as Wagenhals and Kemper, Oliver Morosco, John Golden, Henry Miller, into the allied

THE ANTS TREAD THE WAR MILL IN "THE WORLD WE LIVE IN"

Final Scene in "The Insect Comedy" by the Brothers Capek, Most Ambitious Production of William A. Brady. From a Setting Designed by Lee Simonson

crafts of the theatre owner, the playwright and the actor.

It is Belasco, though, who best represents tradition on our stage. Novice and pioneer in California — quite another and more vital California than that of today; pioneer to patriarch in Manhattan; player, playwright, producer, artist of the theatre; symbol of conservatism in our controversial renaissance, and thereby underrated and overrated by turns. His early days are outside the range of this survey. By 1908 he was already the last of the Elder Showmen. Five years later he was under the combined fire of the rising rebels — an attack to which he has shrewdly trimmed his sails while still maintaining his faith in his familiar strategy. Today, with revolution reorganizing unwisely extended outposts, he is stronger than ever.

Belasco's efforts come clear with knowledge of the man and his philosophy. Patient, gentle, generous; yet persistent, positive, tireless, he looks on life with passive, accepting eyes, finding his satisfactions in sentimental reflections upon the nuances and variations of nature and upon the emotional rather than the intellectual or passionate intimacies of humankind. Life to him is theatrical, raw material for his theatre; rather than the theatre the distillation, the microcosm of life. A sunset in Carthage, a snowstorm on the Steppes, a peddler in Houston Street, are data for his dramatic notebook just as a Dutch sea chest is treasure for his property room.

The peak of his career as playwright and producer, therefore, is " The Return of Peter Grimm," epitome of his emotionally optimistic philosophy; appropriate subject, with its pathetic ghostly figure, for treatment with the finesse of which he is master. Nowhere else are his precision and resourcefulness in his limited, chosen field, so apparent, so germane to the theme. Here he had no bothersome playwright to rewrite, adapt. Warfield understood him and the role he had to play through long and subtly intimate association. Flesh in skin; hand in glove. And finally he had full tether to display his astonishing technical and esthetic knowledge of the functions of light in the theatre — " the immediate jewel of my soul," he has termed it. A jewel which, this year for Mrs. Fiske's sake, he has polished still brighter.

Elsewhere, these specific qualities may be noted, but not in such fitting combination. Elsewhere his limitations are more apparent. His disdain for " literary drama," extending not only to the precious, the affected, the academic, but even to masters of the living theatre like Ibsen, Strindberg, Hauptmann, Tchehoff, Gorky, may be variously explained by fear, by lack of understanding, or by shrewd appreciation of the barriers between these plays and success in America — probably a little of all three. Ironically, the nearest he has ever ventured toward this type of drama, Walter's " The Easiest Way," is the most significant play he has ever produced, attracting him probably by its weakest aspect, its sentimental angle.

Belasco's preoccupation with the idiosyncrasies of life for use on his stage is simultaneous strength and weakness. With " Peter Grimm," " The Girl of the

Golden West," "The Darling of the Gods," it is closely, sympathetically, attuned. Authentic atmosphere here is the play's leading character. With many slight and specious plays, it has saved the financial day. With "The Merchant of Venice," reappearing in exaggerated form though with occasionally great intrinsic beauty after years of comparative abeyance, it stands directly and stubbornly in the path of logical presentation of Shakespeare's double story.

Beyond himself, though, lies one of Belasco's chief limitations. The American theatre with its transient, vagabond existence, has denied him repertory and a permanent company, ready to rehearse at needful length without thought of Equity, and growing under his hand with the passing of the years, into a spiritual acquaintance, indispensable for supreme dramatic art.

Still, though he has lacked the faith, the final courage, the youthful resourcefulness at an advanced age, or the sheer luck to attain this goal, he has served the theatre's art indispensably during emergency years. To the younger generation he has been a lonely example of patience, thoroughness, love of one's work. If some of his critics in and out of print had had their way, the representational art of the theatre would have been sold for a pot of cubist moons. His detractors overshot their mark. At the hands of the Moscow Art Theatre they have rediscovered the actor just where Belasco knew he was all the time — at the center of the stage production. Meanwhile, to balance matters, in the end his apol-

OUR PRODUCERS

ogists have lived to see O'Neill emerge from the despised Provincetown Players; the Washington Square Players bloom into the Theatre Guild; the Neighborhood Playhouse become artistic as well as social center; Little Theatres spring up all over the land to give amateurs a keener judgment of plays and acting; the Theatre in the University provide training schools for the stage which the stage should have provided for itself; Jones, Geddes and Simonson develop a new art of stage design; Morris Gest discover the stimulus latent in dramatic treasuries overseas; Arthur Hopkins lead provocative revolt against tradition, abetted by Winthrop Ames, John D. Williams, Brock Pemberton, William Harris, Jr. and a half dozen lesser figures. Belasco is still Belasco, last of the Elder Showmen and master of traditional finesse. But our theatre has expanded to provide room for many others.

In fact, the room provided is far ampler than the stature and number of those who are ready to move in. A handful of beans rattling around in a giant pod. A fleet of ocean liners trying to bridge the Pacific. Opportunity awaits — opportunity only the producer at his vantage point can seize and realize.

Hopkins, perhaps, has come nearer realization than any single one. Round as Balieff, red-faced as Sitting Bull, reticent as O'Neill. Scanty hint, here, at first sight, of the will and the vision behind the mask. In fact, neither will nor vision existed until Hopkins was thirty-five. Born in Cleveland of Welsh blood, newspaper reporter and vaudeville press agent after schooling that ended early, he had reached a secure position as producer of unusual acts for the Orpheum Circuit, such as "The Light of St. Agnes," with Bertha Kalich, and Everett Shinn's "More Sinned Against than Usual." Smugly satisfied with the American theatre and with his really sound achievement in producing "The Poor Little Rich Girl," he went to Europe in 1913. He returned with a conviction of sins of neglect and a will to expiation. The vision of the way that was to be accomplished did not come at once. It isn't wholly clear yet. But a decade has passed in deliberate and determined quest for a new theatre — deliberate to the point of exasperating his impatient admirers, determined in a degree and toward an end that the rest of Broadway is utterly unable to comprehend.

The key to understanding Hopkins is a kind of optimistic fatalism. Esthetically, this takes the form of artistic evangelism. In his own words in his curiously named apologia, "How's Your Second Act?" he "clings to the belief that the theatre can be a great agency for development — that it can greatly aid in the spread of culture and breeding and the growth of sounder logic — that it can ultimately reach a place where it helps mankind to a better human understanding, to a deeper social pity and to a wider tolerance of all that is life." He would hold a revival among the materialists of our theatre and exhort them: "If there is any way we can make life a little better, a little gentler, a little kinder — we will try to find the way."

Technically, this optimistic fatalism finds expres-

"HE'S PULLED HER THROUGH!"

Scene from Act II of "The Poor Little Rich Girl," by Eleanor Gates, Produced 1913 by Arthur Hopkins. With its Evocative Phrases, it Was Forerunner of the Expressionistic Plays of Today

sion in his theory of unconscious projection. Quoting from the same work: " Extreme simplification — that is what I strive for incessantly — not because I like simplicity. It isn't a matter of taste or preference — it is a working out of the method of Unconscious Projection. It is the elimination of all the non-essentials because they arouse the conscious mind and break the spell I am trying to weave over the unconscious mind. I want the unconscious of the actors talking to the unconscious of the audience, and I strive to eliminate every obstacle to that."

Proceeding from theory to practice, therefore, Hopkins conceives himself as the clearing-house for the younger artists of our theatre — playwrights, actors, designers, musicians. He is satisfied if he can bring them together and say to them, " Now, ladies and gentlemen, here is your opportunity. Get to work and see what happens." This theory and practice might be most admirable if all of those whom the producer had gathered together were adults in their art. Actually, however, they are often mere children, spoiled children, especially the actors, pitifully unfitted to rise to the producer's challenge. Hopkins' opponents, therefore, have some excuse for the charge that the conception of the producer as clearing-house is philosophical alibi for an indulgent and easygoing temperament. If he would refute the growing charge, he must soon bring his experiment to a more successful climax than he has yet done.

Still, despite the apparent flaw in his practical philosophy, Hopkins has contributed generously to our awakening theatre. His theory of "producer's hands off" has worked thus far in the cases of Jones and O'Neill. Without Hopkins as steady sponsor, Jones today might be baffled and even embittered by the struggle to find channel for free expression. It was the magnet of the clearing-house that attracted O'Neill to Hopkins when he had proved himself ready to remain on Broadway. Among the players, Pauline Lord has risen to its challenge. So have the Barrymores on fitful occasion, and several less widely known. Ben-Ami gave promise and then marked time. Numerous others have come and gone without so much as dreaming there was a clearing-house.

I have said that the path of Hopkins' esthetic progress is not wholly clear yet. He is still feeling his way, unwilling to rest at a comfortable half-way house. In close collaboration with Jones, he found a simplified and stylized realism in "The Devil's Garden" and "Redemption"; a sophisticated and stylized comedy in "Good Gracious, Annabelle" and "A Successful Calamity"; an atmospheric and stylized romanticism in "The Jest" and "Richard III"; a stylized but too harshly frugal tragedy in "Hamlet"; a vaguely realized abstraction in "Macbeth," which he admits was not so suitably adapted to such treatment as a new play written deliberately to be so interpreted — as, for instance, "The Hairy Ape."

Of one thing Arthur Hopkins is sure: he wishes to appeal in his theatre to the adult intelligence. "The theatre in America today," he has said, "is adapted in general to the understanding of the eight-year-old mind. It is too much to expect that it can be fully developed at one bound, but at least we are justified in demanding that it measure up to the comprehension of the age of sixteen. The trouble with our present theatre is that it is a ceaseless repetition of a familiar and time-worn formula, a bag of tricks which anyone with skill can play and assure himself a certain amount of success. The whole problem is too easy to stimulate the interest of the audience or the creative imagination of the artist.

"There is no longer any excitement in the experience of playgoing. Everywhere I went in Europe, the audiences were moved to a passionate intensity of interest and stirred to an eager and often violent discussion of the play they were attending. Even in America at the Yiddish Art Theatre, you can see the same clash of feeling and opinion. I want people to leave my theatre actually quarreling about what they have seen. There is nothing more tragic to me than the complacent, unmoved faces that pour out of our Broadway theatres after the play."

In this light, it may be possible to pierce Hopkins' dogged faith in his conception of himself as clearing-house for the theatre's artists, a faith he holds in the face of incredulity and fragmentary achievement. If he believes above all that the theatre is wholly justified only in the white heat of emotional and mental exaltation; that such moments come not by calculation or conscious effort but by the chance coördination of individual talents mutually firing each other

OUR PRODUCERS

to ecstatic creation; that the single time the thing happens is so rich, so rare, so unobtainable otherwise, so supremely worth awaiting that the failures on the way do not matter — then it may pay to be patient with him and see whither his path leads.

Of the other figures in the new generation of producers — new in viewpoint if not always in years — none is so provocative, so fecund, so stimulating, so exasperating, as Hopkins. Winthrop Ames gave promise of becoming such a valuably disturbing spirit early in the period of our survey. The dilettante become expert. The amateur turned professional, and amateur still. The gentleman in the show shop and the gamblers' den, by his very presence making it something other than shop and den. This parabola of paradox playing round Ames the producer was promptly discernible. Proceeding from wealth at home and honors at Harvard to management of the Castle Square Theatre in Boston, he was summoned thence to Manhattan in 1910 by the founders of the New Theatre to become its first director. This post he held through the two seasons that unwieldy infant breathed. Contrary to custom in such crises, Ames was not held responsible for the catastrophe. And justly. The cards were stacked against him. And he emerged from the experience stronger than when he ventured upon it.

Undaunted, therefore, Ames at once built his own Little Theatre, distinguished drawing room of a suave host, and produced therein such fitting fantasies and realities as " The Affairs of Anatol," " Prunella," "The Pigeon," "A Pair of Silk Stockings," "The Philanderer." Not content, he next erected the Booth, ampler in scale but likewise expressive of its owner's taste and refinement. Further step was the shrewdly contrived addition of a balcony to the Little Theatre to make it self-supporting, for Ames' New England frugality is wounded when ends do not meet.

Almost on the heels of these adventures as builder, however, Ames largely abandoned his stages to other producers. For three years he has made but one production a season, and that at times in another's house. To the Winthrop Ames who made a dozen thorough and provocative productions a winter at the New Theatre, we have a right to look in these his riper years for more frequent vital contributions to the dramatic renaissance which he helped to inaugurate. Ames is far too young to be dubbed Cincinnatus, but the current theatre summons him from his reflective plough!

Another of the younger generation who has latterly lived up to few of his prefatory promises is John D. Williams. Trained in the elder showmanship of Charles Frohman but with an attentive eye on to-day's newer, more virile, more ambitious theatre, he made Galsworthy's "Justice" omen of fresh and genuine talent in the producer's field, and gave O'Neill his first foothold on Broadway with "Beyond the Horizon." Without Frohman's knack for carrying on financially despite frequent failures, Williams seems to be in a periodic state of eclipse. His is a

OUR PRODUCERS

gift which a national theatre could use to great advantage.

William Harris, Jr., and Brock Pemberton, on the contrary, appear to be moving forward each year to more secure and enviable positions. From an Elder Showman's family, son of William Sr., silent shadow of Frohman, and brother of Henry B., producer of "The Lion and the Mouse," "The Third Degree" and "The Chorus Lady," Harris entered the theatre only after the loss of his brother on the *Titanic* to continue the family tradition. His sponsorship of John Drinkwater is thus far his chief achievement, but with courage he should go much farther. Pemberton, on the other hand, came from the daily journals by way of novitiate under Hopkins. "Enter Madame" gave him fortunate footing, and thenceforth a strangely halting but persistent kind of courage to explore has brought him to Pirandello's "Six Characters in Search of an Author," with other provocative projects on the horizon.

Struggling upward with variable talents and undetermined prospects is a still newer generation in point of service. Ranks recruited, rating recomputed, from month to month. At the moment may be mentioned: Richard Herndon, patron of the Harvard Prize Plays; Earl Carroll, builder of a plastic and well-appointed playhouse which he knows not how to use; Guthrie McClintic, pupil and protégé of Ames; Gilbert Miller, Henry II, and experimenter with the Frohman boots; Henry Baron, ambitious toll clerk to French bridges.

As for the others, new or old, Lee Shubert and Klaw and Erlanger have become so wrapped up in the manifold and absorbing intricacies of theatre owning, booking and leasing that they will be reserved for Chapter XXII, " The Economic Problems of Our Theatre." With all his orientally extravagant productions of spectacle, Morris Gest has latterly become more significant as dramatic ambassador at large in introducing to our stage the treasures of foreign playhouses and in creating for them sufficient and sympathetic audience; he belongs most appropriately, therefore, in Chapter XXI, " America as Host to Foreign Drama." Likewise, the overlords of our light musical stage — Ziegfeld, Anderson, Berlin, Short, Dillingham, Comstock, J. J. Shubert and their lesser rivals — fit aptly in Chapter XX, " Revue, Variety, and the Dance."

Outside the walls, of course, is that host of experienced and often most gifted stage directors, near-producers who, somehow, lack the constructive and executive force to become producers in their own right: Augustin Duncan, god-father of such widely variant ventures as " John Ferguson " at the Guild; Vildrac's " S.S. Tenacity "; O'Neill's worst, " The First Man "; the initial and indeterminate season of the Equity Theatre. Iden Payne, child of the English and Irish repertories, hampered and unhappy servant of the incorporated heirs of Charles Frohman, director in his own and others' names, finding his major joy and outlet in collaboration with Thomas Wood Stevens in the dramatic school of the Carnegie

OUR PRODUCERS

Institute of Technology. Frank Reicher, able actor, producer for the Guild and latterly for the Selwyns; and his father, Emanuel Reicher, once of Reinhardt's staff in Berlin, and likewise associated with the Guild as well as the Jewish Art Theatre and other projects more fleeting. Adolph Klauber, formerly critic of *The New York Times* and thereafter invisible counselor of the Selwyns. Robert Milton, Russian by blood, American by training, who dreams of a repertory theatre and meanwhile quietly saves many a fading hope for diverse managers. Sam Forrest, Winchell Smith and Hassard Short, who similarly make and remake for others the more ordinary and every-day stuff of our popular stage. Stuart Walker, pupil of Belasco, inventor and proprietor of the prepossessing but ephemeral Portmanteau Theatre, indignant runaway from Broadway's banality to what he feels are the fresher opportunities of the Middle West. Maurice Browne and Sam Hume, projectors of art theatres in Chicago, Detroit and points beyond, subconsciously envious of Manhattan's glamour but hating it and rendering themselves thereby their own worst obstacles in their quest.

Obviously, the producer in our American theatre has a pilgrim's progress ahead of him in order to perform fully his potential service as interpreter of the playwright to the audience, of the audience to the playwright. In his path, as we have seen, stands his own varying ignorance of the theatre as an art. His ignorance, often, of his ignorance. Fifteen years have largely mended this scandal. Fifteen more should erase it. But there are other handicaps, less within his exclusive power to mend. Mutual concession for the sake of the theatre, which is larger than either party, will alone heal the bitter feud between producer and player. Mutual understanding of the problem of rents and real estate on the part of both producer and public and a yielding of the latter's prejudice against pastime far past Times Square are necessary to the solution of the theatre's economic impasse. Settlement of both these problems is essential to any progress toward repertory, genuine experiment, the permanent company, the institutional theatre on a large and efficient scale, the producer as artist of the theatre.

Chapter V

OUR INSTITUTIONAL THEATRES

When in the course of American events, we realize that something isn't all it should be, we immediately start a "movement." Movements are our impulsive and impatient panaceas for ills social, political, economic, material, spiritual, esthetic. Consider America without a club, a guild, a league, a circle, a society, a union, an alliance, an association, a brotherhood, a federation, a fraternity, an institute! By organization, Main Street makes over human nature while you wait. Or benevolently attempts to.

Quite naturally, therefore, when we became convinced a decade and a half ago that our stage needed reformation, we bolted the idea of the institutional theatre as a cure-all. The tradition of the genre, as our fathers knew it vaguely at the hands of Daly and Palmer, persisted with the glamour of "the good old days." Rumors of its invaluable service to the contemporary dramatic renaissance in Europe enhanced its reputation, reinsured its worth. The producer as a group. The individual made impersonal and incorporated in a machine. Mechanism, organization, efficiency. In the theatre. A new field for America's household gods.

But we ignored the fact that the old American stock companies grew slowly to their prime, that the institutional theatre — endowed by city, state or princely patron — was an ancient tradition in Europe, that its fresher forms which we would copy were novel, revolutionary, not in structure but in spirit. What others had taken generations to develop, we would rear over night. The individual producer had failed to give us what we desired. Therefore we would gather several such individuals together, bestow on them plentiful amateur advisers and then expect the miracle to happen, heedless of the law of common denominators.

It is these misconceptions of the infallibility of the group and of the time required to evolve a competent group that have wrecked most of our attempts to found an institutional theatre. Add to these fallacies the frequent abuse of the idea by those who would pervert it to a passing fad, a social ladder, a route to notoriety, and it is small wonder that the net result of fifteen years of experiment is the Theatre Guild, the Provincetown Players and the Neighborhood Playhouse, the three groups whose fortunes the ensuing chapters will relate.

Before proceeding to their chronicles, however, let us examine the idea of the institutional theatre in the light of its models from abroad, its most instructive failures here, its inherent faults, advantages, ultimate possibilities.

Permanence, continuity, freedom from the accident, the error, that incapacitate, lead astray, the individual. Those are the fundamental reasons that lie, consciously or unconsciously, behind the established

IN THE MOUNTAINS OF "PEER GYNT"

The Institutional Theatre's Frequent Fault of Unfused Imaginations Was Typified in This Guild Production, for Which Lee Simonson Designed Cubist Settings for an Otherwise Nondescript Interpretation

theatres of Europe. When the younger generation rebelled from the traditional stages a quarter of a century ago, it usually had the foresight to take over from its elders the form of organization they had tried and proved. A commonwealth of responsibility, of opportunity. An aristocracy of talent. To the extent this delicate balance was respected, preserved, the result was both sustained and brilliant. The Moscow Art Theatre thereby has weathered war, social chaos, famine and the distractions of life overseas. Through assumption of all responsibility himself, Max Reinhardt, absent from his machine in Berlin, has seen it dissolve and, at the height of his career, he starts anew in Vienna, determined by the coöperative method to stimulate his artists through sharing responsibility with them.

A commonwealth of responsibility, of opportunity. An aristocracy of talent. In other words, a fortress with duties and privileges for everyone alike where, in the interests of all, the best men are the commanding officers.

The institutional theatre is no mystic formula in itself. Without the inspiration, the leadership, of great talent — individual producers, *regisseurs,* within the group; captains within the citadel — there is chaos. Without mutual respect between the rank and file and the leadership of talent, there is mutiny. Without sufficient time to fuse free imaginations into a unity in which their freedom is preserved, there is mediocrity.

From one or more of these shortcomings, almost

every attempt to found a group theatre in America has languished and failed or at least has fallen short of its goal. Through its paradoxical poverty in producers, the Theatre Guild, as we shall see, has had to call in outsiders to perform the task for which the Guild exists — play-production — and thus avert chaos or the general discovery of its weakness. Through the scant regard the directors of the Provincetown Players paid to their associates, the tiny but mighty little theatre in Macdougal Street has suffered passive mutiny and at least temporary eclipse.

The most frequent failing we have made in America is to underestimate the time it takes to develop an efficient and richly creative group theatre. Architectural and economic errors were immediately responsible for the catastrophe of the New Theatre, most ambitious of our projects in this field. But behind them was the prior and more responsible error of supposing that such a theatre could be born fullfledged. If its founders had counted on five years or ten for it to discover and know itself, they would possibly have cut their cloth to such a measure that both the architectural and economic pitfalls might have been avoided.

Refusing to learn, even from experience so recent, many of the actors who founded their own Equity Theatre and most of their patrons have been willing to judge the venture on a single season's disappointing experiment. The Equity Theatre is neither a failure nor a success. It is not yet even a theatre. When it develops leaders, organization, an esthetic policy, a repertory, a more or less permanent company, then its achievement as an institutional playhouse can be profitably examined.

A military review of the other failures of the last fifteen years would grow monotonous. Except where mere pastime, social ambition or precious and esoteric motives were involved, the aims of all these ventures were similarly worthy: to provide in lieu of its neglect by individual producers the intelligent production of mature drama for adult minds. Their mistakes likewise were similarly disastrous. Neither the Chicago Theatre Society with its several futile projects, nor the Northampton Municipal Theatre under its successive managements, nor the recent upstart of a National Theatre fathered by the Producing Managers' Association, took to heart the negative lessons of the New Theatre or the positive precepts of the Theatre Guild, the Provincetown Players or the Neighborhood Playhouse.

If it were not for these latter exceptions to a deadly rule of disenchantment, the whole idea of an institutional theatre in America might justly be suspected. Under cover of an impersonal group, energy may be all too speedily dissipated, funds melt away irresponsibly, ambition fire itself into the air like rockets. A polite shell game to mulct the unwary patron and guarantor. Now you see it and now you don't! In time, nothing remains but the dead mechanism of the venture, with secretaries desperately prolonging the life of the organism for the sake of their jobs.

Still, we have the encouraging example of these three

OUR INSTITUTIONAL THEATRES

groups which have achieved in measure. On these three stages there has existed for upwards of a decade an unusual opportunity for experiment, for practice, whether or not advantage has always been taken of that opportunity. Some day, unless individual producers forestall its coming by a thorough housecleaning of their own, which is almost too much to expect, we shall have a National Theatre, an institutional theatre, which will command the loyal collaboration not only of individual artists and of the group stages already existing, but even of producing managers as an opportunity for them to experiment safely with their most cherished and dangerous dreams. When it comes, it will epitomize all that is best, most vigorous and most characteristic in our theatre and our life. It will subject and put to efficient use our genius for organization instead of becoming the slave, on the one hand, of mere mechanism, or on the other of depending blindly on mechanism as a panacea.

It may seem somewhat ironic to turn to the annals of the Provincetown Players, whose future is in the balance, for expression of the inner impulses of the institutional theatre, but the fault of the Provincetowners lay in their haphazard pursuit of their dream, not in the dream itself. In conclusion, therefore, I quote from Macdougal Street:

"That a closely knit group of creative and critical minds is capable of calling forth from the individuals who compose it richer work than they can produce in isolation is the basic faith of the founder of our playhouse. He knows that the art of the theatre can not be pure, in fact can not be an art at all, unless its various elements — playwriting, acting, setting, costuming, lighting — are by some means fused into unity. There are two possible ways of attaining it: the way of the director and the way of the group. Unity in the theatre has been attained, especially in the case of Reinhardt, by imposing upon all the necessary collaborators the autocratic will of one mind — the director's — who uses the other minds involved as unquestioningly obedient instruments. This method of attaining unity leaves room for one and only one free spirit in a theatre.

" It was not so when drama first came into the world. Primitive drama, the expression of the communal or religious life of the organic human group, the tribe, had spontaneously the unity of a pure art. There may be two hundred actors dramatically dancing the conflict of Winter and Spring, but all that all of them do in that drama springs from one shared fund of feelings, ideas, impulses. Unity is not imposed on them by the will of one of their number but comes from that deep level in the spirit of each where all their spirits are one. The aim of the founder of the Provincetown Players, as yet imperfectly fulfilled, is to make all hands work from that level and to do it by recreating in a group of modern individuals, individuals far more highly differentiated than primitive people, a kindredness of minds, a spiritual unity underlying their differences, a unity resembling the primitive unity of the tribe, a unity which may spontaneously create the unity necessary to the art of the theatre."

Chapter VI

THE WASHINGTON SQUARE PLAYERS AND THEIR INHERITORS, THE THEATRE GUILD

The Theatre Guild is the lustiest, most promising and most aggravating of our American adventures in the institutional theatre. It is like a precocious child who won't do what you wish it to do, insists on following its own bent, and then wrings from you reluctant but unequivocal commendation for the way it carries off its perverse escapades. Ever since it emerged from the war-gutted wreckage of the Washington Square Players early in 1919, this group of young mutineers against the established theatre has steered a path far off the course mapped out for it by benevolent friends.

Sponsorship for American drama, the watch-cry of the group's nursery days at the Bandbox and the Comedy? The Guild has produced in five seasons four native plays, twenty-one foreign.

Discovery and development of its own producers, stage directors? Crux, here, of the theatre as an art, unified, effective, adult. The Guild reaches outside its own staff for Robert Milton, Frank Reicher, the Sisters Lewisohn, Agnes Morgan; goes abroad at home for Emanuel Reicher, and actually abroad for the Russian Kommissarzhevsky.

A permanent company, a Guild company? Artists through long and mutually revealing association developing a sensitive and eloquent ensemble? The Guild company is a pleasant fiction. Its "guest" artists — able, unselfish, eager as individuals — far outnumber the home guard. Circles drawn and dissolved. Bubbles blown and broken. Designs carved and shattered.

Repertory — not the sham repertory of the stock company or of a half dozen plays running simultaneously in different theatres or of the occasional revival of past successes, but genuine repertory with a shifting pattern of contrasting plays, keeping patron and performer fresh, eager, alert? Repertory has been in the promises of the Washington Square Players and their inheritors, the Theatre Guild, for nine years. And it is still only a promise.

A permanent home, a Guild Theatre, as contrasted with a Theatre Guild? That prospect seems at last to be on the verge of realization, along with the conceivably simultaneous achievement of several of the other goals. But at what jeopardy to financial, artistic and spiritual independence, time and the stock ticker alone can tell.

And yet, despite the frustrated promises of this group in its dual incarnation, despite its headstrong disregard of patent fact and patient advice, it still commands the respect due to earnest adolescence. Ridiculing and making sport of a youngster dissipates all hope of influencing him. Overpraising him and taking him too seriously turns his head. Leave him

THE THEATRE GUILD

alone. Or better still, show him what he would look like if he could see himself.

Attributing adolescence to the Theatre Guild today may seem to some like a temporal error. Wasn't that awkward age suffered, endured and passed on the Guild's earlier stage? Rather, the Washington Square Players were kindergartners to the restless, assertive youth at the Garrick. Precocious, artistic childhood has been succeeded by the self-conscious pugnacity of the middle years: delight in bravado; ambition to be seen, heard, recognized; desire to achieve here and now at a minimum of preparation, self-counsel, experience; belief in the ability to go out and buy whatever is lacking.

But adolescence passes. Maturity lies ahead. If the Theatre Guild persists — and there can be no doubt that it will, or that it will become adult without the need of a third incarnation — the broader lines of that maturity should be possible to forecast from a careful survey of the formative years.

The Washington Square Players were born spontaneously, just as children don the long skirts and tall hats of their elders and pretend grown-up. There are various versions of the nativity, but the one which is truest in spirit if not in fact discloses in Greenwich Village studio a cross-section of the Village the newspapers and the slummers never discovered. Dunsany's "The Glittering Gate" was at hand. So were Robert Edmond Jones, Edward Goodman, Philip Moeller, Samuel A. Eliot, Jr., Helen Westley and others. Someone suggested impromptu performance.

Jones forthwith made eternity's walls out of window curtains. The rest as promptly became the two thieves, the rocks, the audience.

Shortly after, in the Washington Square Bookshop, then in Macdougal Street, the fact that a new theatre had been founded at that impromptu performance was recognized by the participants just named as well as by Ralph Roeder, Josephine A. Meyer, Dudley G. Tucker, Holland Hudson, William Pennington, Albert Boni, Ida Rauh, Lawrence Langner, and Lucy Huffaker. Amateur playwrights, amateur actors, amateur producers. Impatient of Broadway's standards but even more of its standing lines and outer offices. A theatre of their own! But where? None in the Village. The Bandbox was available at 57th Street and Third Avenue. At thirty-five dollars weekly for Friday and Saturday nights.

There, therefore, on February 19, 1915, the first public performance was given: Maeterlinck's "Interior"; a gastronomic pantomime arranged by Ralph Roeder, "Another Interior"; "Licensed," by Basil Lawrence (Lawrence Langner); and "Eugenically Speaking," by Edward Goodman. The one-act-play not only for its own sake but as first aid to ambitious dramatists.

"We have only one policy," said the first program, "in regard to the plays which we will produce — they must have artistic merit. Preference will be given to American plays, but we shall also include in our repertory the works of well-known European authors which have been ignored by the commercial managers."

Friday and Saturday soon proved insufficient. A third performance was added weekly, and a fourth. By June, forty-three performances of three programs and a review bill had been given, each to 299 spectators, the limit beyond which fire and license strictures became operative. The announced preference for American works was respected by a score of fourteen native to three foreign plays.

The second season — further expansion. The same nursery used more intensively. Nightly performances. Admission advanced from fifty cents to a dollar to permit payment of $25 weekly to the actors, $250 weekly for the theatre and a budget for the house staff in charge of Grace Griswold. Zoë Akins' "The Magical City," Lewis Beach's "The Clod," Alice Gerstenberg's "Overtones," and Philip Moeller's irreverent clownings of history and literature, "Helena's Husband" and "The Roadhouse in Arden" — all classics now in Little Theatre repertories — emerged to encourage faith.

The third season, 1916–17, still further expansion — over-expansion, as outcome proved. From the Bandbox to the Comedy, from the byways to Broadway, from spiritual freedom hampered by material bondage to material freedom hampered by spiritual bondage. Nevertheless, out of the unequal struggle to play Broadway's game, came a rudimentary school of the theatre under Clare Tree Major and still other play candidates for amateur favor the country wide, authentic contributions to native tragedy and comedy in miniature, such as Susan Glaspell's "Trifles," Edward

Massey's "Plots and Playwrights" and Bosworth Crocker's "The Last Straw," as well as the Oriental accident in the Occident, the discovery of the Japanese "Bushido," a one act play-gem set in the interminable reaches of Izumo's "The Pine Tree."

The native playwright began to languish, though. Feeble wings, attenuated imagination. At the end of three seasons the score stood twenty-seven native, twenty-three foreign, stirring Waldo Frank to protest in *The Seven Arts:*

"These spirits of revolt — Andreieff, Wedekind, Maeterlinck — are not true for us. They have not reached up through labored fields that are our own. Absorption in them is a natural growth for their countrymen; for the American it is a dangerous trick. And its consequence must be to cleave us from reality as completely as it intensifies reality for the European.

"We have our own fields to plough; our own reality to explore and flush with vision. Let us do this first; humbly and doggedly as lowly toilers must."

At the cross-roads, then, in the fall of '17: Financial difficulties, the exhaustion of the one-act play, thwarted longing for longer forms, the war. Demoralization, discouragement, dissolution.

And yet, of the Washington Square Players there was residue, leaven, the full worth of which has been obvious only in recent seasons. Of actors, schooled, heartened, encouraged: Roland Young, Katherine Cornell, Rollo Peters, José Ruben, Margaret Mower, Marjorie Vonnegut, Elinor Cox, Frank Conroy and Glenn Hunter, not to mention those like Helen Westley whom the Guild salvaged and held fast. Of stage designers: Lee Simonson, Rollo Peters, Robert Edmond Jones. Of playwrights who have moved out into ampler expression: Zoë Akins, Eugene O'Neill, Lewis Beach, Philip Moeller, Susan Glaspell and Ben Hecht.

Chief residue of the Washington Square Players, though, is the chip of the old block, the Theatre Guild. Conceive, if you can, of the one without the other, of adolescence without childhood, of achievement without experience, of experience without the chance to make mistakes. Out of the adolescent Guild, too, by the same process of mistakes, experience, achievement, should grow a mature Guild.

In the spring of '19 when, as Walter Lippmann points out, no one believed in anything, the leading spirits of the Washington Square Players, minus Edward Goodman who had held the whip hand over the Players for their welfare if not for his own popularity, organized the Theatre Guild. Among them were Lawrence Langner, Philip Moeller, Helen Westley, Josephine A. Meyer, Rollo Peters, Justus Sheffield and Lee Simonson, around whom was gathered an acting company including in addition Augustin Duncan, Helen Freeman, Edna St. Vincent Millay, Dudley Digges and Henry Herbert.

With capital of $500 and a generous lease from Otto H. Kahn to the Garrick, one time home of Mansfield, " Zaza," " The Little Minister," " Sherlock Holmes," " Captain Jinks " and the French Copeau, the Guild spoke the fragile lines of Benavente's " The Bonds of Interest " as its salutatory April 14, 1919.

Six weeks later, with as much timidity as that of the youthful Moscow Art Theatre in reviving Tchehoff's "The Sea Gull," the Guild put on St. John Ervine's dour tragedy of cowardice, "John Ferguson." And like "The Sea Gull," it established the name, fame and fortune of its sponsors.

Four full seasons have passed since then. Langner, Moeller, Simonson and Mrs. Westley remain on the board of managers — a patent lawyer, a playwright, a painter and an actress. An early recruit and a faithful is Maurice Wertheim, of Broadway — the lower Broadway of stocks and bonds. And another is Theresa Helburn, shrewd, taciturn, matter-of-fact, who is properly placed as executive director. At the hands of these, of the divers directors they have hired, of acting company after acting company hurriedly grouped round Helen Westley as resident player, twenty-three other plays have been presented — four American and nineteen from overseas — and all of them originally at the Garrick, although success took nine of them uptown to continue their run and permit the Guild to meet its obligations of six productions a year to its subscribers. Those subscribers have grown from 150 in 1919 to 600 in 1920, 1300 in 1921, 2800 in 1922 and 6000 today — a sound indication of a problem met and a service fulfilled.

Outstanding achievements of the Guild in these four and a half seasons have been Ervine's "John Ferguson," his even more taut and human bit of middle class realism, "Jane Clegg"; Bernard Shaw's symbolic fable of war and after, "Heartbreak

House," his mastodonic and wearying pentateuch, " Back to Methuselah," and the ironic melodrama of his creative youth, " The Devil's Disciple"; A. A. Milne's fantastic farce, " Mr. Pim Passes By "; Franz Molnar's disillusioning but picturesque " Liliom "; Arthur Richman's plodding and sometimes penetrating " Ambush "; Andreieff's half-mood and elusive " He Who Gets Slapped," interpreted gratuitously by the Guild as romantic melodrama and attaining undreamed popular favor thereby; Georg Kaiser's " From Morn to Midnight," anemic partner of O'Neill's " The Hairy Ape " in introducing expressionism to the American stage; and Karel Capek's mordant challenge to our industrial civilization, " R. U. R."

And yet, despite achievement, despite geometrically progressing subscription list — perhaps, rather, because of them — the Guild was not satisfied. It wished a home of its own, " a Guild Theatre for the Theatre Guild." And so, quite simply, just as with everything else it had really wished to do, it went out last spring and got one. At least the promise of one in the form of a bond subscription generously in excess of half a million dollars.

The ease with which the Guild sold its bonds and assured itself of a home, prompts inquiry into its influence, its motives, its methods, its prospects. What sort of a youth is this who at a gesture can command a castle? Who are its friends? What has it done to justify such confidence? What does it propose to do to fulfill that confidence? In short, what is the Theatre Guild and what is it not?

Whatever it may hope to accomplish with more elaborate equipment, the Guild on its record is not an experimental theatre. It has taken no more chances than the average earnest Broadway producer, not so many as Arthur Hopkins, the Neighborhood Playhouse, the Provincetown Players or its own earlier self, the Washington Square Players. Shaw, Milne, Molnar, Ibsen. Mansfield, Daly, Belasco, Mrs. Fiske, were pioneers for most of these years ago. Today, they are names on the cover of the theatre's *Cosmopolitan*, its *Saturday Evening Post*.

Nor is the Guild non-commercial, whatever may be the merits of that estate. It has paid its way from the start without gift or charity. It has paid its working staff a living wage. It has paid its actors — less, perhaps, than the market price, since actors relish its prestige. True, it has turned back into the theatre all its profits. But wherein have Hopkins, Belasco, Ames, Gest, Tyler and numerous others done less?

In what, then, does its prestige consist? How has it won the right to special favor? To call it, as Ervine does, the leading art theatre in the world today is absurd. Ervine is simply paying a just debt, rather awkwardly. The Theatre Guild is not an art theatre at all — at least not yet. It is too young, too inexperienced, too much a creature of changing personnel, of makeshift equipment, of an audience that is only beginning to be exacting, mutually stimulating. Thus far in its progress toward becoming ultimately an art theatre, it is the epitome of the highest common denom-

"THE TRAGEDY OF AN ELDERLY GENTLEMAN"

For the Fourth Part of the Theatre Guild's Production of Shaw's Mastodonic and Wearying Pentateuch, "Back to Methuselah," Lee Simonson Used Projected Light for His Settings

inator of the theatre that can " get by." Miss Helburn, for the Guild, has admitted as much, and it is no damaging admission. Rather, it is encouraging augury. A youth who has no exaggerated illusions concerning his own importance can be much more safely entrusted with a castle.

The Guild, therefore, in its exalted pretensions is the victim of its friends. Sometimes that has been to its advantage. These young men and women are shrewd enough to be coy in the face of the flattery of the press. They have let the critics " discover " them, boast of the discovery and make it their own child who can do no wrong. Thereby the Guild's subscription list grows and with it the power to persist and proceed. Sometimes, however, adulation becomes ironic, embarrassing. Witness Ervine. Or Walter Prichard Eaton. In the July, 1916, *American Magazine,* Eaton wrote: " The Washington Square Theatre started in poverty, and it is comparatively poor yet — thank heaven. We hope it always will be. Then the workers in it will always be its lovers. We don't want them to work for nothing; but better for nothing than for great riches." And yet it was Eaton as chairman who managed the half million bond campaign!

The Theatre Guild probably deserves its new castle if only for the reason that in this phenomenally affluent land of ours, the arts should be treated at least as prodigally as our rivers and harbors and sports. In its castle, the Guild proposes: " (1) To improve the Guild standards of play production; (2) To improve the Guild standards of acting; (3) To experiment to a

THE THEATRE GUILD

greater extent than heretofore, especially with the works of American dramatists; (4) To develop a permanent ensemble acting company; (5) To maintain a repertory of fine plays which shall be presented from year to year; (6) To establish a Studio for all branches of the Art of the Theatre, in which young people of talent may study as an inherent part of the life of the theatre."

An ambitious program, a right program. A program that might inspire more confidence if the Guild in the past had manifested a greater determination to pursue it as far as its resources would permit. By foresight in choosing and rehearsing plays, instead of rushing a production through to fill a gap, it could have improved its standards both of staging and of acting, besides retaining from one bill to the next a larger resident acting nucleus, willing, by virtue of permanent occupation, to devote more than the union limit of four weeks to rehearsal. With a little more alertness, patience and unselfishness, producing talent might have been found, developed and added to the inner circle of the board of managers to recruit Moeller's leaden hand. Rather, this course, than to go in the open market and bid for Stanislavsky, for Reinhardt.

And finally, solicitude for American drama comes a bit tardily. It will not do for the Guild to insist that it is interested in good plays wherever they come from. A policy of come-one-come-all is a tacit admission of preference for foreign product. On even terms, the latter will still crowd out the native ten times to one. What did the Guild do to help O'Neill to his feet?

What effort has it made to obtain his work since he reached that posture? Has the Guild finally after four years and a half awakened to the fact that production of a foreign play can at best be only an approximation of success, that our knowledge of other civilizations is surprisingly limited, and that confidence in place of knowledge is a poor priest in art?

Then, there are those bonds. Whose Theatre Guild, whose Guild Theatre will Guild and Theatre be in case of repeated disaster and default? Is the future mortgaged thereby? Artistic independence in entail? Isn't it possible, on the contrary, that the sense of financial responsibility will make an energetic, headstrong, adolescent Guild into an efficient, far-sighted, mature Guild? The bondholders, after all, aren't the ordinary sort. Let them be a bit stern on occasion, like a wise parent, and their ward may become the pride of our awakening stage.

Chapter VII

THE PROVINCETOWN PLAYERS

If the New York Symphony Society, the Metropolitan Opera House or *The Century Magazine* were to announce to their subscribers: "We are going to quit for a year — rest, recuperation, quickening of faith, freshening of spirit. Come back again seventeen months hence, and we'll greet you once more at the old stand "——. Imagine the gossip, the scandal, the ferreting of ulterior motives!

The Provincetown Players issued this proclamation in so many words at the close of their season, spring, 1922. And the only reaction is a keen disappointment at having to do without them so long, coupled with the observation that, of course, in Greenwich Village, time is not money but duration. More correctly, that is the prevalent reaction for there are some of us cynical enough to suspect and predict that interim is graceful excuse for interment, that this particular group sees its end served, its personnel in need of realignment, rebirth. And yet, with the approach of the date set for resumption, even the cynics begin to wonder whether the Provincetowners didn't really mean what they said, after all! Recall their determination seven years ago to found a theatre in New York on $320 — two-thirds of the Guild's nest egg. The founding of the theatre. Its persistence, growth. Its ups and downs, more ups than downs. Recall, most of all, its unique function as "The Playwrights' Theatre." The gap it has left in interim. The failure of the Guild or anyone else to confiscate that function. The Provincetowners once more? If not, why not?

Meanwhile, whether or not, the posture of circumstances makes narrative, analysis, extremely difficult, embarrassing. Suppose, then, for the sake of clarity, we look upon the first seven years as a completed epoch, destined to lead in time, if not to resurrection, at least to inspiration of a new group.

The Playwrights' Theatre. There is something aptly American in the implications of that title. The age of specialization. Let the producers have as many theatres as they like; the actors, one of their own, if they can get along with each other; the designers, a scenic theatre, if they can make settings an end in themselves. The playwrights care not, so long as they have theirs.

The Playwrights' Theatre. Expanded, that title reads thus in the folder announcing the first New York season: "The present organization is the outcome of a group of people interested in the theatre, who gathered spontaneously during two summers at Provincetown, Mass., for the purpose of writing, producing and acting their own plays. The impelling desire of the group was to establish a stage where playwrights of sincere, poetic, literary and dramatic purpose could see their plays in action, and superintend their production without submitting to the commercial manager's interpretation of public taste. Equally, it was to afford an opportunity for actors, producers, scenic and costume-designers to experiment with a stage of extremely simple resources — it being the idea of the Players that elaborate settings are unnecessary to bring out the essential qualities of a good play."

The Playwrights' Theatre. That, with all respect to the theatre's other craftsmen invoked in the preceding proclamation, has been the Provincetowners' gospel. Captious comment, considering O'Neill as the dominant product of their stage, might on the sly reverse the apostrophe. And yet, despite the preëminence of O'Neill among the alumni of Macdougal Street, despite the fact that to nourish him and pass him on to wider public is in itself sufficient justification for seven years hard labor, the Provincetowners' roster as the Playwrights' Theatre would be notable without O'Neill. In eight seasons — two summer and six winter — ninety-three plays by forty-seven American playwrights were brought to light which the vast majority would never otherwise have seen. Second only to O'Neill with sixteen plays is Susan Glaspell with eleven. To five is attached the name of the Playhouse's director for all but one of its seasons, George Cram Cook. Others more beholden to the Provincetowners than the Provincetowners to them are: Floyd Dell, Alfred Kreymborg, Rita Wellman, Maxwell Bodenheim, Bosworth Crocker, Harry Kemp, Djuna Barnes, Edna St. Vincent Millay, Wallace Stephens and Evelyn Scott.

The Playwrights' Theatre? Yes and no. More correctly, the Provincetown Playhouse became in its latter seasons the private feoff of its founders. They were playwrights, to be sure, but the general significance of the title suffered, and thereby the vitality of its stage. With the graduation of O'Neill to Broadway and the waning interest on the part of those whose first flame was fitful, the group became circumscribed. Through the laxity and irresponsibility dangerously inherent in group organization, there was only a helter-skelter effort to recruit new blood, no adequate play-reading, no intelligent, insistent and persuasive invitation to gifted writers in other fields to try their hand at the theatre. In similar posture, the Moscow Art Theatre did not rest content with Tchehoff; it went out and commandeered for the stage the promising young novelist, Gorky. In time, therefore, few remained but George Cram Cook and Susan Glaspell, with an occasional gift from O'Neill, just for old times' sake. Handwriting on the wall: the life-preserver of the season of 1920–21 was O'Neill's "The Emperor Jones"; of 1921–22, O'Neill's "The Hairy Ape." Cook and Glaspell could not together provide a season's repertory. O'Neill could not be expected to perform missionary service indefinitely. In such an impasse, the logical end of an epoch was at hand, and with it, an opportunity for survey, reminiscence, appraisal, of a group which for seven years in a remodelled livery stable with a capacity of less than two hundred roused and fulfilled more expectations for native American drama than all the other forces in our theatre put together.

ON CONGO'S BANKS IN O'NEILL'S "THE EMPEROR JONES"

Cleon Throckmorton Used the Plaster Horizon of the Provincetown Playhouse with Telling Effect in the Outdoor Scenes of the Tragedy of the Black Monarch

The Provincetown Players were born of the same general impulse and out of the same soil as the Washington Square Players. Both groups crystallized in answer to the same impatient desire of young and insurgent artists in Greenwich Village to have a stage of their own. From the beginning, these two groups were separately organized, each with its own motive, program, personnel, although several individuals were associated in turn or simultaneously with both stages. The proof of divergent motives lies in the courses the two groups have pursued, the widely different goals they have reached. The Washington Square Players by rebirth in the Theatre Guild have permitted an early interest in foreign drama to become a definite if unacknowledged predilection. The Provincetown Players clung to the end to their untiring and often discouraging search for a native American drama. The result has been that two stages, which might have become competitive and in their rivalry extinguished each other at birth, staked off and developed separate claims to the greater enrichment of our contemporary theatre.

Dissatisfaction with some of the judgments of the Washington Square Players resulted in casual experiment in the summer of 1915 on the part of several Greenwich Villagers whom chance brought together in Provincetown, Mass. What Dunsany's " The Glittering Gate " was to the parents of the Guild, two plays — both of them American — were to the rebels. One was " Suppressed Desires " by George Cram Cook and Susan Glaspell; the other, Neith Boyce's " Constancy." The latter's home was turned over to Robert Edmond

THE PROVINCETOWN PLAYERS 95

Jones to convert into impromptu theatre — the same Jones who devised impromptu setting at the birth of the Washington Square Players. An inner room served for "Suppressed Desires"; the portico for "Constancy," with the audience turned about face and with Long Point Light at the tip of Cape Cod for beguiling vista.

Success led to repetition, extension. The Provincetown Players found, or rather made, a Provincetown Playhouse — the Wharf Theatre, once a fishing dock and then when too rickety, a studio. Cook as carpenter superintended alterations, dividing a room about twenty-five feet square and ten feet high into stage and auditorium, with the former opening once more on demand to the sea for background and Long Point Light for vista. Cook as director financed the venture with coöperative contributions of $5 each. The first bill was repeated in the new home and then followed by a second — Cook's "Change Your Style," a satire on Provincetown's wrangling art schools, and Wilbur Daniel Steele's "Contemporaries."

Plans languished through the ensuing winter. Two plays were given at the Liberal Club in New York and repeated at the studio now known as the Samovar. At O'Connor's, where Masefield once kept bar, a committee was appointed — or appointed itself — to make plans for the summer of 1916 at Provincetown. That summer marked progress: Thirty active members; eighty-seven subscribing members at $2.50 each; installation of electric lights and built-in seats; four bills of three short plays each; O'Neill to the stage for the first time as playwright with "Bound East for Cardiff" in the second bill, for the first and almost the only time as actor in the rôle of the negro in his own "Thirst" in the fourth bill; Susan Glaspell scribbling the final starkly eloquent lines of "Trifles" just in time to appease a committee waiting to make up the third bill.

At John Reed's home, then, toward close of summer, the active members met, adopted a constitution and planned transfer of their holiday stage to the rigors of a winter in the city. From play in Provincetown to work in New York. A review bill netted a nest egg of $80; eight players advanced $30 more apiece. Of the eighty-seven subscribing Provincetowners, sixty-four were winter New Yorkers — nucleus of a mailing list. For Manhattan home, Macdougal Street, 139. For steel girder over the proscenium, $200, or sixty per cent of the capital. For program, ten bills at a subscription rate of $4. For fortunate windfall to enable fulfilment of these promises, a lump payment of $1600 from the Stage Society in return for Sunday and Tuesday evening privileges. Regular subscribers, numbering 450 the first year, took the rest of the five performances of each bill — Friday, Saturday and Monday evenings. Attendance was limited to subscribers to avoid the strictures of censorship and the building laws. Critics were taboo. And of this program — amazing for a first season — nine bills were given before the Building Department used unsuspected technicality to close the doors.

An appeased building inspector permitted resumption in the fall. Subscriptions remained at $4 but the number of bills was cut to seven. The best plays of the first New York season had been revivals from the Wharf Theatre. In 1917-18, however, emerged O'Neill's " The Long Voyage Home," " 'Ile " and " The Rope "; Susan Glaspell's " Woman's Honor," " Close the Book " and " The Outside."

Preparations for the third season in the city found America at its deepest engrossment in the war. The Washington Square Players had succumbed to attrition of their ranks. Seven Provincetowners were in the army at home or in France. But the rest determined to persist, raised the subscription to $5, remodelled and moved into 133 Macdougal, and issued this proclamation: " It is now often said that theatrical entertainment in general is socially justified in this dark time as a means of relaxing the strain of reality, and thus helping us to keep sane. This may be true, but if more were not true — if we felt no deeper value in dramatic art than entertainment — we would hardly have the heart for it now. One faculty, we know, is going to be of vast importance to the half-destroyed world — indispensable for its rebuilding — the faculty of creative imagination. That spark of it which has given this group of ours such life and meaning as we have is not so insignificant that we should now let it die. The social justification which we feel to be valid now for makers and players of plays is that they shall help keep alive in the world the light of imagination. Without it the wreck of the world that was, can not be cleared away, and the new world shaped."

O'Neill's "The Moon of the Caribbees" and Glaspell's "Bernice" distinguished that season. Almost nothing — except Milady Millay's "Aria da Capo" — marked the next, which was under thumb of James Light as director, with Cook a hermit on Cape Cod. Light, however, expanded each bill to two weeks playing time to keep pace with spreading clientele.

And then for the first bill in autumn, 1920, two weeks were mere prologue. The Provincetown Players found fame for themselves, made it for O'Neill. Or O'Neill made fame for the Provincetowners, found it for himself. "The Emperor Jones." Week after week it ran in Macdougal Street, with the Players' subscription lists growing geometrically and their season's plans wrenched awry. Finally, Adolph Klauber arranged to transplant to Broadway both play and players, including Charles S. Gilpin, the gifted negro actor whom the Players rescued from an elevator lever after he had closed in "Abraham Lincoln." O'Neill's "Diff'rent" that same season was understudy only to "The Emperor Jones" in its fortunes down town and up.

In the last two seasons of the Provincetowners, the one-act play began to give way to longer forms. In 1920–21, three plays of full length were given — Cook's "The Spring," Glaspell's "Inheritors" and Evelyn Scott's "Love" — while O'Neill's two were practically self-sufficient. In the last season, only a single bill of short plays was presented. Devotees of the one-act form deplored this turn of affairs, foreseeing disappearance of the last stronghold of this particular genre in New York. But the Provincetown Players never committed themselves to the one-act-play as such. They expressed themselves in that way at first simply because it was more surely within their range.

Of the inner group which made and maintained the Provincetown Playhouse for seven unbroken years, O'Neill has already been thrown full-stature on our screen. With a restless, inquisitive, penetrating and sensitive spirit, Susan Glaspell, like O'Neill, has served chiefly as contributing playwright, although, like O'Neill, she, too, gave of her courage, daring and insight to the Playhouse's important decisions. In life and as counsellor, just as in her work as dramatist, a strange, subtle charm vies with the self-conscious hardness of the propagandist, with the result that a rare imagination sometimes bows to the latter and lesser master. Cook's gifts, on the contrary, have been largely executive and inspirational, although he, too, would probably prefer to be looked upon as playwright, and it is this misapprehension of his true function which, as much as anything else, drove the Provincetowners into the blind alley of sterility.

One other stage director besides Cook has emerged from the Provincetown experiment — James Light, recruit in 1917 from the Middle West, whose understanding often outruns his self-confidence. Due in part to its emphasis on its rôle as the Playwrights' Theatre, the Provincetown Playhouse has graduated only a single stage designer of promise, Cleon Throckmorton, and but few actors aside from E. J. Ballantine and Charles Ellis. The administrative side of the directorate —patient and self-effacing souls — comprised M. Eleanor Fitzgerald, Edna Kenton and Harry Weinberger in the theatre's last season.

Just what was the dilemma that faced this staff of eight in the spring of 1922 and persuaded them to announce an interim, is difficult to explain. Need of leisure, lack of plays worth doing — these are official reasons. The situation was more complicated than that. Dismayed by personal artistic failures in the season of 1921–22, and finding route open to holiday in Greece, Cook and Miss Glaspell suddenly took leave in early spring. For the rest, there were several conceivable courses: a choice, from the standpoint of organization, between continuation and reconstruction; a choice, from the standpoint of theatre home, among renewing their lease, buying their premises outright, moving out of crowded quarters into an already existing structure such as the Greenwich Village Theatre or the picturesque old church in Jane Street, now razed, or building anew from the rock up. There was even momentary proposal to recruit Robert Edmond Jones as director, Arthur Hopkins as distant sponsor. Anything, many of the Provincetowners' friends thought, to preserve name, good will, clientele, continuity. Ultimately, the decision lay with O'Neill as youthful patriarch of the board. And with his strange but characteristic combination of sentimentality and fatality, O'Neill could bring himself and the more passive directors to agree neither to radical revision of the structure Cook had reared, to half-hearted " carry-on," nor to frank termination of the experiment with acknowledgment of ends achieved and with hope of rebirth of a new group with new ends — like that of the Theatre Guild, perhaps, from the remnants of the Washington Square Players. Decision of any kind averted, therefore. Interim!

During this interim, what has happened to the minds, the imaginations, the ideals, of Cook, Glaspell, O'Neill, Light? Will others enter the situation to stimulate interest, rouse further questions? On the answer — unpredictable because it is not the individual answers or their sum but the group answer which is important — depends a larger share of the future of our awakening theatre than can be readily foreseen.

Chapter VIII

THE NEIGHBORHOOD PLAYHOUSE

If I were a playwright and had written a courageous play which no one had the equal courage to produce, and if in amazement I discovered thousands of playgoers ferreting out the devious way to a little theatre in a congested portion of the world's most imposing city, where that play was visible nightly for many weeks, I would be tempted, like John Galsworthy, to describe that theatre as " the house where magic has come to stay."

Or if I were mistress of the art of acting and saw in this theatre the fountain head of the finest impulses in my art, I would probably judge it in the terms of Minnie Maddern Fiske: " One of the most stimulating playhouses I know. Rare good taste prevails everywhere — good taste, good sense."

Or, further, if I were a sympathetic observer from overseas, my natural reaction would be that of William Archer: " Perhaps the most delightful of the New York sideshows."

But I am neither grateful playwright, nor artist within the theatre, nor gracious and perspicacious visitor from afar. I am, if anything, simply chronicler and, where possible, interpreter of our dramatic endeavors. And I like to think of the Neighborhood Playhouse of the Henry Street Settlement as a laboratory built securely on the ground floor of an ultimate National Theatre, the superstructure of which is not yet even remotely conceived or planned. The larger edifice may belong to the dim future, or it may be around the corner of time, but down in Grand Street — garish, glutted, guileful Grand Street — behind that dignified, though unpretentious, Georgian façade, is an institutional stage of which it must take account and which it will use as one of its testing grounds when it comes.

The Neighborhood Playhouse has had a home of its own ever since it was born. Silver spoon. That birthday was February 12, 1915, just a week before the Washington Square Players began. What was there in that first spring of world war that begat theatres, our three most significant institutional stages? Probably mere coincidence. For the Neighborhood, at . novitiate dates back to the dawn of the epoch we considering. Eight years before the Neighborhood became the Neighborhood and the esthetic and social soul of its neighborhood, the " festival groups " of the Henry Street Settlement gave seasonal pageants in the gymnasium. For three years, the Settlement's dramatic club had given such plays as Galsworthy's " The Silver Box " in Clinton Hall near by.

" These productions," said the announcement of the first season in Grand Street, " reached a point where the development of the players, the interest of the audience and the response of the neighborhood seemed to demand the erection of this playhouse. It hopes to be a community playhouse, where the traditions of the neighborhood can find artistic expression, where anyone with special gifts can contribute his talent, and where interesting productions of serious plays and comedies as well as the lighter forms of entertainment may be found. By the variety of its program, the Playhouse aims to appeal to a public of diverse tastes, interests and ages, and in this way to share in the life of the neighborhood."

A dual rôle, then: to serve its milieu esthetically, and then, by indirection rather than obtrusion, to serve it socially. Dual in another and more particular sense: to assist its community toward esthetic self-expression, first, through active participation in classes in acting and dancing conducted in the Playhouse's own workshop leading to ultimate participation in performances given on the Playhouse's own stage; and secondly, through the example and inspiration of visiting artists of high attainments. In still a third sense, a dual rôle: to serve its neighborhood first; and then, if patrons were attracted from up-town and out-of-town, to be cordial host to them as well.

No illusion here about creating a national theatre, or even, in its stricter sense, an art theatre. The founders of the Neighborhood knew the limitations of their project. They knew its assets. The assets they cherished and put to work. The limitations likewise, so far as possible, they capitalized. They were simply good architects, building on a difficult plot of ground; and, instead of letting the difficulties baffle them, they were spurred thereby to creation of something new, something unique, something that had never been.

THE NEIGHBORHOOD PLAYHOUSE 105

As something unique, therefore, without a pattern but possible provocative pattern to others, the Neighborhood Playhouse is stimulating subject from the diverse angles of personnel, administration, organization, plant, esthetic point of view, record, residue and prospects.

The Neighborhood is a woman's theatre. No man has anything whatsoever to do with it except by invitation. Alice and Irene Lewisohn, sisters, built it and gave it rent free to the Settlement. Unlike too many founders, they have consistently refrained from autocratic domination, although their generosity has extended to personal interest and participation in the Playhouse's activities. For collaborators in management they have had Helen Arthur and Agnes Morgan; for counsel and coöperation, Sarah Cowell LeMoyne, Yvette Guilbert, Gertrude Kingston and Esther Peck.

To the public, Helen Arthur *is* the Neighborhood Playhouse; to the players, dancers and participants in the Playhouse's varied pursuits, the Lewisohns and Miss Morgan are equally if not better known. For years before formal début in Grand Street, Miss Arthur brought her efficiency and enthusiasm down to the Henry Street Settlement and its dramatic redoubt, Clinton Hall, after a day's work in responsible and exacting post with the Shuberts. As head of their playreading department and confidential secretary, she had learned every phase of the business and administrative side of the theatre, had won wide acquaintance with the personnel and methods of our contemporary stage. In the fall of 1917 she abandoned Broadway altogether for the richer satisfactions of the East Side's first community playhouse.

In administration of the Neighborhood, Alice Lewisohn supervises the classes in acting and characterization; Irene Lewisohn, those in dancing, together with planning the choreographic work of the festival plays. Dagmar Perkins is assistant to the former with the classes in diction; Blanche Talmud, to the latter, with especial charge over the younger children. Agnes Morgan, pupil of Professor George Pierce Baker at Radcliffe and shrewd observer of continental stages, is producer and stage manager.

In novitiate, before the days of Grand Street, the dramatic interests of the Settlement were divided between acting and dancing. At the Neighborhood, therefore, these two phases of self-expression found embodiment in the Neighborhood Players and the Festival Dancers. Admission to both groups has always been guarded, but most democratically. Through the first six seasons, Saturday and Sunday evenings were reserved for the Players, Saturday and Sunday afternoons for pantomime-ballets and fairy plays done by the Festival groups, Monday for rehearsal, and the rest of the week for visiting companies, guest artists and motion pictures as filler, understudy, emergency. In the fall of 1920, with certain dates saved for the Festival Dancers, the expedient of a resident professional company was tried. Intensive example to the student. The student tested, spurred, in minor rôles. Success led to the repetition of this régime through the season of 1921-22. And

point where false and artificial folk-drama has crept into the repertory.

Manifestly, such an institution as this is primarily a school — a school for actors and dancers and a school for audiences, as well. Despite its admirable equipment — self-contained as no other American theatre by virtue of its own scenic and property and costume workshops and storehouses under one roof — it can not hope to rise to first importance as a producing theatre. Its secluded location and its small auditorium stand in the way of an ambition which it has had the discretion to forego. Occasionally, as in the production of Galsworthy's "The Mob," it will add a distinctive chapter to the general chronicle of our theatre at large, but that is only a fortunate by-product of its specific labors. Fortunately, too, the Neighborhood Playhouse does not feel too conscious of its function. The pervasive air of play, of joy in work, of unhampered experiment, of challenging its audiences with plays above rather than beneath their natural expectations and comprehensions, has been marred only on occasion by misplaced faith in a work of deceptive values.

It is a little disconcerting, it is true, to be called on to recite the concrete instances of the Neighborhood's service as an experimental playhouse. The results of this side of its activities seem hardly commensurable, at first glance, with the effort expended in the last eight years. The Neighborhood has yielded no Eugene O'Neill, no Susan Glaspell. It has passed on to the theatre at large from its amateur companies no Katherine Cornell, no Frank Conroy, no Charles Ellis, no E. J. Ballantine, or a dozen others from Bandbox, Guild and Provincetown. In scenic artists, it has produced Ernest de Weerth, Warren Dahler and Esther Peck — promising but not yet the equal of Jones and Simonson, nurtured in its rivals among our group theatres. And in dancers, its single noteworthy talent thus far is Albert Carroll.

And yet, as pioneer, it has again and again brought to our stage numerous significant plays and productions which would not otherwise have reached us. Dunsany, meet America! An introduction which the Irish poet repays by inscribing in the theatre's guest book: "Dunsany, whose spirit was discovered waif-like in Grand Street, an unknown immigrant, about 1915." Galsworthy's "The Mob." Debussy's "*La Boîte à Joujoux.*" Shaw's "Great Catherine," "The Inca of Perusalem." Andreieff's "The Beautiful Sabine Women." For the first time in New York, many for the first time in America. Most exquisitely, most courageously, Charles T. Griffes' festival with music, arranged from Walt Whitman's "*Salut au Monde*" — for the first time on any stage. Guilbert, while still unknown in America; Ben-Ami, thwarted and discouraged ere the Jewish Art Theatre gave him leeway and lift to fame; Tony Sarg's Marionettes; Thomas Wilfred's Color Organ — all these have been welcome guests, lodgers for a night from the artists' long and weary highroad. Then, too, through its classes and productions in ballet and folk dance, it has made its mark upon its entire surrounding community, both

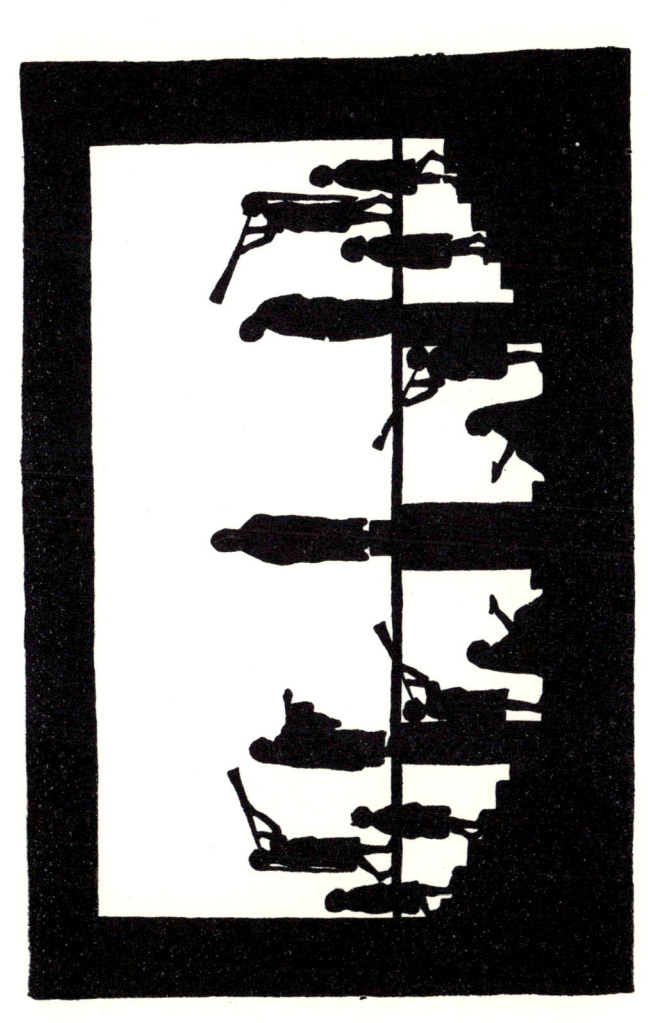

FESTIVAL OF THE TABERNACLES AT THE NEIGHBORHOOD PLAYHOUSE

In the Productions of its Festival Dancers, the Little Theatre in Grand Street Achieves both Social and Esthetic Expression

then came interim — interim wholly different in cause, in motivation, from that of the Provincetowners. Behind closed doors, with staff and classes busy and with the Sisters Lewisohn observant travelers overseas, the Neighborhood Playhouse for an entire year has laid by energy, impulse, creative and executive stamina, in order to advance to new goals with resumption of its public activities this season.

An attempt to deduce the esthetic tenets of this group from a season's record and especially from the entire repertory of the Neighborhood results in the conclusion that the only dramatic theory here is an open mind and a quick sympathy to reach out for vital things, both new and old, an eclecticism rare in these days of positive and blatant affirmation and negation in the arts. Hardly any type of play or manner of presentation is missing, except the more radical and revolutionary phases of the art of the theatre which are not yet of general appeal. In keeping with the social motive of this stage — propagandist never, subsidiary always, subconscious often — folk drama has invariably found a warm spot in the predilections of the directors. Never permitted to crowd out other vital forms, it has been, nevertheless, the Neighborhood's greatest strength, its greatest weakness. The recurring Hebrew festivals obviously fulfil the communal spirit in the Ghetto. Not less socially stimulating have been the miracle and morality plays of the Middle Ages and the folk fantasias from Russia. Such an enthusiasm, however, holds dangers of exaggeration and at times it has dulled the judgment to the

Chapter IX

THE LITTLE THEATRES

Out in the suburbs of the idea of the producer as creative agent between playwright and audience is the Little Theatre. What is a Little Theatre? And why? These are questions that have fed the column writers of the newspapers handsomely ever since, a little over a decade ago, Maurice Browne applied the term to his tiny experimental stage in Chicago.

What is a Little Theatre? Just because the wits have provided smart answers that beg the point, just because the wide range of paradoxical and heterogeneous specimens complicates satisfactory and inclusive answer to the question, are no reasons why we should not attempt serious definition. The Little Theatre is no longer a mere social fad, a whim, a passing fancy, a toy of the moment. Sometimes it is, but when it is, it need not concern us. Frequently enough, it is something more. And it has come to stay — to stay or to grow into something else not always readily discernible.

In that aspect of transition, there is hint of a definition. If we can not yet phrase it more particularly, we can at least admit that the Little Theatre is the institutional theatre, which we have been considering in theory and in example, still in embryo. Just as the embryo does not always develop to maturity, especially under severe and unfavorable conditions, so the mortality among the Little Theatres is high. The fit survive, giving us in time the Theatre Guild, the Provincetown Players, the Neighborhood Playhouse.

With this understanding of what the Little Theatre is, its reason why also becomes more apparent. Dissatisfaction with the established theatre is the cornerstone: revolt — especially in communities distant from New York — from the infrequency and inadequacy of travelling companies and the dull, impersonal monotony of the motion picture. But a theatre, no matter how little, consists of something more than a cornerstone. And besides, we have Little Theatres near New York, in New York, where these causes for their existence are inoperative. Other stones, therefore, are added, the stones of individual ambition, of desire for self-expression in acting, in designing, in playwriting, in producing. Contributions, in variety if not in reverence of spirit, like the carved stones brought by the artisans of the community to the making of the medieval cathedral. And finally there is the keystone, the capstone, of one or more directing personalities, bent on preserving the structure as reared, on extending it if possible.

As the common or garden variety of the institutional theatre, the Little Theatre is particularly subject to the American passion for "movements." In five years after its inception, the Little Theatre had become enough of a movement to rouse the frightened and

THE LITTLE THEATRES 115

scornful wrath of Belasco, the same Belasco who, with the further relentless spread of the movement, gracefully agreed to bestow the prize last spring on the winner of the first Little Theatre Tournament.

The Little Theatre movement, in fact, has run away with itself in these United States. In a decade its original impulses have been greatly altered; its direction has swerved from the esoteric to the popular. And from this more readily comprehensible direction, the movement has gained an impetus which has carried it from coast to coast. Little Theatres in the larger cities — sixty or seventy groups within commuting distance of Times Square — where the established theatre, especially in its richer contemporary development, might have been expected to forestall such activities. Little Theatres in the smaller cities where, under pressure of motion picture competition and prohibitive railroad rates, the "road theatre" has dwindled to insignificance. Little Theatres even in the towns and villages whose acquaintance with drama never before extended beyond the ten-twenty-thirty thrillers exposed to wondering view the week the county fair made a miniature metropolis out of each court house community. Today it is a perverse municipality, a listless Main Street, which hasn't at least one Little Theatre.

The early aims which dominated the movement tended to make it aloof in nature. *Editions de luxe*. By appointment to His Majesty. *Triple Sec*. *Crême de la Crême*. Exclusive named varieties. 99 44/100% pure. None genuine without the signature. The Lit-

tle Theatre was to be an art theatre, the utter pole of
the commercial stage in financial organization, in plays
chosen, and in the manner of presenting and interpreting those plays. It was to set for itself a difficult,
impersonal and all but unattainable ideal under which
the theatre was to be as rigorously self-critical as any
of the other arts. It would subsist by endowment or,
if its independence were sufficiently guaranteed, by
subscription. It would consider only those plays
which had stood the test of the art theatres of Europe
or native works of similar worth and quality. It
would be boldly experimental, scorning conventional
and traditional manners and makeshifts of production.

The Chicago Little Theatre, under Maurice Browne,
professed many of these aims. Founded in 1912 and
housed in a nook in the Fine Arts Building seating less
than a hundred, it set out to create " a new plastic
and rhythmic drama in America." Yeats, Schnitzler,
Strindberg, Ibsen, Shaw, Wilde, W. W. Gibson and
others, chiefly from oversea, figured in its repertory.
On Gilbert Murray's translation of Euripides' " Trojan
Women," Browne bestowed his best work in rhythmic
interpretation. Women of Ilion, in the Greek chorus
rediscovered by him, dominated not only the interludes
but the entire course of the tragedy — praying lips of
the world's torn soul in the early years of the war.
For five years, Browne clung to the hope of finding
root for his theatre in Chicago, but it was doomed
from the start by a false economic basis and by pre-
maturely precious ideals.

Most of the other Little Theatres that followed

WALT WHITMAN'S "SALUT AU MONDE"

Peak of the Neighborhood Playhouse's Festival Activities, with Music by Charles T. Griffes and Settings by Esther Peck

esthetically and socially. And most of all, it has built up from the foothold of kindly curiosity a distinct and group-conscious audience whom it can trust to follow it wherever it goes.

If someone says that the Neighborhood Playhouse could and should mean more than this, it would be well to remind him that a laboratory takes on added zest and enthusiasm and creative impulse when it realizes that it has stimulating outlet. Which is to say that the little theatre down in Grand Street, whether it is aware of the fact or not, is patiently awaiting the founding of a substantial and authoritative art theatre in America along the lines of that of Moscow to which it can stand in relation of Studio Theatre and workshop.

THE LITTLE THEATRES

immediately in the trail of Browne's were similarly ambitious, similarly esoteric, similarly weak in material foundation. Each of them after a futile struggle had to give up, either yielding entirely or shifting to more popular gear. The Philadelphia Little Theatre, the Toy Theatre in Boston, the Indianapolis Little Theatre as founded by Samuel A. Eliot, Jr., followed one or the other of these courses.

Residue, then, from those early days: amateur groups like that at Hull House in Chicago, antedating Browne's venture by over a decade and hardly a Little Theatre in the strict sense, belonging rather with the Theatre in the College; and those less precious projects which established and maintained contact with their public and grew in time into our Institutional Theatres.

Just how far the Little Theatre movement of today has deviated from the esoteric aims of these pioneers is evident from a glance at any one of the bulletins on the subject issued by the New York Drama League, at any issue of *The Drama* or at the list revised and published monthly by *The Billboard*. The mere number of these groups is indicative of a certain relaxation of the ideals of the pathfinders. Stage directors and producers of the calibre at first contemplated are not numerous enough to go around. There are not enough auditoriums and stages properly equipped to make possible the realization of those ideals. Plays? Enough, if foreign sources are acceptable, to make up any number of repertories. But the apparent tendency runs either toward imitation and emulation of Broadway at its middle-best or toward the development of a Little Theatre tradition, slavishly obeyed, which is based on the widespread repetition of such pleasant but inconsequential plays as " Suppressed Desires " or " The Florist's Shop."

Whereas the original Little Theatres were little not simply because funds were scant but rather from a deliberate restriction of the auditorium for the sake of intimacy and aloofness, the Little Theatres of today are little simply because they are not yet big. The old desire for a taut, intense atmosphere like that of Reinhardt's Kammerspiele in Berlin, has yielded to a multiplicity, a vagueness, of desire, motive, dramatic theory. Little Theatres are easier to start than big ones. That's all! The new groups have popularized the old ideals. They have built up a new emphasis, a new significance, for the movement of which they are parts.

The nature of this new emphasis, the implications of this new significance, need not be wholly disconcerting or discouraging to those who originally put their faith in the Little Theatres as agencies for aiding and developing our awakening stage outside established channels. It was too much to expect that America was ready for the construction in every community of an art theatre, austerely and impersonally conducted. Nor had the founders of the first Little Theatres any right to hope that they could contain the movement they had started within circumscribed limits. At any rate, the movement, once under steam, has broken those limits and has gone its own way — as movements

ANDREIEFF'S "THE LIFE OF MAN"

As Produced by the Washington Square Players, Pioneer among the Little Theatres, in January, 1917

always do, irrespective of leaders or of original impulses — according to the natural instincts of those who have been attracted to it.

Positively considered, the Little Theatre today is a stepping-stone not so much to an art theatre as to a people's theatre, a popular theatre, a theatre in which men and women can satisfy their suppressed desires to walk and talk upon the stage. The pioneers proved how simple a thing, though at times how costly, it is to present plays outside traditional channels. By their example, they gave a new impetus to the instinctive desire to " dress up and act." They struck the shackles off the stage-struck. And the stage-struck struck back at the ideals of their benefactors. When have children and beneficiaries done less?

The result has been that many of the Little Theatres have grown up simply as more ambitious and more efficient amateur acting societies. Sometimes they have paid directors to help them satisfy their greater ambition and their desire for finer efficiency. Oftener, they are content with leaders from within their ranks who display the gifts of direction and administration. Their amateur nature is evident, when they gather at banquet or in conference, through the topics that enlist their attention: elementary problems of lighting and stage-setting, costume and make-up. These young stage directors, for the most part, are beginning at beginnings. They are eager to learn. And until they have learned fundamentals, they can not be expected to develop new and valuable ideas for the established theatre.

In effect, the impulses of those who began the Little Theatre movement have been thinned and spread out over an unexpected expanse of ground, just as Roman civilization was diluted to permeate a continent of barbarians. For the moment, just as in the Dark Ages, the finer motives may seem to have been lost. Patience and a far view, however, lend body to the hope that these motives have not been dissipated but scattered, that their sum total is not less but greater than a decade ago, and that when they have had time to work as leaven in fresh and eager soil they will emerge again to justify their apparent disappearance.

Even now, under cover, often unconsciously, these motives are contributing to the education and development not only of players and playwrights but of audiences. Stern and salutary potions administered between layers of social orange juice. Genuine talents holding to their self-appointed tasks on the town-hall platform while the merely stage-smitten fall one by one through the sieve of trial, experiment, rehearsals, that begin as play and end as hard labor. From these talents — actors, designers, directors — and from the playwrights whom failure fails to discourage, will come the backbone of our next dramatic generation, when the real stage, greatly aided by this early schooling, has had time to give them intensive training. And from these audiences, particularly from those who participate in a measure but forego a professional future, should come an enlightened and exacting clientele for our awakening theatre.

What the Little Theatre movement in this country

needs today most of all, is an efficient, responsible clearing-house, a coöperative organization, through which widely scattered groups can keep in touch with each others' work and methods of administration and through which interesting plays developed or discovered by one group can be passed on to a wider audience and thereby add variety to the monotonous repertory which prevails at present in so many communities. Thus far, the Drama Leagues have been the heralds, the bulletin boards, the scout leaders for the movement, through their publications, banquets, conferences, Little Theatre Tournaments. To be most widely and stimulatingly effective, though, this work should be in the hands of a coöperative association of the theatres themselves.

Meanwhile, the fecundity of a rabbit hutch. A corn field on a smotheringly sultry night in August, crackling with life of its own but reckless of the field across the road. There is nothing quite so like the Little Theatre movement in America as the spontaneous outburst of peasant theatres in Russia after the Revolution — hundreds of them, scattered throughout the span of the old empire, inspired vaguely by stories from the capitals but dependent chiefly on their own devices. Vitality there. Vitality here. Rude at times, imitative often, banal on occasion. But the raw material of renaissance.

Chapter X

THE THEATRE IN THE COLLEGE

Out beyond the suburbs of the producer in his institutional guise is the Theatre in the College and University, the School of the Theatre wherever it is — on secluded campus, aloft of the city's roar; adjunct to seat of learning, struggling " on its own," studio and workshop attached directly to its parent stage. Only incidentally is this theatre a producing medium, a phase of the producer as group or institution. In it, production is a means, not an end in itself — a means for instructing its students practically in action rather than by precept. But before completing the survey of our theatre from the angle of the producer as intermediary between playwright and audience, it is well to pause here; for a study of the School of the Theatre, not only in its incidental aspect but as trainer in the component arts of production, illuminates the problems and progress of our awakening stage.

A School of the Theatre. Where better than in the theatre itself? The Comédie Française: the Conservatoire. The Moscow Art Theatre: the First, Second, Third, Fourth, Operatic, Studios. But we have neither Comédie Française nor Moscow Art Theatre. Without parent, no child. Left to its own devices, our theatre has always trained its recruits like a mother trailing seven smudged and squalling children to market through the push-carts of Rivington Street. Actors, designers, producers, playwrights, dragged up rather than brought up amid the slums of Broadway. The slender, the fragile, are crushed. The fittest survive — the exceptional few hardened, polished, perfected, by the process; the rest stunted and seared.

One of the sure signs of our awakening theatre was the realization about a decade and a half ago that this process wasn't quite civilized. But what could be done? The children couldn't be left at home. The marketing had to be done. And you had to have children. At least, preservation of the race said so. Of course, there were doctrinaire boarding schools like the American Academy of Dramatic Arts and countless courses in elocution. But the theatre, like the telephone company with the graduates of Miss Frear's Finishing Seminary up the Hudson, usually refused to take their products seriously.

At this juncture the university volunteered. The college of liberal arts, shaming its perennial and professional detractors, rose to the emergency. The Theatre in the College? Heresy! Just a hundred years ago, Timothy Dwight declared at Yale: " To indulge a taste for play-going means nothing more or less than the loss of that most valuable treasure, the immortal soul." And now the colleges were proposing not merely to condone the monster but to nourish it!

For years in the more liberal colleges, for not so long in the more sedate, the students had been giving class plays. The names of Shakespeare and Sophocles mitigated the offense to Puritan tradition. In the new, active, vital rôle which the college was to play, Harvard took the lead. Not so much Harvard, either, as one man at Harvard, Professor George Pierce Baker. For Harvard gave grudging and niggardly support to his dreams, still denies them adequate realization, although for ten years their soundness has been apparent, proved.

Where Harvard — or Baker decked with Harvard's crimson hood — led, the rest followed. Like the American newspaper, the American college. " All the views that are fit to teach," with Harvard as arbiter. The old course in Shakespeare, taught as literature rather than drama from Rolfe's pedantic scholia, soon found such rivals in the curriculum as " The Drama in England from the Restoration to Modern Times," " The History of Greek Drama " presented in English for wider appeal, " The Forms of the Drama," " The Theory of Poetry and Drama " — all recognizing, to the extent of the intelligence of the professor in charge, the fact that plays were written by the Greeks and Shakespeare as well as by George M. Cohan for the express purpose of being performed on a stage in the presence of an audience. The metamorphosis has been so thorough, the revenge of the Greeks upon our Puritan morality is so complete, that from Athens, Ga., to Olympia, Wash., from Corinth, Miss., to Sparta, Wis., no son of a Methodist bishop can be graduated without knowledge that there is and always has been and probably always will be such a thing as a theatre.

A thorough survey of this movement — for it is a movement of typically American purpose and extent — would require a volume to itself. Almost without exception, Shakespeare today is only the starting point for dramatic reading and discussion. Increasingly, practice is added to precept on the university stage. There are almost as many Little Theatres in the colleges as there are outside them. Thus far, the movement has seldom carried the idea beyond amateur experiment — helpful to the experimenters but not immediately to the theatre at large. Thus far, we have but two dramatic departments approximating in thoroughness of organization and in concrete results the other professional schools that make up our institutions of learning — those at Harvard and at the Carnegie Institute of Technology in Pittsburgh.

To set these two apart and to examine them in some detail, is not to hold lightly the work that is being done at Yale — Phelps, Woolley, the Dramatic Association with its proud record of pioneer production often revealed to New York and other cities; at Wisconsin — Thomas H. Dickinson's *The Play-Book,* the Wisconsin Players, Zona Gale's novitiate; at the University of California — the Greek Theatre, productions therein by Margaret Anglin and others, varied practical use of it under the direction of Sam Hume and Irving Pichel; at Smith College — student energies crystallized, pointed to ambitious ends, by the energetic, inquisitive, headstrong Samuel A. Eliot, Jr., charter member of the Washington Square Players and first director of the Indianapolis Little Theatre; at the

THE THEATRE IN THE COLLEGE

Agricultural College of North Dakota — the Little Country Theatre of Alfred G. Arvold, esthetic melting pot and preceptor of the prairie's varied peoples; at Columbia — home of the annual Pulitzer Prize award, though still under the hopelessly academic shadow of Brander Matthews; at Hull House in Chicago — in courses and production under Laura Dainty Pelham, the predecessor of Harvard and Carnegie by many years; at a score of other centres just beginning to grow a radius.

Still, Harvard and Carnegie, each in its own way, are thus far without parallel — Harvard in the record of work done in the actual theatre by its graduates; Carnegie in an institutional and material equipment under one roof superior even to that of the Neighborhood Playhouse in New York.

Claiming for Harvard's honor and Professor Baker's renown all the playwrights, producers, actors, scene designers and critics who have lived in Cambridge long enough to vote, is like a political party assuming credit for seasonable weather and abundant crops. O'Neill, Ames, Hampden, Jones, Macgowan might have been head waiters, golf instructors or tree doctors — if it hadn't been for Harvard. But the chances are they would be just where they are now — in and around the theatre.

What may be asserted reasonably about Baker and Harvard-Radcliffe is that under their paternal auspices successive groups of youthful imaginations innately predisposed toward the arts of the stage and particularly toward playwriting have gathered together to receive from their mentor the disciplinary compulsion to express themselves; and from each other, mutual spur. Birds of a —

George Pierce Baker is just the man to do just this sort of a job. Naturally, for instead of falling into his post, he created it step by step. A snail's house, a snail's patience, persistence, though not a snail's pace. A clean, decisive mind — Baker's "Argumentation" antedated "Dramatic Technique" and English 47. An easy adaptability to academic processes; a refusal to be bound by them; a consequent tactical grip not only on the unreal world of the university but on the hard-boiled burghers of Broadway. For years, while Sheldon, Ballard, Kinkead, Knoblock, were writing successful plays to a more rather than less traditional formula, Baker accepted in silence the charge that he was training soldiers for review, pigs for market, rather than artists for the free pursuit of their calling. Then, last year, there was produced in course "Welcome to Our City" by Thomas Clayton Wolfe, a play as radical in form and treatment as the contemporary stage has yet acquired. And suddenly it became evident that Baker had been frowning on new forms simply to prevent their being used as mere novelty. Yankee caution, reserve, self-possession, without its bigotry.

By way of Shakespeare and the historical courses in drama expanded therefrom, Baker created his course in playwriting, English 47, informally at Radcliffe and then in 1905–06 formally there and at Harvard. Crowded at once so that difficult tests were erected as barriers, it had to wait until 1912 before the university deigned to give it the 47 Workshop in Lower Massachusetts Hall as home. Even yet, its only stage for the six productions a winter made with alumni contributions is in Agassiz Hall, Radcliffe — miniature, makeshift, mockery. Here, before an audience of 400, picked for "critical standards and helpfulness of spirit," the best plays written in course are given and judged in relentless questionnaire.

Most tangible mark of the respect in which Broadway holds Baker and his work at Harvard, notwithstanding occasional disparaging bravado, is the $500 prize first offered in 1911 by John Craig, then manager of the Castle Square Theatre, Boston, to the best play written in English 47. Snatched up by Oliver Morosco upon Craig's relinquishing of the contest, it has latterly fallen to Richard G. Herndon, who has termed it the Belmont Theatre Prize and who guarantees production of the winning play within six months. At least four of the Harvard Prize Plays, all of which are listed in Appendix III, have been among the hits of their respective seasons.

And yet, Harvard dawdles — official Harvard. Whoever controls policies and finances is ignoring one of the most unusual opportunities an American university has ever had to make vital and immediate contact with contemporary life. Baker has caught the attention of the practical theatre. With a stage, auditorium and experimental scenic and electrical workshops as elaborately and scientifically equipped as Harvard's laboratories and museums in chemistry, biology and medicine, Cambridge could be made the authoritative post-graduate retreat of all the earnest craftsmen in our theatre. Confidence in Baker combined with a full set of the theatre's tools would lure to Harvard not only promising but practicing playwrights for experiment with their maturer work; producers, designers, even actors, for experiment with their more dangerous dreams. Ames, Hopkins, O'Neill, Geddes, Peters, Woollcott, as special students, fellows in research. Craig, Appia, Reinhardt, Stanislavsky, Mei Lan Fang, Baiko, as visiting lecturers. Students as lecturers, lecturers as students. The atmosphere, the stimulus of the medieval university. The exhilaration of being on the threshold of something. The excitement of the new learning that is old but freshly rediscovered. The new learning of the eternal theatre adapted to the occasions of today, just as the new learning of the schoolmen lit the fires of the renaissance.

All this is no idle dream, chimera, but a conceivable eventuality, for the theatre in America in the last few years has absorbed, obsessed, the minds and imaginations of men and women more broadly, more generally, than any cultural or esthetic agency in our history. To realize it, however, Harvard must act and act at once. Baker is still in his creative prime. Whatever he is permitted to build into the university's academic structure would have the permanence which universities alone seem to be able to vouchsafe to us. Harvard gambles. The next Baker may rise at New Haven, Chicago, Morningside Heights.

Meanwhile, not in New Haven, Chicago or Morning-

THE THEATRE IN THE COLLEGE

side Heights, but in Pittsburgh, a similar dream is already in process of fulfilment. Carnegie Institute of Technology and the head of its dramatic department, Thomas Wood Stevens, are not so well known along Broadway and to the public which reads newspapers and magazines as Harvard and Baker. Perhaps that is because — well, Pittsburgh! Can any ——— ? Chicago is nearer New York. The most real reason, though, is that Stevens has never bothered with sandwich-men, has never desired, sought nor had publicity. Neither has Baker sought it, but then there is the megaphone of Harvard's far-flung, faithful and conversational alumni.

With half the apologists, Carnegie would be twice as well known as Harvard, for, though Stevens has not had the gift, the fancy or the fortune to father playwrights like Baker, he has had in generous measure the equipment Baker wants and has put it to workmanlike use. Carnegie's dramatic department is not a mere school of acting or elocution or a correspondence course in playwriting or an appendage to a college of scientific or liberal arts, but a full-fledged school of the theatre with a faculty, an auditorium, a stage and workshops of its own and a four years curriculum leading to the degree of Bachelor of Arts in Drama. Its ill fortune is that it is hopelessly distant from our dramatic capital. In or near New York, the mutual give-and-take between school stage and real stage might be multiplied ten-fold.

But Stevens hasn't let this handicap worry him. Rather, he has capitalized it, put it to work — for

Pittsburgh. In lieu of the travelling company which travels no more, Carnegie is Pittsburgh's theatre. On an average of seventy-five to a hundred nights a season, anyone in the steel city may see a performance, more nearly professional than amateur, of a play, classic or modern, foreign or native, comic or tragic, familiar or original, for the price of his street car fare to Schenley Park and the trouble to make his desires known in advance. In nine years, nearly 210 plays have been presented thus for a total of twelve hundred public performances, fifty of which have been new works, seen for the first time on any stage.

Pittsburgh's gain, of course, has been simply a by-product of Carnegie's prime purpose: to teach young people by thorough extensive and intensive practice as well as by precept the various component crafts of the theatre. Practice under as rigorously professional conditions as possible. Practice extensive, assuring familiarity with all the crafts, their requirements, difficulties, potentialities. Practice intensive, permitting the student in his latter two years to concentrate, specialize, in the craft for which he has shown most aptitude.

All this has happened so quietly, so unobtrusively, so unbeknown to all but prospective students who have besieged the limited roll of fifty or sixty with persistent waiting list, that it is difficult to believe the school's life dates back nearly a decade. According to a plan laid out by Stevens and the late Russell Hewlett, which was approved and ordered by President Hamerschlag, the Department of Drama of the College

MAETERLINCK'S "THE DEATH OF TINTAGILES"
As Produced by Chester Wallace at the Carnegie Institute, Pittsburgh. From a Design by David Mudgett

of Fine Arts was opened in February, 1914, with the first performance in the theatre on Shakespeare's birthday two months later. Building extension two years later gave ample room to design, construct, paint and store scenery, to cut, fit and lay by a generous wardrobe, including the gift of William Poël's priceless Elizabethan collection, to rehearse three plays at one time. No sabotage here as at Harvard, but the most perfect coöperation between executive and administration.

All this has happened so quietly because Stevens is a modest soul. A painter by training, an instructor in painting by early profession, a pageant master, collaborating with MacKaye in the St. Louis Pageant and author of the Red Cross Pageant which was given throughout America in 1917 and 1918, he has preferred rather than blazon his work at Pittsburgh to let it be its own reward, an agreeable surprise to those who come upon it by accident. To him in his busy hermitage in the theatrical woods have come not only Poël to produce Jonson's " The Poetaster " but B. Iden Payne, Hubert Osborne, Whitford Kane, Donald Robertson and John Galsworthy. From this hermitage have come Woodman Thompson, scenic designer of the Equity Theatre, and two or three score other designers, players, producers, who have modestly but with confidence born of practice entered into the manifold life our stage.

The School of the Theatre. What is its future? Disinherited by the theatre itself, awkwardly tended by private samaritans, it has been adopted by the college and university. Until we have an institutional theatre with stability, authority, tradition, the theatre itself is not likely to reclaim its school. A shiftless parent destined to see others bring up its young. Nor is the path of the private samaritan easy. Without an adequate and permanent home, without enormous endowment, a school is dependent on the missionary spirit of those who conduct it and those who counsel it.

On the college and university, therefore, seems to depend the immediate tomorrow of instruction in the stage's crafts. Collegiate organization and finances seem peculiarly adapted to the task, provided those in control have evolved beyond Puritan bigotry. Not every college will have its school of the drama. Exaggeration. Surfeit. In time, though, the rudiments of appreciation of dramatic art will be available in all of them. While in others, a chance and chosen few, the theatre will be taught in practice as thoroughly as architecture, medicine, law and economics.

Chapter XI

OUR ACTORS

The playwright and his play. The producer in any one of his many guises. And then the actor. The first act of a play is not its first act, but the tale of the producer's efforts to find players to fill its various rôles. An unwritten act, secret — unless the press agent capitalizes it — but often more complicated, interesting, than the play itself.

This primal position of the actor among the producer's collaborators is so obvious, so rational, so axiomatic through twenty-five centuries of recorded occidental drama, that it is difficult to see how it could ever have been questioned. But it has been questioned, doubted, denied. Opponents of the actor — usually misguided apologists for the scene designer — have talked a deal about the necessity of dismissing the actor from the theatre, of putting in his place the super-marionette, abstract moving and changing forms, lights, sounds. Even Duse — she who could say it without suspicion of envy if anyone could — has declared: "To save the Theatre, the Theatre must be destroyed; the actors and actresses must all die of the plague; they poison the air, they make art impossible." Indeed, the greater part of the last fifteen years of progress has been a case of two steps forward and one step back — two steps really forward and one step back toward this mysteriously engaging heresy. The designer has run away with the contemporary theatre, partly because he has been strong, partly because the actor has been weak.

When the time came about a year ago for the inevitable reaction to set in against this fallacy, it was an actor who was not weak who led the way. The Russian. The Moscow Art Theatre. If it accomplished nothing else in its first American season, Stanislavsky's company gave point, impetus, to this reaction. Here was a group playing in a foreign tongue, so foreign that even the play receded into the background, leaving the actor alone in the sun; a group scorning elaborate scenery for its own sake, getting on with an absolute minimum in a spirit which in others would have seemed bravado. Through these Russians, the actor once more regained his birthright of respect, consideration. If in America he is not yet able at once to live up to this birthright, he has at least had an object lesson, an inspiration, a spur to bestir himself, which the challenge of the designer failed to give him. His title, his name, are cleared, his head held up, his temperamental ambition encouraged.

If and when he wishes it, therefore, the actor may be once more the pacemaker of the theatre. If and when he wishes that post rather than the aimless puppet-like existence he has led the last thirty years — cast monotonously for type rôles, sealed up alive in the tomb of the long run — he must be willing to work, to think, to forego personal reward, material luxuries, gratification of his vanities and idiosyncrasies. Pacemaker and pioneer must live the life of the pioneer. No sedan chairs, cog wheel railways, Rolls-Royces. Walk! Climb! Fall down, pick up, carry on!

The new attention devoted to the actor today will do him more harm than good if he doesn't realize these facts. Few of them will. The artificiality of their life, the lingering vagabondage of their material existence, give them a near-sighted and specious view of reality. They live in a world of their own, self-sufficient, circumscribed — orchids nourished by one of the strangest and strongest of human whims. The idler, of course, is hopeless. So are the merely vainglorious. But even the earnest, when they have achieved success, fret to become their own managers, their own producers, resenting the fact that an " outsider " shares their rewards, forgetting that in our specialized life today, even the theatre is specialized, that the actor's is one of its crafts which demands concentration, and that the producer is free, potent, only when he can maintain his objectivity, perspective.

Still, the actor is not — or should not be — a mere automaton, a dumbwaiter, convict No. 6724. We see the results of this other extreme too often even today. In the stereotyped actors trained like trick dogs by the régime that succeeded the old stock companies. In the persistent type-casting that condemns a player to flex the same muscle, to make the same grimace, to drone the same tone, that first commended him to public favor. Bidden and guided and broken in spirit by greedy and stupid and unsympathetic overlords, our

OUR ACTORS 139

actors too seldom yet have the temerity to glance beyond their prompt books or at most to long vainly for personal opportunities in plays already outmoded by an onrushing art.

In between these extremes of wayward license and spiritual bondage lies the ideal ground for the actor. Freedom to create, to grow, in his art. Freedom from primitive solicitude for material things. A wage commensurate with ability, paid throughout the year. Subtle interrelationship with other players, won by years of effort together. A spur to keep fresh, to broaden, deepen, one's art by being cast for various rôles. Freshness and eagerness kept by rivalry, too, unselfish rivalry, heedful only of results, cheering one another along like the Russians!

All this, of course, means nothing less nor more than repertory, the institutional idea applied to the company if not to its management. Repertory, the permanent company, were difficult in the old days when the road counted. Today, with New York self-sufficient, with the road left stranded until it wakes to realization that it must become self-sufficient, there are no insuperable bars to repertory and the permanent company but inertia and selfishness. Inertia on the part of the manager. Selfishness on the part of the player. A panicky selfishness, partly justified but fanned to unwarranted proportions by unfortunate circumstances.

For this repertory company, seen to be so desirable, so simple, by example of the Russians, we have an embarrassment of riches, raw material, unassembled parts. Enough not for one company, but for six or eight equal, after time elapses for ripening, coalescence, to the three best in Moscow, the one in Petrograd, the four in Berlin, the two in Vienna, the three in Paris, the — well, is there even one in London?

Let us see. It is hopeless, of course, to name everyone who might serve. Homer's catalog of the ships would be no more deadly. Representatives, therefore. First, of the old guard, those who could not be expected to do anything strikingly different but whose expertness in familiar fields is invaluable. Links to tradition, these; present everywhere — Lucien Guitry in Paris, Albert Bassermann in Berlin, Hugo Thimig and Ida Roland in Vienna, Sumbatoff-Youzhin and Yermolova in Moscow. Second, of those known to more or less fame fifteen years ago, who are still capable of assimilating, adapting themselves, to new ideas. These are the Stanislavskys, who, however old, are always tolerant of youth, young themselves. And third, of the new generation on whom, here as everywhere, most depends.

Compatriots and contemporaries of the Elder Showmen, this Old Guard — William Gillette, expert in verbal thrust and parry; John Drew, bland gentleman of the world; David Warfield, past and present master of sentiment; George Arliss, inherited of England, conjurer of the saturnine and insinuating; Mrs. Leslie Carter, *grande dame* of the passions; Otis Skinner, veteran romancer, a trifle soured by fate's buffetings; E. H. Sothern, child of artifice and asset whenever the artificial is demanded, as in the quibbling Benedick in "Much Ado"; Julia Marlowe, Shakespeare's composite heroine of our generation, unless Jane Cowl decides to try to wrest from her the crown.

Chief of our Stanislavskys, of our youthful elders, is Mrs. Fiske, still restless, insurgent, stimulating, after forty years of public favor, epitome of the actor's rarest gift — the power of sustaining a personal and an impersonal rhythm simultaneously. I recall an evening when with two friends I sat in the first row while she played "Erstwhile Susan." That entire performance she gave explicitly for and at us. And yet no one else in the crowded theatre knew she was doing it. It is such powers less strictly held in check that marked the masters of the old *commedia dell'arte*. If Mrs. Fiske were twenty-seven today, instead of fifty-seven, what might she not do to lead and spur the player in relay race with playwright, producer and designer!

Less varied in genius but endowed with more potent personal charm, Maude Adams in fickle retirement withholds an influence and a leadership which would still be irresistible. The Barrymores, too, fall short of their conceivable stature and service — Ethel, by indulging ambition unwisely with remote Rose Bernd and too juvenile Juliet and by returning thence perforce to the easy rote of her great ladies; Lionel, by dalliance with the motion pictures and a stab-in-the-dark manner of picking plays; John, by over-indulgence in personal ills and whims such that no one but William Shakespeare is willing to trust a valuable dramatic property to him. All three of the Barrymores, in fact, are nervous victims of our wasteful stage, able, when the time for leadership is at hand, to lead with only partial efficiency.

After them come — well, actresses rather than actors. Henry Miller on occasion dares something as original as " Pasteur." Frank Craven plays as well as he writes but that is not so important. Holbrook Blinn paddles in the shallows of satire in " The Bad Man," hesitant whether to plunge in. George Marion endows O'Neill with sound tradition in " Anna Christie." Leo Ditrichstein frets futilely at the bonds of matinee idolatry. But for a Miller, a Craven, a Blinn, a Marion, a Ditrichstein, there are a dozen women among matured players. Jane Cowl, pulling herself up by the boot straps from thriller and the paper flowers of false sentiment into the exacting realm of Shakespeare with a Juliet surprisingly simple and sheerly beautiful. Blanche Bates, in her youth picturesque in " The Darling of the Gods " and " The Girl of the Golden West," in her maturity mistress of nimble wit, which no one has the foresight to write for her. Grace George, educated at a prodigious cost to be a comedienne for whom contemporary plays are all too dull and wooden-tongued. Frances Starr, who found " The Easiest Way " difficult to duplicate but not to revive. Margaret Anglin, ambitious for she knows not what, so that her audiences, as well as the Greeks, suffer instead of sitting spell-bound by a contemporary Lady Windermere. Doris Keane, both blessed and cursed by the perennial Cavallini. Laurette Taylor, unfortunate in her deviations from her husband's manuscripts

for half a dozen companies, any one of which under competent direction and five years mutual association might stand up to the Russians.

Consider, then. Among the women: Pauline Lord, mordant, illuminated with an inner fire, attaining her own in " Anna Christie "; Jeanne Eagels, bitter-sweet, arriving finally in " Rain " after years of wandering; Eva Le Gallienne, starkly simple and stoically earnest; Clare Eames, regal, dominant, with the psychologic power to overtop any group on any stage; Lenore Ulric, with an unplumbed native fund of passion and vitality; Carroll McComas, sensitive delineator of homely subtleties in " Miss Lulu Bett "; Helen Mencken, whirlwind of the emotions, still without worthy channel for their release; Katherine Cornell, wise interpreter of all-too-wise youth; Margaret Wycherley, mistress of the elusive borderland between smiles and tears, between instinct, reason and unreason; Emily Stevens, inheriting from her Fiskean aunt both talents and mannerisms; Elsie Ferguson, painter of prim and picturesque pathos when she takes her art seriously enough; Alice Brady, daughter of her Irish father who has yet to find rôle worthy of her power to characterize; Margalo Gilmore, roseate, ecstatic, tending to the over-sweet; Estelle Winwood, incisive, nervous, voluptuous; Helen Hayes, naïvely and southerly in earnest; Violet Heming, southerly but not so earnest; Winifred Lenihan, coy and demure; Ina Claire, graduate of the revues, with a glib and shimmering wit and charm; Gilda Varesi, example of what intelligence without emotional appeal can accomplish; Phyllis Povah, pert purveyor of the younger generation's impudence; Martha Hedman, intense, exotic; Margaret Lawrence, a quiet mouse, deft at depicting sentiment and caprice; Genevieve Tobin, wistful and wide-eyed; Ruth Chatterton, by turns ardent and vivacious; Helen Westley, vicious shrew and crusty grandmother; Madge Kennedy, expert in the sly points of farce; Marjorie Rambeau, lioness of the broader emotions; Mary Nash, tigress of the same; Lynn Fontanne, crisp caricaturist of the commonplace; Florence Eldridge, seductive interpreter of "the beautiful and the damned."

It is not so easy to characterize the newcomers among the men. A lap behind their sisters in art in the long run, most of them await a more intelligent régime to reveal their individual powers. Some of the most interesting of them have come from abroad, if that is pertinent definition: Ben-Ami, soul of his tortured race, inheritor of the Russian genius for the stage, narrower in range than his appraisers at first surmised, but awaiting the opportunity, if he does not in the meantime grow morose, to leap to peaks of tragic expression; Schildkraut, father, likewise constrained by age, training and local prejudice, to limited channels; Schildkraut, son, bad boy of the Theatre Guild, startling at the premiere of "Liliom," a poser while its run was still young, and irreverent mockery as Peer Gynt, an undoubted talent demanding the steel hand of a Reinhardt to realize its bounds; Roland Young and O. P. Heggie from England, both possessing an individual personality, droll and refreshing,

JANE COWL IN THE EXACTING REALM OF SHAKESPEARE

Rollo Peters played Romeo to her Juliet as well as Designing the Settings for the Production

and driven back thereby to their dull futility. Lucille Watson and Effie Shannon, extracting the last ounce out of the small favors vouchsafed them in a mad world. Billie Burke, forgetful if her public is not, of sound beginnings made in Pinero's "The 'Mind-the-Paint' Girl." Henrietta Crosman, emerging too fitfully and unfortunately to preserve her earlier reputation for a saucy tongue. Louise Closser Hale, tethered to elderly termagants.

But the hope of the American theatre on the score of its actors lies not so much with mature leaders who refuse to lead or lead in fitful and diverse directions, as in the younger generation, those who have forged forward since new impulses began to impinge on our stage a decade and a half ago. In these ranks, the men more nearly restore their balance with the women, though the latter still predominate in talent if not in numbers. All of them are still pliable enough to answer any challenge of a new dispensation. Many of them by force of character have snatched breadth of training out of forbidding conditions.

Consider, then, these disregarded forces of youth — youth not always in years, for some of them have come to us within the period of our survey in full-fledged maturity but with a youthful spirit, lacking which they wouldn't have taken the trouble to come. Leaves in the wind. Dancers in the dark. An armada scattered and impotent in fog. With an arbitrary limit of thirty women and thirty men, all of whom were in fact or to us mere futurities fifteen years ago, we could rig the effective nuclei of ten players each

OUR ACTORS 147

which has wider outlet with us than in Britain; Dudley Digges and Whitford Kane, opposite as the poles, the former matter-of-fact, the latter with a vein of whimsy, but both trailing the sound impulses and precepts of their cradle, the Irish Players.

But we have our own, too, blood of our blood: Rollo Peters, with a flare for romance; Dennis King, diversely gifted and tsar of his every muscle; Henry Hull, intense, florid, but desperately in earnest; Lowell Sherman, suave expert in finesse; Sidney Blackmer, handsome and much more; Charles Gilpin, the Emperor Jones, tied by his dark skin to a chance rôle now and then; Augustin Duncan, freed at last from being known as the brother of his sister not only by his skill as producer but as creator of John Ferguson and other rôles; Henry Herbert, with a penchant for the grotesque; Wallace Eddinger, richly versed in the seriocomic; Robert Ames and Tom Powers, adroit expositors of the average youth of today; Walter Hampden and Fritz Leiber, journeymen Shakespeareans; Leslie Howard; Otto Kruger; Grant Mitchell; Allan Dinehart; Alfred Lunt; Glenn Hunter; Charles Coburn; McKay Morris; Gregory Kelly; George Gaul.

Beyond all these, of course, are the clowns and dancers, the comedians and comediennes of our lighter stage. Their turn will come in Chapters XVIII and XX, " The Theatre of ' Let's Pretend! ' " and " Revue, Variety, and the Dance."

To glance back over these sixty names, familiar to few beside their owners in 1908, it may seem as if the deadly virus of " type " were already at work on their reputations. True. A few adjectives place them, define their known orbit. Ten years more like the ten years past and they would revolve for life in those orbits. But the next ten years will not be like the last ten if this younger generation among the players has its way. And it will have its way, thanks to the assistance of the same younger blood among the playwrights, the producers, the designers. A fund of undeveloped treasure here, unmatched by any continental capital. But scattered, unattached, ineffective. That it will remain thus powerless for long, considering the vitality it possesses, is unthinkable. Whether it organizes or is organized into four companies or ten or twelve is immaterial. There is enough to go round, with the addition of the elders to insure that the best fruits of the past be retained.

That this younger generation will remain thus powerless for long is unthinkable — if only one obstacle could be removed. That obstacle is not the esthetic inertia of the producers nor the lethargy of the playwrights. It is the selfishness of both the players and the producers. The ominous growth of the determination on the part of both to look upon the theatre as a trade to be regulated by the deadly class warfare of the labor unions is the most disturbing factor on our American stage. Material in nature, though with broader implications, this problem will be reserved for Chapter XXII, " The Economic Problems of Our Theatre." Until it is settled — by understanding and not by might — there can be little prospect for any of the workers in the theatre, least of all for the actor.

OUR DESIGNERS FOR THE STAGE 159

ting not like a picture but resembling rather a picture puzzle with the essential elements withheld until the meaning of the play is disclosed as a whole. Such a play in such a theatre, he believes, might consist of a few hundred scattered words and page on page of stage directions. In all this, Jones is struggling to formulate a theatre which will leave the utmost possible to the imagination of the spectator. He is interested not in carrying over an emotional reaction from the stage to the audience, but in compelling the audience subjectively to create its own emotional reactions under the stimulus of significant suggestion.

Almost contemporaneously with Jones, arrived Lee Simonson. Harvard, too. But New York in place of New England. The self-consciousness of the Hebrew instead of that of the Puritan, manifesting and relieving itself in explosion outward rather than inward. And the painter in the theatre, proud of the fact. Paint, though, was not Simonson's first deity. In college he was known as "the best writer of English Harvard had had in ten years." And so when he came to the Washington Square Players in the spring of 1915 by route of Julian's studio in Paris and sketching expeditions to Corsica and the Midi, he had no narrow, bigoted conception of the painter in the theatre. What he craved and what he has largely realized as the strongest creative asset of the Washington Square Players and the Theatre Guild, was the opportunity to apply his feeling for brilliant color, his sense of the exotic and the grotesque and his faith in scenery as static and interpretive background rather than as pure form or as plastic and dynamic accompaniment for the dramatic action.

These principles Simonson began applying to "Pierre Patelin" and "The Magical City" at the Bandbox. With greater esthetic economy and poise he has used them at the Garrick, notably in "Jane Clegg," "The Faithful," "Heartbreak House" and the last scene of "The Power of Darkness." With the growth of the non-realistic and frankly expressionistic drama he has kept pace, acquisitive but making his acquisitions his own, concerned less with theory than with practice, a step at a time. In this newer vein, he has wrought most effectively for "Liliom," breaking shrewdly from realistic to expressionistic at the death of the circus-barker; for "Back to Methuselah"; for "From Morn to Midnight"; and, outside the Guild in service to Brady, for the ant-hill scene in the Insect Comedy, "The World We Live In." Occasionally, as in "He Who Gets Slapped" and "Peer Gynt," he has let his penchant for the exotic and the grotesque run truant from the true import of the play — paradoxically enough, to the advantage of the Guild's box office — but for the most part he has lived up to his conception of scenery as background rather than foreground.

In keeping with his respect for the practical and his indifference to theory, Simonson disagrees with Jones' latter-day apathy toward intricate physical appliances for the stage. "I have no patience," he says, "with Gordon Craig's scorn of mechanism in

Chapter XII

OUR DESIGNERS FOR THE STAGE

ENTER the Stage Designer, Karl Marx of our dramatic revolution. "Workers of the theatre, unite! You have nothing to lose but your chains! You have a world to gain!" Not in the spirit the actors have taken it. Equity Shop and all that. But rather the coöperation, the self-effacement, of the Russians. Unite! Everyone! For the Theatre! And the rest shall be added unto you.

It is the ironic fate of all earnest reformers that the stage designer in his rôle of prophet should be accused of self-interest, that his o'erweening apologists should claim for him post and importance he would be the first to deny. Prodigy of his profession, summoning his fellow-craftsmen — playwrights, producers and actors — to push on to the goal he has seen of a theatre so old that it is new, he has been charged with the attempt to make scenery paramount in the art of the stage.

For a few years after he got his hand in, he did make it paramount. The designer dominant. Play and player suffocated by exquisite but obtrusive stage settings, just as relentlessly as they had been suffocated by the banal and obtrusive stage settings against which the new designer had protested. Play and player occasionally carried to specious and unmerited favor by the virtuosity of the designer. Sometimes play and player stood up to their precocious rival, answered and matched his challenge, but public curiosity had made him a god and there he was, still in the saddle. The designer dominant. And if not deliberately, maliciously, why then?

The negative reasons I have cited: playwright and player remained content with the old theatre long after the designer had thrown it overboard and had started making a new one. But there are positive reasons. The art of the theatre is largely visual. There can be no theatre without the eye. Given the eye, the other senses are luxuries. When the modern theatre lost its vitality, therefore, and when that loss became apparent in Europe about twenty-five years ago, in America about fifteen, the symptoms of illness were visual symptoms: a painfully cluttered stage, a stage without simplicity, emphasis, balance, form or suggestion. Regarded at first as the illness itself instead of mere indications of deep-seated disorder, and entrusted accordingly to the designer for correction, they were soon found to stem from something more serious. The whole structure of the theatre required rebuilding: not only its settings but its plays, its acting, its administration, its theory. But the designer had a head-start. He understood his patient. And besides, his task was easier. Painting had already cleaned house. And he could make instant use of many of the experiments tried and proved by the painter. To correct the theatre as a whole,

OUR DESIGNERS FOR THE STAGE 151

though, has required more time. It is an art unique, unified, not a composite, with laws differing from those of its component crafts. Without a parallel, it must grope its way slowly, step by step, with now one craft and now another slightly in advance.

No one regrets this adventitious notoriety more than the designer himself. There are exceptions. But not among our American designers. Although designers by training and viewpoint, they see the theatre whole and they cherish the theatre whole, beyond their particular craft in it. If they thought that the theatre would be more the theatre without scenery, they would abdicate and at once enlist in one of its other crafts.

What, then, is this precocious individual to do? As Robert Edmond Jones asked me in a moment of impatience and discouragement several years ago, " What is the future of designers of scenery who have caught the spirit of the new theatre? Must we quit for a while? Sit back and wait for the playwrights, producers and actors to catch up with us? "

That, of course, would be no solution. Either they must wait patiently for plodding comrades, or themselves learn and practice the other crafts of the theatre, particularly that of the producer. As a matter of fact, the designers have followed both channels the last few years. Waiting has been rewarded by the emergence of O'Neill and other promising playwrights, by the indication of a new spirit among some of the players, and by the increasing readiness of the producer to experiment, now that he finds that public curiosity makes it pay. In the other channel,

Jones has received more responsibility in collaboration with Hopkins, and Geddes has by himself projected an entire grandiose production of Dante which has several times just missed realization. One thing is certain: The vitality of the American designer, vouched for by Reinhardt with an enthusiasm doubly significant after his wide experience with the master designers of Central Europe, insures his continued presence as a prime factor in our awakening theatre.

Where did this American designer come from, this precocious pacemaker of our stage? Why did he come so late, a decade and more after his brothers in Europe? Who were his preceptors? How did he shake them off and become independent, self-sufficient? His arrival was undoubtedly deferred partly by the sound and thorough practice of traditional methods by Belasco in such imposing productions as those of " The Darling of the Gods " and " The Girl of the Golden West," partly by the lavish hand of the American producer in matching increasing public demand with increasingly extravagant settings of the old order long after conservative continental managers had to cry quits and admit themselves defeated.

Then, too, new movements in art permeate America slowly. Once we grasp them, we sprint and catch up, but lethargy has been our esthetic middle name until very recently. We required, therefore, the repeated rumors of Craig and the Russians and Reinhardt, the visit of the latter's " Sumurûn," the arrival of Urban, Barker, the Diagileff Ballet, to tilt our nose in the air. A pioneer of our own was the artist John W. Alexander,

arrived late at the party. But he has already caught up and is eating meat with the rest. He has matured so rapidly, in fact, that when Reinhardt came to New York to look over our theatre preparatory to entering upon active work on our stage, he picked Geddes for scenic and architectural collaborator as, in his mind, the most vital, fecund talent, the most original and arresting imagination among our native designers.

Geddes is more American than even Jones. He ran across Craig and the "new movement" long after he had copious ideas of his own about a new theatre. He "discovered" Europe with amusing naïveté only last summer and was disappointed with what he found. Born in Detroit, he turned from high school to a year of art study in Cleveland and Chicago, and then went to work. With a commercial art syndicate. Designing covers for periodicals. Editing and writing himself a magazine, "Inwhich." Making relief maps. Writing "Thunderbird" as an Indian pantomime, as a play, inducing Cadman to provide a score, building a model stage to contrive settings no one else would provide, stumbling thereby into his future profession, for Aline Barnsdall saw the model and induced him to come out to her Little Theatre in Los Angeles and design settings for her.

Unlike Jones and Simonson, Geddes has had no Hopkins or Guild for a homestead, a mother ship. He has had to shift for himself. A pugnacious disposition and an early tendency to scale his designs to burst the normal proscenium, were handicaps to easy progress and quick reward. These qualities were offset, until experience tamed them, by a fund of practical common sense and ingenuity. Indigenous. Of our native stuff and character. If Jones paints tapestries with his own hands, Geddes makes them out of oilcloth, burlap and lights. He has known how to adapt himself to conditions without losing his integrity.

"I believe," he said to me several years ago after he had made an exquisite "Erminie" for less, as he put it, than the price of the original production back in the low-cost-of-living days of 1886, "that the ideals we are striving to attain can be applied honestly and effectively with a small expenditure of money. The thing that counts is the spirit in which the work is done. If the artist lacks full means to a perfect realization of his ideals, there is no reason why he can not use the means at hand to prove in part what he is trying to accomplish. The producers and the public must be educated to accept, appreciate and understand what we are trying to do, and if we start showing them simply, they may ask us to tell them more."

If today he is not so readily in a mood to show merely the half, it is because both producers and public have asked him to tell them more and his missionary years are over.

One of Geddes' most successful compromises has been his school, an ingenious life-line through difficult days, rendezvous for dilettantes as well as earnest novices in stagecraft, enabling him with student help at a minimum of expense to construct to the

OUR DESIGNERS FOR THE STAGE 153

who gave fresh and shimmering beauty by rather complicated means to Maude Adams' " Chantecler," but his untimely death cut short his service.

When Joseph Urban came to America from Vienna over a decade ago, at the call of Henry Russell to design the scenery for the Boston Opera Company, the first enduring factor in our new stagecraft became operative. It is easy today in the presence of rich native talents to forget the service Urban performed — how he came to New York on summons from George Tyler and F. Ziegfeld, Jr., to design " The Garden of Paradise " and " The Follies of 1915," how he made something brilliant, vivid, artistic out of our oldest annual pagan revel, how he turned later to waken the somnolent Metropolitan slowly from coma. If his chief concern today is with the film, that is no reason why credit should be grudged, as it is too often, for his pioneer example to artists and producers, for his emphasis on the use of light as a plastic medium, on broken color to make flat surfaces throb with life, on the importance of form and design in interpreting the mood of a play, on the necessity of conceiving the entire production as a unity.

First on the scene of our native designers was Robert Edmond Jones. Whether he has been, is or will continue to be first in importance is of no moment either to him or to his chief rivals, Norman-Bel Geddes and Lee Simonson. All three work in a spirit of coöperation and mutual respect, thus releasing all their energies into creative channels.

Jones. That's the American language. Milton, New Hampshire. Thirty-five years ago. Village violinist. The white church; rows of straight-laced communicants — bewildering the latent artist. Schoolmaster, then, as stile to Harvard. Harvard? Why? New England. Harvard. Education, inspiration, not in Cambridge but in Boston's theatre galleries. Aristotle? No, Valeska Suratt. Student, then instructor, in painting. But two dimensions were too tame. Therefore, the theatre's three. Via the Harvard Dramatic; window dressing; a "lift" to New York by Morris Gest; a year abroad chiefly at Reinhardt's Deutsches Theater in Berlin, unobserved but observant.

On his return, Jones' work really began. The Stage Society hired him to do France's "The Man Who Married a Dumb Wife," and Granville Barker had the good sense to retain him. Almost forthwith he and Arthur Hopkins discovered each other and for eight years they have been inseparable. Largely owing to this good fortune in finding a producer as collaborator who would give him steady employment, free rein to do, go, as he liked between tasks, a seat and a voice at the most reticent council table since Carlyle — Jones is still the naïve, shy, eager, flaming person he was when he first let his Van Dyke grow.

Jones is essentially an artist of the theatre — not a painter like Bakst and Roerich who carried predispositions and innocence of the stage's pulleys, props and wires to their scenic sketches. There is something unfinished about his designs and even his models

"HAMLET" ON THE STAIRS

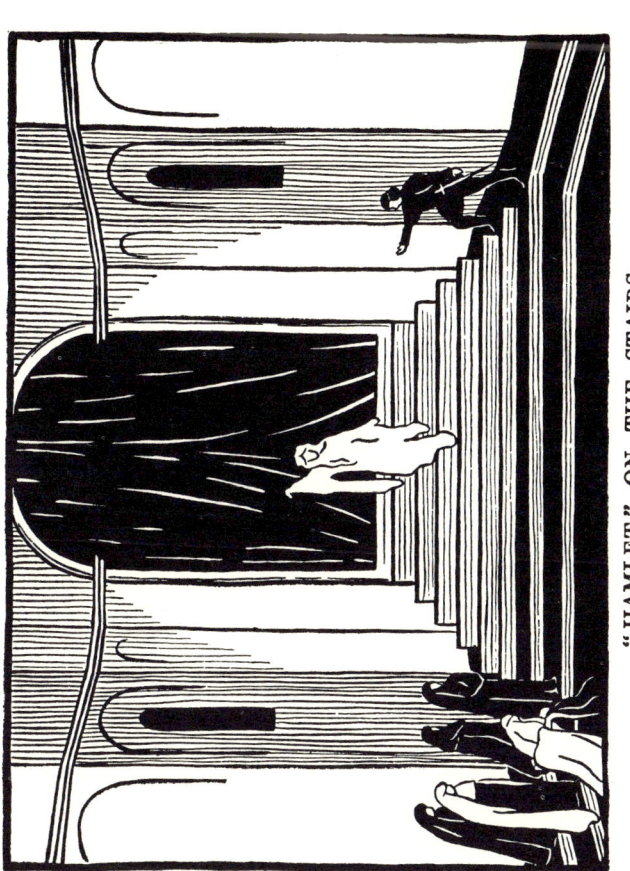

The Mad Scene of Ophelia from Arthur Hopkins' Production, with John Barrymore and Rosalind Fuller, for Which Robert Edmond Jones Designed Imposing but Rigidly Confining Setting

that worries and baffles the connoisseur of mere pictures. They are sketches in reality as well as in name — working plans to be fulfilled only in the stuff and media of the theatre — fulfilled oftener than not by his own hand as manipulator of shears, needle and brush. He wants a texture, a pattern, that exists only in museums or in his own imagination? He makes it. There is something almost ironic in the fact that he has become one of the most dangerous opponents of the old ways in the theatre. Eight years ago, beleaguered tories like Belasco retorted that the impulse toward a new theatre, arising on foreign shores, could have no significance on American stages, that its proponents were mere intruding amateurs from the other arts lugging their unwelcome and impractical theories into the theatre. Today they are compelled to face the fact that a young man with the unmistakably native cognomen of Jones, whose entire apprenticeship and labor have been wrought within the confines of the "commercial" stage, has turned out to be one of the most formidable protagonists of the despised impulses and theories. In practicing them, of course, he has had his ups and downs, but, rather disturbingly for his opponents, the ups have usually been when he has largely had his own way, the downs when in goodness of heart he has agreed for Hopkins' sake and against his better judgment to do an "Idle Inn" or to race "Romeo" against the Selwyns.

What are those impulses and theories of the new stagecraft as far as he is personally concerned?

OUR DESIGNERS FOR THE STAGE 157

There is stylization, of course, borrowed from the Continent, but turned by him to fresh uses. He is fond of knitting the various scenes in a play together by a firm but unobtrusive bond. Border designs were the keynote of the costumes of " The Birthday of the Infanta," an incisive reiteration of the Moorish heritage in Spanish art. The Tower of London loomed behind every scene in " Richard III," as it must have done in the minds of all who dreaded its power in the days of Plantagenets. A flight of steps, an arch and wall of ominous grey stone stood sentry over all the troubled scenes of " Hamlet," less successfully than the Tower in " Richard " because too rigidly confining.

Then, too, there is abstraction. More nearly his own than stylization. He is less sure here, feeling his way but experimenting courageously, persistently. Undaunted by the cat-calls, the condolences, that greeted his " Macbeth," he pulled up, caught his wind and proceeded to " The Hairy Ape." These are studies, landmarks, not only in stage designing but in dramatic theory, and their consideration belongs in Chapter XVII, " The Revolt against Realism."

For a third theory, to take as illustration only one more out of several significant aspects of his work, there is luminosity. That luminosity is distinctly of the theatre, not merely a trick of brush and paper. Recall, for eloquent instance, only the studio scene in " The Claw," the first act in water front saloon or the second in fog of " Anna Christie." In his own words, Jones aimed in the former — and arrived with telling success — to achieve "the profoundly quiet, pale, melancholy light of early winter filtering through high windows — the light seen and recorded in the poignant prints of Hiroshige and Hokusai where knots of people come out to view the first snowfall. A cool delicate touch of light like a gentle hand on a fevered brow."

"I choose light," Jones continues, "not only to bring out elements of 'character' by a slightly unfamiliar color and value just below the threshold of conscious appreciation, but also to make the players swim in a luminous, shadowless aether, the ideal poetic atmosphere. They exist, so to speak, self-luminous and radiant — important, heroic."

By use of light, therefore, Jones has made something new, more richly expressive, revealing, out of realism. He is not content with that, however. Side by side with his labors as designer for the existing stage and existing plays, he has been applying a keen and original imagination to the task of foreseeing what the theatre of the future may be like. That theatre, he thinks, may disclose a poet who expresses himself not necessarily in words but by those media which give a sense of significant form: color and light; detached, evocative words; the beginnings of gesture; masks; less of character drawing and more of the embodiment of abstract passions; characters depicted as larger than life — not über-marionettes nor supermen, but groups of men, viewed as from an airplane, forgetting themselves as individuals, with everyone lost in a common pursuit; and scenic set-

LILIOM ON THE BRIDGE

Most Effective Setting in the Theatre Guild's Production of Molnar's Tragedy of the Circus-Barker. From a Design by Lee Simonson

the theatre or with the impression which seems to prevail in this country to the effect that we can develop our art of the theatre without mechanical equipment. We pretend to be superior to mechanism and yet we are constantly suffering from the lack of it. Because of that lack, we approach all the physical problems of the theatre the long way round instead of simply and directly. The extensive and costly mechanism of many Continental stages is seldom used for ambitious realistic and pictorial effects as it was when it was installed. But the point is that it is there to be used when desirable. You never have to think of how you are going to accomplish an effect, whether it is simple or elaborate, and that is a great advantage.

" It is something more than merely getting the desire for elaborate mechanism out of your system, although that is not a point to be ignored, for as long as we do not possess it, it is a case of suppressed and troublesome desires. It is something more than that, after the analogy of the spinet and the piano. As long as we do not possess a perfected instrument, we shall call in vain for playwrights to bring to the theatre the material to be interpreted in a new manner. A few of us may discern what is possible in the theatre without mechanism but we can not communicate it to others. The mechanism of the German stages has been a stimulus to the new group of playwrights just as the bettered piano was a stimulus to Liszt and Rubinstein."

Five years Jones' and Simonson's junior, Geddes

PATTERNS OF LIGHT THROUGH MULLIONED WINDOWS
From a Setting by Norman-Bel Geddes for Winthrop Ames' Production of Clemence Dane's "Will Shakespeare"

minutest detail working models of new stages, entire theatres and grandiose productions like his proposed Dante.

From Detroit, Geddes went west, young man, to come east not much older. In Los Angeles, Dymow's "Nju" for the first time in America, Zoë Akins' "Papa" for the first time anywhere. Yeats. Schnitzler. D. H. Lawrence. Then at a gesture from the discerning Otto H. Kahn, he was summoned to court at the Metropolitan to mount the hopeless "Shanewis." Thereafter in quick succession came a round of hack jobs for Brady, decoration of the Century Roof under Gest's first tenure, more work for the Metropolitan, for himself in collaboration with Jones through a Milwaukee summer, 1918, for the Chicago Opera. Through doldrums, "Erminie" and his school, Geddes carried on until, within the last two years, he has been able to pick and choose his tasks.

With all this work behind him at thirty, Geddes' major projects remain unrealized. Not unborn, for he has worked them out to the most infinitesimal minutiæ — "Pelleas and Melisande" in mystic gauzes alive with light; "King Lear" in archaic simplicity; Dante in, on, around and above a vast bowl of steps, varied miraculously by the play of light; a whole series of theatres and stages, each numbered like a composer's opus. Theory bothers him very little. So does his future, the future of the theatre. That portion of the future he sees, he at once executes in model and blue print. Neither can theory synthesize, define him, unless it be the theory of the grandiose, the overwhelming. And that leaves out many of his exquisite miniatures. His first opportunity to carry into fact his taste for that which awes, astounds, will come this winter in association with Reinhardt on " The Miracle." Here will come into play his gifts in architecture, in the devising of a stupendous mise-en-scène, in lighting, in the designing of costumes that live, in providing formal and atmospheric setting for episodes realistic and unrealistic — all the facets of a talent whose future can no more be predicted than the day after tomorrow of radio-energy.

After Urban, preceptor, and these three young native patriarchs, we have an imposing second string of stage designers: Herman Rosse, from The Hague; Willy Pogany, from Vienna; Boris Anisfeld, from Petrograd; Rollo Peters, sensitive to the emotional value of line and color; Ernest de Weerth, known best thus far through Margaret Anglin's " The Trial of Joan of Arc " and chosen by Reinhardt as his personal assistant; C. Raymond Johnson, who caught the spirit of symbolic and rhythmic form in setting and lighting for Maurice Browne at the Chicago Little Theatre and then perversely abandoned the stage for the easel; James Reynolds, daring manipulator of color and curve for the revues; Robert McQuinn, who failed to heed the warning of his " Watch Your Step " and dropped into oblivion; J. Woodman Thompson, designer to the Equity Players; Ernest Gros, faithful satellite to Belasco; Watson Barratt, handy man to the Shuberts; W. T. Benda, who naïvely woke the mask to new life; Tony Sarg, happy with his marionettes; Warren Dahler and Esther Peck, protégés of the Neighborhood Playhouse; Cleon Throckmorton, collaborator with Jones on "The Hairy Ape" at the Provincetown Playhouse; John Wenger, Robert Locker, Livingston Platt and Claude Bragdon.

There are, of course, the imitators. On occasion a few of those just named have been guilty. Usually, though, it is the old "commercial" studio that commits this clumsy flattery, unwilling like Robert Bergman to collaborate proudly, sympathetically, helpfully, in executing the designer's sketches. In nothing else is the progress of fifteen years more evident. Honey and kind words and a peering over the shoulder to catch the secret, if possible, have taken the place of deep disdain; and a certain wariness and a practiced eye are sometimes necessary to distinguish between the shrewdly imitative and the stuttering first notes of a genuine talent. After all, it is just possible that those who ape the ways of the new stage arts are unconscious and unappreciated builders toward a new day. We would hardly return to their predecessors if some calamity should rob us of the genuine talents whose shadows they are.

Chapter XIII

OUR AMERICAN PLAYHOUSE

For the play, a playhouse, a home. If not a workshop where dramatist and producer, actor and designer, can perfect their coöperative task, at least a gallery where they can exhibit to the public their completed labors. That playhouse may be in the open, enclosed; natural, man-made; simple, elaborate; chiefly an auditorium with a mere frame of a stage as on the Greek hillsides; chiefly a stage with spectators herded on the street corners, as with the pageant wagons of the medieval Mysteries; an intricate and sensitively balanced development of both, as in the best of the modern Continental theatres.

Thus far in America the homes of our plays are little more than boarding houses, ranging from the counterpart of a tenement in Broome Street to an apartment in Park Avenue. Any play may rent them if it can pay the price. Destined for any play, they are often badly suited for a particular play, especially if that play possess decisive, unusual or original character. With the exception of the Plymouth, hearth of Hopkins, the Belasco, the Guild's Garrick and some of the revue palaces, none of our playhouses is committed to an enduring policy. With the exception of the Belasco and Ames' Little Theatre, none is fully equipped to perform the functions demanded of it.

It is not lack of money that makes our playhouses inadequate for our needs. Enough fortunes have been thrown away on the theatres erected in the last fifteen years to build as many perfect playhouses, each intended, planned and accoutered for one of a rich variety of uses. Money has made the typical contemporary American playhouse at its best a standardized refuge of comfort and passive good taste for the audience, a cramped sweat shop, too often, for the actor. We have travelled far from the horseshoe, the ubiquitous post, sightless stage boxes, prosceniums crusted with stucco symbols of mythology, the garish pomposity of red plush and gilt. In New York, for instance, the Selwyn, the Apollo, the Music Box, Henry Miller's, the Booth; in Chicago, the Apollo. Money and something more made the New, now the Century, and Earl Carroll's; but that something more — a vague idealistic attempt to build for all forms of drama simultaneously and for no one in particular — doomed both efforts in advance. The extra ingredient besides money in the case of the Neighborhood Playhouse and the Beechwood Theatre at Scarborough was more specific, less pretentious, with greater success resulting; but inaccessible location, though hindering their community service not at all, seriously reduces their general efficiency.

What our builders of playhouses in America need is vision to see what the oncoming drama is going to be like, and to erect for it varied but specialized homes in which it will not only have elbow room to do as it likes, but tantalizing stimulus to further development.

THE CENTURY THEATRE FROM THE PARK

Imposing Façade of the Structure Idealistically Built as the New Theatre for All Forms of Drama Simultaneously and For No One in Particular

Many kinds of homes for many kinds of drama: Simple, severe, intimate homes for the inevitably continuing realistic drama. Gay cottages for the light, the frivolous, the fantastic, with stage extending like a platform into the audience to heighten the sense of contact, participation, on the part of the spectator. Tall church-like structures for the plastic drama of rhythm and ritual. Mansions of steel and concrete for the drama of masses, of crowds as characters. Outdoor arbors for lyric evenings. Broad sweep of hillside, water and vista for the pageant, the expression of the civic soul. And all equipped with the essential — but only the essential — mechanism and especially the lighting facilities to make them fully eloquent.

For this task we are short-handed not only in managers, boards of directors, with vision to command and advertise for bids, but even more in architects to take a hint, fulfil the command and improve on it. We have no Max Littmann, no Henry Van de Velde. We have few practicing architects who faintly suspect that the art of the theatre has moved a step since 1900. The Architectural League opens up the walls of its exhibitions to the new stage designers without dreaming that the problem of the theatre concerns their craft as well and that by entering the theatre more than casually they could materially advance its solution.

The structural solution of the new theatre, therefore, devolves upon the designers themselves, upon the theorists. "Good!" say the tories, "maybe that will keep them out of mischief for a while!" But

OUR AMERICAN PLAYHOUSE 173

it won't. For they thrive on problems, solutions. The fecundity of revolutions is miraculous. Geddes, Rosse, Simonson, Sheldon Cheney, Kenneth Macgowan, Irving Pichel. To these, our theatre is beholden for stating the theatre's architectural quest, for charting unprofessionally but provocatively diverse solutions.

Statement of the quest is nowhere clearer, more suggestive, than in the words of Herman Rosse, Dutch by birth, architect by training, internationalist by experience, stage designer by desire, until recently head of the department of design at the Chicago Art Institute by profession:

" We ought not to borrow all our working traditions from one or two types of stage only, but we should build on wider foundations.

" As the engineer gathers a tradition of working principles in construction, so in the same way we ought to analyze the real underlying constructional principles of the theatre.

" We ought not to take for granted that the modern city theatre is the only basis on which to start work. For all we know the circular theatre is better. For all we know it would be safer for us to start from the methods of the European circus, with its elevated stages, its circular transparent scenery, its stylistic accessories, its visible stagehands. Some theatrical methods carry with them the creative efforts of generations. Some may be valuable. We should always be looking for those working rules which are dictated by necessity of construction.

" Just as the Western antique stages have been

mostly studied from an archaeological point of view, so have those of Japan, China, Java, and other foreign countries been studied only from an ethnographical standpoint. What is needed now is a close analysis of the valuable working principles which they involve. It matters little in which particular way a principle of stage production is applied; it is the principle as type that is of value. The Oriental theatre no doubt offers principles which carry in them suggestions for improvements in our Occidental theatre. . . .

"We ought to question the very shape of stage and auditorium. To expect a new art of the theatre from a change of only one or two of the elements constituting the theatre is futile."

For statement of the particular problem of location and mechanism, Simonson is eloquent:

"For the purposes of our American theatre, it seems to me that the stage of two levels has most significance. Our high ground-rental prevents spreading out. But there is nothing but the blasting of the rock underneath our stages — a problem which has never halted the builders of our skyscrapers — to stand in the way of extending our working space downward into the cellar. From what I have seen in Europe, I summon the American theatre into the cellar. Every advantage seems to point in that direction. We are working against gravity by lifting all our sets today. Why not enlist gravity to work for us instead of against us? By lowering a set into the cellar where it can be replaced through the devices of the sliding stage with the next set, we would not only be enabled to shift our scenes more rapidly and build them more substantially (for they would not have to be taken apart), but we would release the space overhead for free use of our lighting mechanism."

Geddes, however, is the first to command the incredulous eye and respect of practicing architects for his revolutionary, soundly practical and minutely detailed projects. There is a whole series of them. Theatre No. 6 broke into *The Architectural Record* a year ago under the elucidating pen of Claude Bragdon, a structure seating 866 people designed for a plot a hundred feet square, with stage in an angle, instead of at one side, under the same great dome as the auditorium and no curtain to intervene; with seats arranged in quarter circle, all commanding a perfect view of the stage and a strange intimacy with it and each tier an aisle; and with a stage on two levels, moving by hydraulic power to the basement where new scenes can be substituted on platforms in twelve seconds time. An adaptation of this project whereby the scenes for an entire season's repertory can be set and left standing is under consideration for the Theatre Guild's Guild Theatre.

Another square theatre, project No. 14, worked out in Geddes' characteristic detail, seizes the motive of the boxing ring, stylizes and exalts it by the use of steps rising all round to a platform thirty feet in diameter, with an audience of 672 entirely surrounding the stage. Still another project, likely to reach life this winter, is a narrow transverse stage bisecting a huge auditorium like an armory, with half the audience facing each side of it and the dramatic action proceeding two-dimensionally in view from either end of the hall.

And then, of course, Geddes' reconstruction of the Century Theatre, auditorium as well as stage, for "The Miracle" under Reinhardt amounts to the designing and erection of a new playhouse — New York's most banal because most pretentious theatrical palace made over into a Gothic cathedral, more genuinely Gothic than any of her actual churches. After examining the artist's blue prints in Salzburg last summer, Reinhardt wrote to Gest: "I must say that the whole prodigious work represents the most tremendous thing ever done anywhere, up to this time, for the theatre. I am overwhelmed and inspired to the highest degree . . . I am convinced that all connoisseurs of the theatre will make pilgrimages to study this *chef d'oeuvre* of the contemporary stage."

Of course, at every step of this revolution in our American playhouse, the pioneers will have to encounter and wear down or circumvent not only managerial and critical and public lethargy and suspicion but the grotesque red tape of the building regulations. All this, however, will only prove the mettle of revolt, test its convictions, fortify its foundations, hold it back from too hasty growth, assure its future.

Chapter XIV

OUR CRITICS OF THE THEATRE

It is time for a new style in criticism, a style more fluid, sensitive, appropriate to its subject. Not a new theory. Theories in criticism are all very well to give order and point from diverse angles to discussion of drama as well as of literature and the other arts. They are the charted channels retracing the artist's route back from the port of execution to the port of conception. Rocks in this sea, shallows, whirlpools. But many channels. Historic, biographical, moral, social, psychological, impressionistic.

The trouble is not the lack of variety among the channels but the monotony with which each pilot plies his chosen course day after day. The same course, the same speed, the same gestures in tacking and wearing. Rote, livery, abracadabra. No matter what his cargo — light as cork or heavy as coal, common as cotton or choice as Chippendale — he treats it all alike.

How often does the fresh output of dramatist, producer, scene designer, actor, receive varying treatment, changing style? Very seldom. One critic establishes a reputation for philosophic analysis and, faithful to his repute, he bestows the same ponderous and important verdict on the latest edition of the Ziegfeld "Follies" as he does on a provocative revival of "Rosmersholm" or on the disturbing implications of

O'Neill's " The Hairy Ape," thereby reading mysterious intents and pretences into what is simply the lavish indulgence of a modern Sybarite. Another who is convinced he holds his clientele by his less or more witty sallies, finds sharp tongues in trees, jokes in the running brooks, satires in stones and folly in everything.

The question reverts to the critical process, ably dissected over twelve years ago by Arthur Bingham Walkley in his critique on Spingarn's " The New Criticism " in the light of Croce's philosophy of esthetics. The work of esthetic creation, Walkley points out in paraphrasing Croce, proceeds by the following steps: A) impressions; B) expression or spiritual esthetic synthesis; C) hedonistic accompaniment or pleasure of the beautiful (esthetic pleasure); D) translation of the esthetic fact into physical phenomena (sounds, tones, movements, combinations of lines and colors, etc.); E) the " Work of Art." The critical process, the process of esthetic judgment, is simply the reverse of this: E) the physical stimulus (the " Work of Art"); D–B) perceptions of physical facts (sounds, tones, mimic, combinations of lines and colors, etc.) which form together the esthetic synthesis, already produced; C) the hedonistic accompaniment, which is also reproduced. " Thus," says Walkley, " what we call works of art are nothing but physical stimulants of reproduction, the means by which the spectator is enabled to place himself at the artist's point of view, to become for the moment one with the artist. . . . Criticism is the evaluation of C."

The whole course of criticism, therefore, is postu-

suprematism of today, the most incautious and self-sufficient connoisseur often has to ask someone behind his hand what it's all about, for fear he'll miss something perfectly simple.

Today, therefore, a somewhat stunned and startled public admits the need, next to a group of thoroughly equipped artists, of a body of equally equipped critics. In addition to artists, of course, an audience. But the most obvious way to make sure of that audience, is to have a corps of dependable scouts, chart-makers, interpreters, who will scrutinize the experiments of the artists, find out with open mind and broad sympathy what they are trying to do, judge strictly but without rancor the success of the attempt and finally convey to the public this entire process of appraisal in terms both intelligible and interesting. Such a corps of critics could serve the public by explaining each new step the artists take, simultaneously or even sometimes in advance of the taking, thus assuring a competent and sympathetic and intelligent hearing for the strangest and most revolutionary developments in the art of the theatre.

We have no such corps of critics in our theatre. But we have moved. In 1908 we had a fighting Jimmy Bennett on the *Chicago Record-Herald,* an inquisitive Walter Eaton, an H. T. Parker feeling his way toward world horizons. The rest, for the most part, were more jaded and tired than the tired business man for whom they wrote. The cursory daily newspapers were almost their sole channel; the bookstalls were private property, keep out! Today a dozen editors and publishers bid

182   OUR AMERICAN THEATRE

for whatever the critic has to say. And what he says is usually vitalized by that keen curiosity which characterizes our entire theatre, even if it is not yet always equipped to judge between the genuine and the spurious and often yields to the easy lure of self-conscious smartness.

New pens, young pens. Pens well-worn, spurred to new life by the vitality around them or impervious to its stimulus. The justices of our theatre. On the newspapers, the Court of Common Pleas. On the magazines, the Court of Appeals. In theatre lobby, on distant editorial desks, in managerial offices, in the motion pictures, the retired justices. Suppose we review them. The critics criticised. The court on trial. Alphabetically, if you please, gentlemen, within your jurisdiction!

New York City. Common Pleas. Night Court. Heywood Broun, brown bear of the *World*, tamed and chained to the dramatic desk by his managing editor when he would rather report prize fights, but achieving in capitivity an amazing midnight fluency colored by intensely human if not dramatically erudite reactions. John Corbin, Oxonian oracle of the *Times*, tethered like Broun to his task, but sedate, learned and plodding complement to him in all other respects. Alan Dale, crotchety clown of Hearst's *American*, retailing Broadway's idle gossip, harmlessly now when the theatre's public has something more to think about than it did fifteen years ago. Percy Hammond, personally timid but professionally temerarious thesaurus of the *Tribune* transplanted in medial forties from autocratic

lated on divining the nature of the work to be criticised and on keeping contact with it step by step until it is traced back to its origin. And how can that contact be maintained more vividly, more trenchantly than by suiting the style as well as the thought to the subject in hand?

This new, fluid, sensitive, invariably appropriate style, therefore, is not merely a matter of style. But of styles. A style made up of the alert, acute, ever-changing adjustment of manner to content — now placid and simple and direct, now deeply moved and stirred and assuming a more ponderous or a more excitable quality, now stimulated to badinage, now to the light and fanciful, but always maintaining contact in manner as well as in mood with the shifting subject.

I would have the style of criticism, therefore, as eloquent as the verdict it expresses. Ideas and concepts illuminated and made clear and emphatic or purposely kept uncertain and aloof by their outer and immediately visible wrappings.

What if this means a parallel in criticism with the various attempts, most of them vain, in literature and the other arts to enrich form itself with significance, regardless of content? What if we reap from it thwarted abstractions like the Jones-Hopkins " Macbeth " or criticisms in the vein of Gertrude Stein? We can afford much that is inept, inchoate, inarticulate, for the sake of stirring criticism once more into a sensitive, vividly interpretative life.

It may seem a little premature to ask for such a sensitive, congruous, pat expression of critical verdicts when our verdicts themselves are as sophomoric, careless, uninformed as they often are. But for all their immaturity, possibly just because of it, our critics are not petrified, impermeable, blasé, except for purposes of sportive pose. And possibly if they can be persuaded to learn to ply a pertinent style at the same time they are learning to arrive at an illuminating judgment, their maturer service will be the richer. The touch system. Languages, manners, voice control, acquired in early youth.

Every American who has ever entered a playhouse feels competent to pass judgment on the traffic of its stage, to record in all seriousness the results of his soul's adventures among masterpieces. We are all critics, from those of us who scorn the supreme justices of esthetics and gloat in our knowledge of what we like though we don't know anything about art, to those of us who check up our verdict on the sly with that of the established courts.

That is, we were serenely sure of ourselves until the other day when something happened in the arts, and in the theatre in particular, which we're not so sure we comprehend. With the traditional art and letters and drama it was easy to appear wise. All we had to do was to like or dislike what the artist had done and sneak behind the defense of unaccountability in tastes. There was never any question of whether we understood the artist and his works. With the growth of numerous modern tendencies, from the once-suspicious impressionism and the still-unwelcome cubism to the expressionism, the vorticism and the

loneliness in Chicago, but finally taking root in gregarious Gotham, knowing the theatre better than the drama and its people and passwords better than either. Burns Mantle, mentor to the stenographers of the metropolis through the *Daily News*, indulging the ambitions he has preserved from early Chicago days in a well-edited year-book of the theatre. Alexander Woollcott, Sentimental Tommy of the Court, a good actor gone wrong but not so wrong but that the *Times* threw out Shubert advertising a year for his sake and prized his un-Timesly wit until Munsey stole him for the *Herald*.

New York City. Common Pleas. Day Court. James Craig, novice on the *Mail*, open-minded, on his way. Charles Darnton, deliberate and concise chronicler of the *Evening World*. James Metcalf, war horse of *Life's* feud with the Syndicate, reinstated to service by the *Wall Street Journal*. Arthur Pollock, shrewd and penetrating theatre-taster of the *Brooklyn Eagle*, scanning Manhattan at times with a truer perspective than its natives. Stephen Rathbun, Playgoer of the *Sun and Globe*, ready to think the best of everything in the best of possible worlds. J. Ranken Towse, tenacious veteran of the *Evening Post*, living obstinately in his past. Robert G. Welsh, patient paragrapher of the *Evening Telegram*, who husbands his rare sense and nonsense for his friends rather than waste them on readers of want ads.

Common Pleas. Outside New York. Sheppard Butler, courageously risking a race in Hammond's shoes on the *Chicago Tribune*. Charles Collins, canny professor of the *Chicago Evening Post.* Amy Leslie, amazon of extravagant and ecstatic phrase on the *Chicago Daily News.* O. L. Hall, "Doc" of the *Chicago Journal,* learned and perspicacious. H. T. Parker, journalistic god-father of the new stage arts, patron and publicist of the theatre of the world through the pages — yes, pages, not columns — of the *Boston Transcript.* Ashton Stevens, Green Room sheik of the *Chicago Herald and Examiner,* gay, lovable, and eternally youthful *raconteur* of the theatre's contemporary memoirs. And a dozen others patiently writing their way to recognition in Cleveland, Philadelphia, Baltimore, San Francisco,—

The Court of Appeals, then, practically all of them appointed within, not the last fifteen years, but the last eight, five, three. On the weeklies, the monthlies, the quarterlies. Permanent appointments. Piece work, free lance. Robert C. Benchley, Puck of *Life,* cherub of the Algonquin's Vicious Circle, refined essence of America's unrefined humor. Sheldon Cheney, free lance champion of realism's opponents and founder of the *Theatre Arts Magazine,* unofficial guide to an insurgent stage. Walter Prichard Eaton, long ago promoted by a still unregenerate daily press to the more leisurely bench of appeals. Ludwig Lewisohn, the *Nation's* inborn and often prejudiced protagonist of dramatic rather than theatric revolt, unwillingly trailing his despised academic atmosphere behind him, but writing far more cogently withal than less handicapped justices. Kenneth Macgowan, of the once-upon-a-time *Globe,* forced fortunately by its de-

OUR CRITICS OF THE THEATRE 185

mise to the higher court where he already held a *Vogue's* gallery seat, extensive rather than intensive, swayed by enthusiasms, the invaluable exhorter, evangelist, of the new movement, its Billy Sunday, Pussyfoot Johnson. George Jean Nathan, most brilliant, provocative, caustic, of our critics, sublimation of the intellect warped to a poser's whims, safely caviar to the general on the *Smart Set*. Robert Allerton Parker, lucid, sagacious and sensitive stranger in the *Independent's* A B C pages. Gilbert Seldes, mental pantaloon of the precious *Dial*. Stark Young, the *New Republic's* esoteric analyst of the theatre's philosophic fringes and fundamentals.

A word, then, in conclusion, for criticism's lost sheep. Lost, strayed or stolen. Kenesaw Mountain Landises of the court. The list is long and the losses widely variable, but I challenge these as penance to write at least one article a year for the magazines from the vantage ground of new professions about the theatre they once loved: James O'Donnell Bennett, war casualty of Chicago; Ralph Block, Clayton Hamilton and Louis Sherwin, deserters to the films; Francis Hackett, whose trenchant Irish pen was averted by Ireland's woe; Frederic Hatton, who varies playwriting often enough to pay the penance; Lawrence Reamer, hermit in the peace of the *Herald's* editorial rooms; Adolph Klauber, invisible adviser to the Selwyns; and Hiram K. Moderwell and Arthur Ruhl, who find desperate Europe a more engrossing drama.

Ten years ago, even three years, the temptation to lecture these justices on their shortcomings at a safe distance was strong. Today, there is in them such a pace of growth, such a spirit of inquiry, of where-do-we-go-from-here, that the chief warning, after that of a pertinent style, should be to remember Clive Bell's argument that " a critic no more exists for artists than a paleontologist does for the Dinosaurs on whose fossils he expatiates, and that, though artists happen to create those exciting objects which are the matter of a critic's discourse, that discourse is all for the benefit of the critic's readers." The time has passed for worry about insularity. A few pioneers have shamed the rest into travel, study or silence. The time has passed for worry about the hasty judgment of newspaper criticism. The open door of the periodical has solved that problem, and hardly a justice of Common Pleas who doesn't sit *pro tempore* as well in the higher court. The time has passed for worry about whether the critic must be interesting under all conditions. He can hardly help it when his subject is a theatre as interesting, as vital, as ours today.

Chapter XV

OUR THEATRE AUDIENCE

In our house that Jack built, the play has reached the audience. The critics have given it seven days, ninety, indeterminate sentence. But the court of last resort, the ultimate critic of the theatre, is the audience. No one in the theatre can long forget the audience or the audience will forget him, and then there will be no theatre. But the audience is coy about being remembered. It prefers to make its own discoveries, resents remembrance too apparent, paternal.

The potential audience for an adult theatre, even for an art theatre, exists today in America in greater numbers than in the days of Booth before its compact group was dispersed and driven into virtual exile by the commercialization of our stage. But that audience is disorganized and lost among the millions who have swarmed into the playhouse for the first time in their lives under the lure of the motion pictures, the musical comedy and the bedroom farce, diluting the general average of intelligence and lowering the standard of demand. The coefficient of our actual contrasted with our potential audience, therefore, is low, but there are unmistakable signs of recovery.

In New York, at any rate, the childish taboos of our awkward age are disappearing. No longer is the star the sole or even a sure guaranty of financial success. There must be a play, and if there is, there need be nothing but its title in electric lights. Hopkins spelled O'Neill's name in incandescents over the Plymouth for " The Hairy Ape." The Russians may sit patiently through " Humoresque " for the boon of Laurette Taylor. But we are less tolerant, more exacting, even if inferior as connoisseurs of sheer acting. Going, too, is the bugaboo of tragedy. " Beyond the Horizon," " Diff'rent," " Ambush." The happy ending is not only not demanded, like the cake of Pears' on the bathroom floor, but it is even under suspicion. Misreading O'Neill's meaning, many complained that he had warped the conclusion of " Anna Christie " to make a marriage-broker's holiday. As for the new, the original, the unconventional, there is today a premium on it instead of the old-time penalty. And, thanks largely to the example of the Moscow Art Theatre, repertory is nearer than ever before, retarded not by public prejudice but by purely mechanical considerations.

The audience outside New York is tardier. But it has had scant chance to grow. For a time, ten or a dozen years ago, it seemed to be more alert, discriminating, exacting, than its city brothers. At least it knew what it didn't wish, and under its boycott the good old road days of the atrocious second company began to fade. Efforts were made at replacement, at fostering positive rather than negative good taste. But before anything substantial could be accomplished, nature — economic nature — put an end to travelling companies good and bad. At the moment, the only solution seems to be for the road to make its own theatres, which, as we have seen in discussing the Little Theatres, it is proceeding to do at a phenomenal gait. And in making its own theatres, it will incidentally and automatically make its own audiences. Meanwhile, the audience in the city unfolds, expands, with an expanding theatre. It is proper that leadership should repose there, for the modern theatre is a sophisticated art. And sprinkled through these audiences in the metropolis are the visitors of a continent, visitors who will return home with surer taste and broadened horizons to apply to their local stage.

" The theatre is irresistible," said Matthew Arnold. " Organize the theatre! " Klaw and Erlanger, the Shuberts, the Producing Managers' Association, have seen to its economic organization. The Actors' Equity Association has taken care of its professional organization. Both have over-organized, for they have organized for themselves, not for the sake of the theatre. Thus far, however, the audience has failed to organize on any effective scale. There are obstacles. Audiences resent being organized by an outsider; they are dilatory about performing the task themselves. Spoiled children who must burn their hands before they recognize fire. Tenement dwellers outraged by the well-meant interference of superior social workers.

It has been this suspicion of paternalism that has balked the various Drama Leagues and Societies. Organized in 1910 in Evanston, Illinois, the Drama League of America has spread until it has centres from coast to coast. Proposing to hold up the hands of the best in bulletins issued by its playgoing committees, the League found itself thwarted by slow growth and cramped resources after a certain point had been reached, by reversion here and there to purely social ends with the visiting players lionized at luncheon rather than patronized in the theatre, by the gradual disappearance of any kind of a theatre in most of the centres. Besides, why should Drama League dicta be taken seriously when the New York and National branches could not compose their administrative differences for the larger sake of the theatre? Today in New York there is no longer serious need for organizing audiences. And outside, the League will have to organize theatres before it bothers about audiences.

More successful in the explicit organization of the audience from the outside has been the expedient of subscription. Subscription not only indirectly endows the theatre but makes class-conscious playgoers — an organized audience. *Our* theatre! Haven't you heard about it? You must come over! The Provincetown Players thrived on this course from birth. So has the Theatre Guild. The Neighborhood Playhouse, too, has adopted it, and the Equity Theatre. The continued success of subscription, the permanence of this organized audience, are postulated on continued delivery of the goods, but that in turn is reasonably insured by the back-log of the subscription fund. No small secret of the success of this plan is the audience's conviction of independence. They subscribed of their own free will. Nobody is telling them where to go!

Opposed to this efficacious mode of organizing an

audience unawares, the measures the managers themselves have devised have been singularly short-sighted, infertile. Theatre advertising is the cheapest — and most expensive — our journals carry. Only two or three producers have learned anything since Barnum. And few really know their Barnum. That vaster field of the regular columns of newspaper and magazine, inestimably more potent because indirect, lacking the taint of self-interest and backed by the judgment of the editor, has scarcely been touched. This is the domain of the press agent, a legitimate profession which has fallen into disrepute through the ruses of shade and chicane it has employed. In crowding our less principled and wary journals with false and sensational tales, the press agent does more harm to the theatre than all the honest and able critics can repair in twice the time. Good taste offended, public confidence betrayed, the sand bags of a champion heaped on a two-year-old, a rusty can tied to Fido's tail.

But the use of the public prints for the intelligent and interesting discussion of the theatre's manifold topics is wholly justified. Who is O'Neill? How does he work? Who are his masters? What is his theory of the theatre? What is the theatrical life of Prague out of which the brothers Capek grew? What is Geraldy's personal philosophy of love, marriage, the family? What are the expressionists trying to do? And why? Answers from Kaiser, Toller, Rice, Lawson. What was the reception accorded " The Beggar's Opera " when it was first produced? Did Ibsen ever mean " Peer Gynt " to be played? How would Shakespeare be likely to stage " The Merchant of Venice," " Romeo and Juliet," " Hamlet," if he were alive today? Or to write them?

All these are legitimate questions, each within the range of at least a dozen editors. Public curiosity craves, demands, answers to them. The theatre thrives on discussion. So does the press. The latter with few exceptions is eagerly hospitable to this kind of informative publicity. But most of the managers thus far have failed to take the cue, accepting what the daily and periodical press in its amazing alertness does on its own account in this field, but seldom appreciating the service thus performed.

Play insurance, I like to call this use of the highways of the Fourth Estate to inform the public in the ways of the current theatre. Backgrounds, interpretation of motives, are beyond the range of critics engrossed in the play of tonight. And yet, especially in the case of strange and revolutionary ventures, it is vitally important to an ambitious theatre and an openminded public that these aspects of the new project be revealed in advance, for after the premiere, in view of the ponderous pace of our leading magazines from copy desk to news stand since the printers' strike of 1919, it may be too late.

Our American theatre of the last fifteen years is a graveyard of failures that might have paid the experimenter at least his stake even if they had not become hits, provided those projects had been thus brought to discriminating attention. Insured. The insurance of an intelligent, well-planned publicity campaign might have made the Hopkins-Jones "Macbeth" something more than a baffling shot in the dark at a new theatrical technique. It wouldn't have corrected the production's faults, though I'm not so sure that such exacting self-inquiry as the campaign would have necessitated might not have mitigated many of them. But it would have precluded that ghastly atmosphere of perplexity at the premiere which robbed the experiment of its reasonable rewards. Such insurance would have kept "The World We Live In" on Broadway for a year, Geraldy's "To Love" for at least half that time. Conceived and planned almost a year in advance and placed in operation in June prior to the premiere in January, such a campaign insured public acquaintance and curiosity concerning the Moscow Art Theatre sufficient to hold the Russians a total of 177 performances before a public that understood no single word uttered on the stage. Through the magazines, all the magazines. Through the newspapers, all departments of the newspapers. Through books, pamphlets, lectures on platform and over the radio. Through translations of the plays.

For a mature and efficient theatre, our American audience must be organized. It can not be coerced, no matter how benevolently, into organization. It prefers personal experiment and explorations. But it can be lured, persuaded into fascinating excursions, thinking and thinking rightly that it is making its own choice, by the methods which the Guild and Gest have had the shrewdness to conceive and apply.

Chapter XVI

REALISM ON OUR STAGE

The test of a stage really awake, mature, is its variety of theories of the theatre, the clarity with which they are understood and the rivalry which accompanies their practice. By this test, our American theatre is still wanting. A gay, charming, precocious youth, with an eager and beguiling personality, raising hopes for a brilliant future until the damaging secret escapes the bag that he has chosen no profession, has no preference, isn't particularly worried about it. But he will choose in due time; he has too much vitality to avoid choice. And if he hits upon the manufacture of furnaces for vocation and the collecting of Dickens first editions for avocation, the range of his interest would be no wider than the likely lot of our stage when it has had time to think and work through to clear-cut theories of theatric esthetics.

Our theories of the theatre. In so far as they are few, vague and rudimentary through lack of time to develop them, we are fortunate. Theories annexed, commandeered, in full-fledged form are domineering servants. An ill-fitting suit of ready-made clothes. Spectacles bought from a peddler in Second Avenue. Theories before practice are carts before horses. First the blade of experiment, then the ear of theory. Theories, if they are to be something more than pretentious and confusing toys, must be the statements of the ways things are done, formulated after those ways have been discovered, cultivated and approved by use.

To the reverse of this logical process is largely due the maze of hifalutin phrases with which contemporary discussion of a new theatre is beset. Careless thinking has hidden behind a pseudo-philosophical terminology. And even those who know their esthetics as a pilot the routes of the harbor, who are impatient to await the results of constructive stumbling and who hope fondly to spur progress by exhortation, have taken no pains to describe their intentions in clear and unmistakable language. We have heard successively of representation and presentation, of objectivity and subjectivity, of realism and symbolism and impressionism and expressionism and abstraction, until we might as well be gazing on an Egyptian hieroglyph, an Alaskan totem pole or a Japanese ideograph.

Roughly, the parties to the controversy have been tradition, on the one hand; hydra-headed revolution, on the other. Realism, the attempt to imitate and copy life, vs. numerous mutually conflicting opponents. Let us examine the most familiar first.

We have never been wholly without a conscious theory of the theatre in America, but almost so. The theory of the pioneers of our stage — of Booth, the elder MacKaye, Boucicault, Palmer and Daly — was largely an instinctive affair, the continuation of a tradition arising on the European continent and reaching its full flower in the achievements of Irving in London, of the Comédie Française in Paris and of Prince Sumbatoff and the Small State Theatre in Moscow. The theatre was the theatre, and that was all there was to it. You took a story, put it on the stage, and made it as convincing and effective as the means you had at hand would permit — gas light, painted canvas and the actor. To the extent that any theory was deliberately pursued, it was the theory of realism, of creating the illusion of life on the stage. If a considerable share of an elder and artificial technique remained to rob the result of perfect illusion, there was no one to gainsay, correct or disentangle the hybrid. At least, there was no one until Belasco arrived to rouse this instinctive realism into consciousness and self-questioning. Others followed his lead, whether they understood it or not, with the result that, wholly apart from any new movement in the theatre, our stage today is more materially thorough, more exacting in its superficial standards, less beholden to archaic customs than the strongholds of the tories anywhere else in the world.

And yet, when we examine our record as practitioner of realism against that of Ibsen, the Meiningen Company, Brahm, Antoine and the Moscow Art Theatre, there is no denying that our efforts have been callow, accidental, immature. Callow in those numerous cases of reformers who turned to the stage as platform for airing their hobbies. Accidental, as in the case of Eugene Walter and "The Easiest Way." Immature, when we have to place our chief dependence on O'Neill, who at any moment may abandon the realistic technique he has plied so effectively in "Beyond the Horizon," "Diff'rent" and "Anna Christie" and go over wholly to the opposing camp with whom he has already consorted boldly and without shame in "The Emperor Jones" and "The Hairy Ape."

Most discouraging aspect to those who put their faith in realistic plays and corresponding interpretation on the stage is the fact that in his day, even with a play of the impact of "The Easiest Way," Eugene Walter stimulated by contagion no group or school or individual follower to rival or repeat his performance. The other Eugene can hardly be so classified, for not only has too much time intervened to derive such a connection, but O'Neill's writings have proceeded from within his own imagination, tossed and tried by life itself, rather than from any imitation, conscious or unconscious, of other playwrights. It is too early, of course, to say what will happen as a result of the presence of O'Neill and his plays on our stage, but thus far they have yielded imitation rather than inspiration.

The trouble with our dramatic realism is simply this: we have not taken it earnestly enough. We have toyed with it in a naïve, schoolboy way ever since the first forge and the first sawmill in action were set upon the stage to whet the melodrama of the eighties and nineties. It did not particularly matter that the emotions were not deeply stirred thereby or that these expedients served illusion inconstantly, so long as they fanned the less noble fires of curiosity and brought audiences into the theatre. The movement, if it may be so called, took two forms. On the one hand it descended to the brazen stunts of Lincoln J. Carter — mechanical tricks that finally grew to impossibly huge and costly proportions, although they still recur at infrequent intervals when some producer betrays a fond but futile hope that life is not yet wholly vanished from old idols. The motion pictures, however, have sublet most of this realm of realistic blood and thunder, and the theatre is well rid of it.

Rising from its crude and naïve and startling beginnings, the movement on the other hand developed into the more discreet and mannerly make-believe of David Belasco — the oft-cited Childs' Restaurant of " The Governor's Lady " or the rowdy bar of " The Girl of the Golden West." Still, even in Belasco's hands, it concerned itself chiefly with externals, with the meticulous copying of actual and visible details. Except in the stark challenge of " The Easiest Way " and the subtler implications of " The Return of Peter Grimm," there was little of that sterner representation of life which cuts deep below the surface, which the European realists mastered, and which alone justifies realism as a method of artistic expression.

There was none until " The Easiest Way." There has been little intervening between the two Eugenes. Blind to Walter's profounder implications and heeding only his surface thrills, his successors — and even Walter himself in his later plays — set out to tell everything as baldly, as plainly and as completely as possible. No reservations! Every detail set forth with photographic precision. A slice of life is a slice

THE SHADOWS OF PETER GRIMM HAUNT THE REALISTIC LIGHT OF LIFE

A Scene from David Belasco's Production of "The Return of Peter Grimm," Epitome of His Mastery of Stage Illumination

of life, with the seeds left in the melon and neither pepper, salt nor sugar added to bring out a hidden flavor. If sensitive souls, aware that life is something more than its outer appearances, rebelled against this process, they were reminded that facing facts is a noble and courageous pastime.

Morally sensational realism, though, has gone the way of the physically sensational. The propagandist in the playhouse has been unmasked for the artist he is not. Here and there is evidence that playwrights are becoming aware of the existence of "The Easiest Way" and the more varied fruits of O'Neill's pen. With O'Neill, Zoë Akins realizes, especially in the first act of "Daddy's Gone a-Hunting," that selection is the soul of art, that the whole story can be told more eloquently by a part of the details than by all of them, and that reticence if used with intelligence and feeling is one of the surest doors to intimacy and understanding. Without the aid of O'Neill, Craven has found his own way into the homely purports of the American family. With or without O'Neill, Zona Gale has penetrated to exciting significance beneath that same smug exterior.

Moreover, Owen Davis could never have written "The Detour" and "Icebound" without these same objects of emulation, or Arthur Richman, "Ambush." The results are variable in the two cases. It is one thing — and Davis's products are commensurate — to say: "Well, people have said I could write like that if I tried. Go to, I will try." But emulation by the deliberate and exterior process is seldom effective. It is far better if, as in the instance of Richman, the impulse comes by second nature, if a stimulating example simply wakes latent powers, startles them from disarray into definite form as steel dust by a magnet or an electric current. It is interesting in Davis's minor tragedies to note how much can be achieved by studious imitation — and, after all, how little. His scenes, his characters, his casual manner, are after O'Neill. But when he tries to give deep and searching significance to the casual, he falls far short of his younger master. The framework is there, the outer aspects. Davis has gone some distance beyond his earlier patchworks of familiar and effective situations, although he lacks the vision to abandon those situations entirely. Rather, he accepts them because he knows none other and tries to present them without the strain and exaggeration he once bestowed on them. The result is superficially admirable but finally dissatisfying, for the heart and soul are missing.

"Ambush," on the other hand, can be traced to no definite American progenitor. Richman apparently has neither consciously nor unconsciously imitated anyone. Still, with all its virtues as an honest and fearless piece of observation, told in cumulative and arresting sequence, it is easy to doubt whether it would have come into being except through the stimulus of its predecessors. It is too plodding, too obviously the result of effort, too lacking in spontaneity, to have come to pass of its own accord.

After all, therefore, we are compelled to fall back on "The Easiest Way" and O'Neill as the signposts toward a realistic drama in America. O'Neill and his plays we have already considered at length. A word, then, on Walter's masterpiece. In the light of years, the tragedy of Laura Murdock holds its head high. All that was adventitious in its original engagement has now vanished. Its morals are no longer questioned. It has to stand on its own merits. And it was able to do so on its revival two years ago. There is just a suspicion of " journalese " in the opening act — the quick staccato of single words, of phrases chopped short. A trick of the newspaper writer which Walter carried over from the reporter's room to the stage, a trick of which O'Neill is fortunately ignorant. But once the story is under way, this artificial idiom is dropped and the latter acts of " The Easiest Way " are just as powerful, just as poignant, just as pertinent and convincing, as if they had been written today about the latest aspect of an eternal situation. Consider for a moment how infirm " The Third Degree " would appear in revival in this year of our Lord. And yet, it first saw and conquered Broadway in the same season.

If we still lack a rich body of realistic drama on our native stage, we have observed enough of it from abroad to detect its drawbacks. As a method of artistic expression, even when utilized with the patience and thoroughness and insight of Stanislavsky, realism appears to have ingrained in it a double defect: the inevitable element of approximation and the lack of symbolic gesture and rhythm amounting to an unavoidable loss of significant form. From the standpoint of its defect through approximation, William James has indicated the nature of the psychological problem: "Just as an artificially imitated sneeze lacks something of the reality, so the attempt to imitate an emotion in the absence of its normally instigating cause is apt to be rather 'hollow.'" And the revolt of Meyerhold and the Kamerny Theatre from the traditions of the Moscow Art Theatre in Russia, of Reinhardt from his earlier moorings, and of more than one stage artist in America before our realism is fairly of age, is testimony to the dissatisfaction arising from the latter defect. Can it be that realism is a paper doll, and that before we have really learned to enjoy it, to become familiar with its satisfactions, expert in its methods, we have come to demand something more difficult, more emotionally satisfying?

Walter Prichard Eaton has answered that query most effectively: "Realism may not have beauty and wonder, but it has a common sense actuality and a capacity for intellectual comment that not only will not be given up, but should not be given up. The theorists of the new theatre, searching for something lost, forget what has been found. . . . Realism, except in the narrowest definition, is not a fashion. It is a hard won accomplishment of the writing craft. In the theatre, perhaps elsewhere, it has been won by too exclusive a devotion, granted. The theatre has many values, some of supreme effectiveness, which realism ignores. They must be rediscovered. But realism is too integral and too important a part of our modern civilization to be, in its turn, cast aside. . . . Besides, true realism in the American theatre has hardly begun as yet. Most of us haven't had time to get tired of it."

If we haven't yet had true realism — and there can be little doubt of it; " Beyond the Horizon," " Anna Christie " and " The Easiest Way " are degrees below the best of European realistic drama — what forms is our realism most likely to take as it develops under the searching rivalry of newer theories? One thing is certain: we shall not be satisfied with the repetition of the surface naturalism, the clever imitation of the obvious, the prepossessions of the propagandist, all characteristic of realism's youth. In their stead, we shall demand the spiritual realism disclosed to us by the Moscow Art Theatre, the vivid and psychologically accurate revelation of the mystic and subconscious recesses of the human soul, adapted, of course, to the peculiar repressions and intensities and idiosyncrasies of our American life and character.

Chapter XVII

THE REVOLT AGAINST REALISM

In the larger sense, there is no opposition, no distinction, between realism and its several opponents. There is none, there can be none. And this is why: All artistic creation, as we have seen from Walkley's paraphrase of Croce, proceeds from the artist's impressions of the world outside his body, inside his imagination; these in turn become ordered, synthesized, giving the artist a pleasurable sensation which he forthwith translates into physical phenomena for the sake of giving the same pleasurable sensation to others. These physical phenomena — sounds, tones, movements, combinations of lines and colors, etc. — are not in themselves the artist's original impressions, his pleasurable sensations. A mental, an auditory, a visual conception preceded them. They are the translation of this conception in terms comprehensible to others. They represent the conception. Thus far all art is representative art. Thus far there is no minor realism from which to revolt. All is realism.

If we understand and accept this larger unity of all art, we can at once recognize without prejudice and with keener enjoyment the various means and methods the artist uses to represent his vision, to convey it to the public, to transmit to that public the illusion of its reality. He may, of course, like the so-called realist, be content with holding the mirror up to nature, with copying the outer, obvious, material details. For five hundred years, artists have been using this method of self-expression, with infrequent variations — artists of the theatre along with the rest. For a hundred years, they have been using it more and more intensively, more and more baldly, more and more expertly, perfectly, and at the same time more and more unworthily. In the hands of the naturalists, the 100 per cent realists, the process became an end in itself. Cleanliness, health, held no interest, no sensation. Dirt therefore, scandal, disease, the abnormal. In the hands of a Gorky, the lowly way to exaltation, ecstasy. Usually, however, for its own sake. Resulting in a boomerang — Frankenstein, Juggernaut, Golem.

It is easy to see how the narrower realism thus brought discredit on the process, hung itself with its own tether, roused the sleeping dogs of older and at the same time fresher methods, brought on the revolt against itself which is shaking the dull bones of yesterday's theatre into life once more. Despite the meager supply of our sheer realism on the American stage, we have had enough that is native but inept, enough that is imported and skilful, to understand out of our own experience this reaction against realism. When it had not burrowed squint-eyed into a corner of human existence, losing sight of the larger, more inspiring themes of life, it had made faint ges-

THE REVOLT AGAINST REALISM

anything in it worthy to replace the realism that our age has brought to perfection as its characteristic mode of self-expression. It is too early to say that they will not do so in time, for there is in them an amazing vitality, and fecundity; and theoretically they can prove what they can not yet practice. Meanwhile, a glance at some of our efforts to give these theories body, to make them work and live, may clarify their outlines, their uses, their prospects. The theatre of "Let's pretend!" I shall withhold for a separate chapter. Likewise, the theatre of mass characters belongs in Chapter XIX, "Our Civic Theatre." For example of pioneer experiment in general and a foray into the fogs of abstraction in particular, "Macbeth" comes first to mind.

Upheld by the imaginative vision of Jones, Hopkins in this production was bold enough in the midst of Broadway to put to shame all the pretensions of the secessionists who affect scorn for the commercial theatre, by out-experimenting the experimenters. Unsatisfied to dally with expedients or evolutionary processes, he advanced at one leap into a new esthetic, confident of his goal but strangely heedless of the encumbrances he was carrying along with him from the old.

This new esthetic may be defined as an attempt to appeal to the emotions and the imagination through the abstractions of mood and feeling, and to portray these moods and feelings as the background for the action of the play rather than to particularize that background in the guise of either a literal or a symbolic representation of *locale*. At the pole from photographic realism. Far beyond the symbolic theatre where typical and generic objects still represent specific things and places. The theatre of abstraction has nothing whatever to do with things as the physical eye sees them. It seeks not the illusion of reality. It is not interested in the picture-puzzle technique of symbolism; it demands no speculation as to whether a crooked stick is intended to be a tree or a gallows or a cross. It is concerned merely with the mood and feeling which its visible and audible instruments can arouse.

Just as in any form of esthetic expression, the artist who uses abstraction as his medium must convey his meaning to the audience. He must induce them to feel as he has felt. He must make his intentions clear without the use of dictionary or guide-book. Naturally, he can not expect an indiscriminate audience to comprehend him readily. We have thought too long in terms of a narrowly realistic ideology to turn quickly and easily and without self-consciousness to the imagery of abstraction.

In the light of the impelling motive of Hopkins and Jones, as thus stated, their " Macbeth " assumes significance. Brilliant illumination against dark shadows stimulated the emotions. Distorted suggestions of wall and doorway and throne, used not for their own sake or as symbols but as stimuli to a mood, guided the aroused emotions into the channel of ominous dread of impending tragedy. That, indeed, has always been the mood of " Macbeth." Hopkins

THE REVOLT AGAINST REALISM

tures at renascence from within itself through the related medium of symbolism — the use of metaphors, similes, on an extended scale to avoid naming outright the common, the vulgar, the unnamable. Specious gloss, pretentious mystery, mawkish sentimentality. "The Servant in the House," "Experience," "Everywoman," "The Fool."

But a healthier renascence has come. From outside. To revive values too long neglected by the theatre and all the arts. To stir realism, in the stricter sense, to defend itself by showing its best, its right to live. The forms of that renascence are varied, some of them simple and clear, others vague, uncharted — all still in that experimental state from which the unexpected may emerge any moment. Instead of the artist copying the outer, obvious, material details in his attempt to give tangible body to his vision, he resorts to other attributes of that vision.

To the representation of the emotional background of his vision in place of its physical length, breadth and thickness: abstraction. To the frank recognition that it is a vision which he wishes to share with others and not something to be conjured into an illusory imitation of life, presentation vs. representation, in the limited sense understood by the American *Commedia dell' Arte* in its production of Blok's "The Show Booth" and by others who have theorized without practice, though it must be evident that this is simply another way of *representing* the artist's conception. To the theatre not only frankly recognizing itself as theatre but summoning the audience to participate: the theatre of "Let's pretend!" To the crystallization of the subconscious, the telling of a story by the representation of actuating motives on varying planes of consciousness, as Sheldon Cheney puts it in "Modern Art and the Theatre," rather than by the mere narration of the outcome of those motives: expressionism, a term that has been used thus precisely as well as in general to comprise all the rebels from realism. To the reduction of the story, the drama, to its boldest outlines, with groups of men as characters: the circus as theatre; Reinhardt's Theatre of the Five Thousand; MacKaye's community masques — as they might be, almost were but not quite; Geddes' Dante. To the simultaneous recording of a succession of events in time or space, without regard to actual temporal or spacial order but attempting thereby to illuminate their dynamic relationships: futurism, as in Dreiser's "Plays of the Natural and Supernatural," and particularly in "Laughing Gas," effectively produced with its concurrent action in several planes of consciousness by the Indianapolis Little Theatre. To the theatre of masks, of moving scenery, of emotionally attuned but unrealistic lighting, of light used as an abstract medium for its own sake — expedients valuable to more than one of the revolutionary methods just cited.

These channels of challenge, of revolt from photographic realism, are still dimly apprehended, even by their protagonists. They have not yet accomplished all that they may; I say "may" because none of them has thus far demonstrated certainly that it has

THE REVOLT AGAINST REALISM

and Jones merely tried to emphasize it and make it potent in a new way. The witches were made into abstractions of fatalism by appearing in masks, a note stressed by the spectacle of three colossal silver masks in the black void above. Irregular screens at one side of the stage, pierced by pointed arches, connoted not so much the castle as the mood of minds distorted by murderous ambitions. Their placement at increasingly toppling angles in succeeding scenes suggested the intensifying of this mood. The leaning, unsymmetrical shapes behind the throne and the candlesticks askew on the banquet-tables seemed to imply the crumbling of Macbeth's power. The pointed white screens, cross-barred and transparent, which stood about the stage in the sleep-walking scene, were less decisive in their abstract ideology, but by their resemblance in shape to the arches of the earlier scenes they seemed intended to emphasize the pent-up terror of Lady Macbeth shut within her bloody memories. Probably the most impressive and intrinsically beautiful image in the entire production was the tall, tapering white pillar enclosing and rising above the ember glow which revealed the witches and apparitions of Macbeth's final seance, implying, perhaps, the king's devotion at a ritual fire and heightening the feeling of his dependence on fatalistic guidance.

As an étude in abstraction, however, " Macbeth " fell short of its ambitious goal in two chief respects: one of them remediable, the other inherent in the material chosen. In a perfect fusion of all the elements in the art of the theatre, the acting would have been keyed to the setting and therefore to the fundamental note of the production; it would have been removed from the realm of imitative realism into a fantastic and impassioned world of controlled exaggeration. But it wasn't. Therefore, disaster. The inherent difficulty lay in the play itself. "Macbeth" is probably as amenable as any of Shakespeare to interpretation by abstraction, but, like all the rest, it has become so encrusted during three centuries with custom, usage and tradition that as violent a break as this only confuses.

What Jones and Hopkins should have done for their first major attack upon the intrenchments of realism was to have chosen a play deliberately written to be interpreted abstractly. But "The Hairy Ape" didn't exist yet. Nor others for alternate choice. When abstraction and expressionism finally found mouthpiece through O'Neill, the advance into new grounds was made much simpler. Jones and Throckmorton designed forecastle bunks and prison-cell in distorted perspective, denaturalized Fifth-Avenue promenaders with masks and mechanical gait, and those who rejected "Macbeth" accepted it. Partly because its material was adapted to such construction; partly because as abstraction it was a less radical break with the past; partly because "Macbeth," though a failure, had taken the curse off the stranger. Not wholly, though, for in the case of weaker examples, like John Howard Lawson's "Roger Bloomer" and Elmer Rice's "The Adding Machine," tradition used their frailties to disparage their class.

MASKS AS STIMULI TO A MOOD

The Apparition Scene from a Design by Robert Edmond Jones for Arthur Hopkins' Abstract Production of "Macbeth"

Masks, then, moving scenery, light. Tools, properties, servants, of an insurgent theatre. Tending, if not watched, to get out of hand, to usurp undue prominence. Eldest of the drama's accouterments, the mask was rediscovered as a practical implement of our contemporary theatre in early Autumn, 1920, when John Murray Anderson, producer, and Margaret Severn, dancer, scented in the playthings of Wladislaw T. Benda, artist, an intriguing decorative value for "The Greenwich Village Follies." By strange irony, the artist who had built up his masks out of thousands of bits of paper simply to decorate his studio, had never heard of Gordon Craig, apologist for the revival of the mask for twenty years, and he was only vaguely aware of its venerable historic background. And by still stranger irony, the public which knew even less of the theatre's past, insisted on denominating them, not masks, but Bendamasks. Reborn in the Aristophanic revue, the mask in the hands of Rosse, Jones and Geddes is regaining its serious, satiric and even tragic heritage as sublimation of the spirit, epitome, seeking not to copy life, but to get at the heart of it.

The device of moving scenery has been pondered more fully by Rosse than anyone else. He shares the feeling of many others that the present scenic setting is an encumbrance to the art of the theatre in its tendency to remain static and immovable while the rest of the elements of the art flow in rhythmic and plastic line. To overcome this discrepancy, therefore, he proposes a stage on which the scenery

THE REVOLT AGAINST REALISM

moves as well as the actors, in relation to the shifting moods of the play. Conversant with the difficulties which innovators in lighting encounter when the mechanical expedient draws attention to itself from the *mise en scène,* he realises that his path is beset with obstacles, but he is confident that after a period of adjustment to this new convention it will be accepted in the spirit of the other conventions of the theatre and that a return to static scenery will be impossible. The means whereby he hopes to accomplish these ends are still in embryonic development, but for one thing he suggests the use of projected light, with its source behind the proscenium, after the manner of the animated cartoons of the motion pictures. Other expedients with which he hopes to experiment are actors disguised as elements of the scenic setting, finely corrugated surfaces which will reflect changing lights in varying aspect, canvas spotted with numerous colors, after the manner which Urban introduced to the American stage, but carried to more intricate application, and various types of moving or apparently moving floors.

Adjunct to a spiritual realism in the hands of Jones, as well as to Rosse's plastic scenery, light latterly seeks an independent place in the sun. Thomas Wilfred experiments for years with mechanism to project abstract designs in mobile color on a glass screen. He perfects the mechanism, the Clavilux or Color Organ, exhibits it publicly at the Neighborhood Playhouse. Perversity in the form of practical human psychology balks him. The red makes one woman weep as if her heart were breaking. Some discern in the changing shapes ninepins, safety razors, tennis-rackets, Turkish coffeepots. Others persist against their will in seeing the mechanical cause back of the artistic effect, and illusion departs. Time, perhaps, will correct this, break down the slavery to realistic ideology, develop comprehension of abstraction. But for a long time light is likely to be invaluable vassal rather than lord of the manor.

The mechanical and psychological impediments to effective emotional reaction which mar these several proposals for a new theatre are probably sufficient commentary and welcome condemnation in the eyes of those who deplore mechanistic expedients in art. In general, it must be obvious that whenever the thought of mechanism obtrudes, whenever the audience gives the slightest heed to the *way* an effect is achieved, forgetting even momentarily the course and content of the play, then the expedient becomes a mere trick and defeats its purpose. The arbitrary and unrealistic use of light, for instance, especially the rapid change from one color to another, such as Maurice Browne and some of the Russians are accustomed to utilize, must have almost superhumanly expert control to avoid this pitfall. Such a difficulty is not prohibitive although it is extremely restrictive. Another impediment to effective emotional control appears when expressionistic methods are pushed so far along abstract lines that a key is necessary to avoid confusion. Until we escape more fully from the habit of looking for photographic imitation of physical objects in our art and drama, the newer forms will have to remain in the realm of plane geometry, reserving the sphere of conic sections for the more esoteric audience of tomorrow.

Another misconception of revolutionary ways consists in the delusion that they are easy, that their technique is simple, that technique, in fact, is not essential to their practice. Impromptu. Spur-of-the-moment. Improvisation. Sketches, outlines, no need for bothersome detail. Trust to the inspiration of the moment. Wasn't that the secret of the *commedia dell'arte,* the last incarnation of the spirit abroad in the theatre today?

But the appearance of impromptu, spur-of-the-moment, doesn't mean lack of preparation. Art concealing art. Years of learning and forgetting lie behind the most effective simplicity. A vast fund of experience, familiarity with ways and means, a reserve fund on which maturity may draw without strain, anxiety, self-consciousness. Until we have a body of artists — playwrights, producers, actors, designers — trained by long experience in the newer esthetic forms, we can not hope for actual impromptu, improvisation. The revolutionary and apparently go-as-you-please technique requires just as close, if not closer, association, mutual understanding and adjustment among its creative participants, as the elder realistic technique. If Stanislavsky and Belasco spend two years preparing " The Lower Depths " and " The Return of Peter Grimm," the rebels can not escape the necessity of devoting even a longer time, until they know themselves and each other better. Otherwise, they will justly deserve a verdict of unpreparedness and endanger their whole position with a public which is more than tolerant. When Reinhardt proposes to leap at once into modern experiments with the *commedia dell'arte* at the Josephstadt Theater in Vienna, he does so with the assurance that his collaborators, reassembled from the scattered staff of his Deutsches Theater in Berlin, will have a quarter of a century of mutual association and understanding behind them. And where do we have at most two artists who have worked together that long, or a half, a third, a fifth the time?

Deeper than this delusion that revolt and reconstruction are easy, but allied to it, nevertheless, is the whole spirit of the "Younger Generation," demanding today, not the freedom to express itself which it craved when it emerged a dozen years ago, but the license to insult, outlaw and ostracize everything but the new, the "modern," the revolutionary. Not this way does true progress lie. Only confusion, bitterness, jealousy, bigoted refusal to accept them when they do achieve. " The real young man," says Croce, "is he who in good faith hopes, and in good faith strives, to be as wise and well-considered and sagacious as the old, who perpetrates immature trifles and imagines them equal to the best and most famous, who is almost offended when he is called young because, he says, he wishes to be judged by the value of his work and not by the number of his years, and who alternates these boasts with profound de-

promptly banishes from the playhouse illusion, cold reserve, and all the other bodyguards of the traditional theatre. In their place he puts warmth, cordiality, zest, alert expectancy, and the spirit of play. His quaint and unconventional introductory remarks amount simply to saying "Let's pretend!" He does it a little less baldly and more provocatively. But he has established an intimacy with his audience that could not be heartier or more friendly if he had called from midstream in leafy August, "Come on in; the water's fine!" The mood of reserve is broken. The spirit of challenge is forestalled. The chip on our shoulder is forgotten. The circle of entertainers has been extended to include the entertained. We have shaken imaginative hands with the captain, and his game is ours. He has made us participants, willing and morally responsible participants. And if the result isn't satisfactory, the fault will be partly ours, just as the credit will be partly ours if everything goes well.

There are three collaborating elements in this strange theatre; the entertainers who provide the stimulus, who toss the ball in the air; the entertained who stand ready and expectant to receive the stimulus, to catch the ball and toss it back; and the coach on the sidelines who directs the play and keeps the excitement at fever pitch.

I half suspect that when we are better trained, when we are more familiar with the rules and the tricks and the fine points, we may be able to dispense with the coach in person. He will be there in spirit, the subtle influence of his personality will pervade the theatre from the moment we cross the threshold; but his physical presence may not be necessary. Meanwhile we have Balieff in fact and numerous others waiting around the corner to serve as amiable guides to uncharted pleasures.

We have Balieff, but just who else is there? Who, aside from mere imitators — and there have been a dozen of them — could create interesting variants of the Chauve-Souris? What are the unconsidered trifles, the neglected and disdained institutions, forces, instincts, customs, predilections, which all bespeak our natural adaptability for such a theatre? How can we overcome intervening obstacles, coördinate these forces, make use of them as foundation stones, apply the selective principle of the artist to them, change them from unconscious to conscious forms of expression? What can we find in the rich and varied past of the theatre to serve as spur to our imaginations today? And what are the ultimate possibilities of this sort of theatre? Is it limited to the gay, the ephemeral, the trifling? Or has it potentialities for deeper, more profound expression, for appeals to the more exalted emotions of ecstatic passion, reverence, self-sacrifice?

The chief obstacle in America to a theatre in which the audience participates is the American audience itself. As Arthur Hopkins has put it, we go to the theatre with icicles in all our pockets. We take ourselves, our work, our play too seriously. We are a childlike people at heart. Witness our ex-

lization, and which persists today unhonored and unrecognized in numerous humble byways and backwaters of our contemporary scene.

Like a poor relative, this theatre has been banished from the artistic calendar. The dons and the signors of our esthetic aristocracy will not deign to notice its existence. It is common, vulgar, trivial, beneath contempt. What has the clown in the circus, with his slap-stick and his practical joke, to do with art? Art is refinement, austerity, reserve. Where is the refinement of our musical comedians? And what have the Billy Sundays, the William Booths, the Vachel Lindsays, and the athletic cheer-leaders to do with the theatre, not to mention the high calling of the artists?

The reëstablishment in grace of this despised vagabond has been a difficult task. It would be about as effective to try to convince most composers that a worthy musical tradition can emerge from jazz or to persuade most artists that the billboards and the comic supplements can yield a significant sense of design, as it is to insist that art could spring from circus and revival-tent, from variety stage and foot-ball field. We had heard of experiments of Meyerhold in Petrograd and Reinhardt in Berlin with a theatre in which the audience participated, though it all seemed rather difficult in theory. We ourselves had numerous potential examples in our revues and on our variety stages, but we lacked someone to call our attention to them — until Balieff came.

With the droll countenance of the born clown and the mock dignity of the clown as artist, Nikita Balieff

quires something more even than sympathetic and tolerant observation. It demands participation, cooperation, mutual creation on the part of both spectator and performer, a natural, instinctive blending of the functions of entertainer and entertained, with the former in the rôle of pace-maker.

Analyse the theories cited in the previous chapters and two main concepts emerge. On the one hand, there is the theatre of illusion, the theatre largely as we have known it in recent times, but perfected and enriched by new appeals to the intellect and the imagination. The theatre of illusion is an objective affair, and its success is measured by the extent to which we forget that it is a theatre at all. It may be realistic or symbolic or abstract. It may copy and represent the superficial and fundamental facts of life, or it may seek out and present the hidden soul and halo of life. Its distinguishing feature is that it is nominally self-sufficient, that it would be the same with or without an audience, and that its audience is a passive and receptive factor in its existence. To this theatre belong the drama of ideas, the literary drama, the drama of persuasive story, the drama of impressive fantasy, even much of the expressionistic drama.

But there is another theatre, — one that makes no attempt to disguise the fact that it is a theatre, which glories in that fact and sets out unashamed to make the most of it. It is not a new conception, this theatre of "Let's pretend!" In reality it is the oldest form of dramatic art known to man, a form which has recurred periodically throughout the course of civi-

RUSSIAN BABI IN BALIEFF'S CHAUVE-SOURIS

Under the Conferencier's Ingratiating Command of "Let's Pretend!" the Folk Tunes of the *Muzhik* Enlist the Audience as Participants in the Performance

travagant enthusiasms, our susceptibility to panic, our flaring newspaper head-lines, our flaming magazine covers, our fads of apparel and carriage and speech. But we like to pretend that we are very staid and grown-up and self-possessed. Our incessant busy-ness, whether real or artificial, induces a tenseness and a strain which admits of no genuine relaxation even when we have the opportunity for it. What we need when we go to the theatre is to let loose, to give our minds, our emotions, and our imaginations full rein, to yield ourselves to the playwright and the player not passively and dumbly, but alertly and creatively, as so much sensitized paper on which they may record their message.

And if we need this unwearied, unprejudiced, wide-awake, creative audience for the traditional theatre, how much more essential it is for the theatre of "Let's pretend!" An audience unhampered by lassitude on the one hand or by callousness on the other is absolutely requisite if it is to participate in the game of make-believe. No wonder, then, that it has taken a Balieff with the intriguing fillip of a foreign reputation, the provocative persuasions of novelty, and the arresting stimulus of an unusual personality to jolt us out of our rut, to reveal to us the unsuspected satisfactions of a new pastime, and to call our attention to our own undeveloped resources in the field of which he is master.

What are these resources, after all? Let us examine them in the light of this provocative object lesson from Russia. Our light musical and vaudeville stages

THE REVOLT AGAINST REALISM

jection, regarding himself one day mistakenly as a great poet and the next with no more truth as a complete imbecile. Out of these young men will come the wisdom and power of the next generation."

Chapter XVIII

THE THEATRE OF "LET'S PRETEND!"

Come with me to the theatre of "Let's pretend!" Nikita Balieff's Chauve-Souris from Moscow will suffice until we construct one of our own. Maybe it will seem strange and confusing at the start. We are accustomed to sitting aloof in the playhouse. We let the actors do all the pretending, and we ourselves maintain a bleak and rigid detachment. We take our seats in the auditorium with chips on our shoulders, as much as to say: "Fool us, if you can, into believing what you tell us. Kindle our emotions, break down our complacency, if you dare. And convince us, if you are smart enough, that this is a slice of life we have come to see." We are so used to this attitude of challenge and non-participation that it will take a considerable wrench to lift us out of the rut. But the fascinations of the theatre of "Let's pretend!" are sufficiently alluring to tide us over any initial period of awkwardness and self-consciousness.

The Theatre of "Let's pretend!" Simply one in which the audience takes part — an eager and active part. It is an ancient axiom of the theatre that no play is a play until it is acted before an audience. But this theatre we are considering requires something more than mere passive attendance. It re-

THEATRE OF "LET'S PRETEND!" 227

abound in talents that need not fear comparison with the company and the repertory of the Chauve-Souris. To cite at random, there are: Ruth Page among the dancers and, if she would submit to rigorous guidance, Margaret Severn; Rosalind Fuller in old English melodies and dances, assisted by Constance Binney; John Alden Carpenter's jazz ballet, " Krazy Kat," with Fred Stone or Leon Errol in the leading rôle; Ruth Draper in anything her fancy favors; the Rath Brothers, acrobats; almost any one in Benda masks; the Three Legrohs; Joseph Cawthorn, with his accordion; and the Six Brown Brothers. And a dozen other groupings from the varieties.

Robert Edmond Jones, Norman-Bel Geddes, Lee Simonson, and Herman Rosse are ready to enter the lists as rivals of Balieff's artists. Robert Benchley, Brian Hooker, Alfred Kreymborg, George Jean Nathan, Heywood Broun, Don Marquis, Franklin P. Adams, George S. Kaufman, and Marc Connelly are a few of those who might be drafted to write lines and compose sketches equal to the unexpectedly ludicrous episodes by Tchehoff which Balieff has disclosed. If they didn't in " The Forty-Niners " — and they didn't! — it was because they obeyed no Balieff. And such lilts as " Swing low, Sweet Chariot," " Nobody Knows the Trouble I Has," " Inchin' along like a Poor Inchworm," and scores of other hauntingly beautiful negro spirituals; or the secular melodies, " De Massa Run, ha! ha! " and " Massa's in de Cold, Cold Ground "; or even such collegiate chorals as " Bingo Farm," might hold their heads high in the presence of the ballades of Glinka and the folk-tunes of *muzhik* and Gipsy.

But all this, admirable as it might be in skillful combination, is not enough. It is not sufficient to set on the stage these snatches of song and dance and pantomime and episode, no matter how dexterously, if the audience remains aloof and detached. To sit through an evening with these Russians is to realize how diverse is the resulting satisfaction, how different the same material can be, when it is merely placed before an audience impersonally as in the traditional theatre and when it is presented intimately with an invitation to the spectators to be participants. The gaiety of light-hearted moments is more buoyant, more sparkling, more spirited. The gravity of a sober episode is more tender, more sympathetic. Every one in the theatre, therefore, must be enticed into the game of " Let's pretend! " And inasmuch as we are novices at the game, we must have, at least, in the beginning, a mentor, a guide, a coach — a Nikita Balieff.

Probably, those who have dismissed our revues and our vaudeville as vulgar and trivial pastime outside the range of art have begun to wonder since the coming of the Chauve-Souris whether they haven't neglected something. Certainly, the devotees of the various idols of our light musical stage are ready at this point to suggest to me candidates for Balieff's post in our own Chauve-Souris. I hear, for instance, the name of one of the Russian comedian's staunchest admirers and steadiest patrons, Al Jolson. Raymond Hitchcock is placed in nomination? Yes. And Will Rogers. And

THEATRE OF "LET'S PRETEND!"

Frank Tinney. Remember "Watch Your Step!" And Ed Wynn and Fred Stone. A member of the Lucy Stone Club suggests Elsie Janis and Fannie Brice. Admirers of our guests and visitors from abroad will propose Mme. Guilbert, Sir Harry Lauder, Albert Chevalier. But haven't we enough of our own? Personally, I am inclined to trust Jolson or Rogers. Who knows what they might do if they had half a chance? How about Stephen Leacock or Vachel Lindsay, if salt could be placed on their timid tails? And I am not so sure we could not trust one of those swaying comedians from "Shuffle Along," that throbbing and vibrant example of the negro's instinct for the theatre.

America is ripe for the experiment, riper and readier than staid and conservative and formal France and Great Britain and Germany. It is riper, even, than Balieff's own Russia, where the *Intelligentsia* share the inhibitions of western Europe and where the peasantry are still groping their way, though with virile instinctive equipment, toward a conscious appreciation of art of any kind. It is we who have created the modern circus, we who permit the clown to penetrate the stands and play practical jokes on us. It is we who have dramatized religion and carried it from the formal pulpit and the mysterious shadows of the cathedral into the tents and the tabernacles of Moody and Sankey and Billy Sunday. It is we who have made our athletic sports into huge dramatic spectacles, with the spectators as active participants, a custom which, with the exception of the Spanish bull-fight, requires a trip back to ancient Rome for parallel. Few if any modern popular and variety stages can show as many undeveloped talents as ours for a theatre conceived in this same spirit.

Why, then, have we not taken these talents in hand, applied the process of selection to them? Why have we not borrowed the impetus of our other mass expressions of the same spirit and applied it to the theatre? Why have we not made these forces conscious and deliberate and pointed, instead of letting them go to waste as random and contemptible by-products of our civilization? Why, in short, have we not garnered in the playhouse these virile and deep-seated emotional reactions and made them obey the rules and perform the services of art? Is it because we disdain the familiar? Have we so pedantic and artificial an idea of art that we can not conceive of its springing from the market-place, the music-hall, the foot-ball field, the church? Or is the Puritan tradition still so potent that we yield to the theatre only a grudging attitude of detached observation and refuse to release therein a free and creative spirit?

Whatever be the reason, it seems as if we were on the eve of correcting our neglect. A new spirit is moving in the theatre, and this theatre of "Let's pretend!" is likely to be one to which we Americans will pay heed at least as much and possibly more than to the subtler forms which delight the esoteric and intellectual audiences of Europe. Balieff has broken the ice. He has brought to a head a swarm of vague, unconscious desires, hitherto suppressed. And if we really mean our enthusiasm over the Chauve-Souris and really wish to construct our own, there is plenty of evidence at hand waiting to guide us, such as the records of the experiments of Meyerhold in Petrograd and of Reinhardt in Berlin. They need not be recounted here, for they are at hand in books. Equally available for those who wish to carry their research further are the chronicles of the theatre of "Let's pretend!" as it was practised at the dawn of the drama among the Greeks, before the chorus became the vicarious participants with the actors, in place of the audience who had originally fulfilled the rôle of chorus. And within still easier reach is the story of the *commedia dell'arte* and the medieval theatre in Europe, progenitor of Balieff's Chauve-Souris.

I for one am not willing to stop with the Chauve-Souris as an instance of the theatre of "Let's pretend!" The program that follows Balieff's introductory hand-clasp might be any one of many kinds of program. He happens to choose a light, highly amusing, and diverting program, because that is the expression of his own personality. But the range of this theatre is not limited to the droll and the humorous, although that is likely to be its most popular and prevalent aspect, considering that humankind is humankind.

There is no inherent reason why the guiding spirit should not be satiric or philosophical, passionately esthetic or patriotic or religious. Prokofieff's opera, "The Love for Three Oranges," might have been the bridge from the comic to the satiric theatre of "Let's pretend!" if it had had a personal master of ceremonies, or if we were yet ready to dispense with the presence of a Balieff. The experiments of Percy MacKaye and Harry Barnhart in such productions as "The Will of Song" are groping steps toward a passionately communal theatre of "Let's pretend!" And think of the opportunities in wartime to lift an entire people to sublime heights in such a theatre! Remember Paris in August, 1914. Recall the *Lusitania,* the draft, the armistice! Any phase of human experience can be dramatized, and within the framework of this theatre it can be made a creative instead of a passive experience by enlisting the participation of the audience.

It would be absurd to claim for the theatre of "Let's pretend!" that it will displace the traditional theatre. There is room to spare for both. With its development, however, our tense and constrained modern life will find a gracious and effective servant. Instead of a sedative for overwrought nerves, it will provide a source of spirited relaxation, a refreshing stimulus to new endeavors. Instead of an audience passively and inertly accepting its pastime on a platter, as in the ordinary motion-picture and the ordinary stage-play, it will train up an audience responsible for its own entertainment, an audience keenly alive to life.

Chapter XIX

OUR CIVIC THEATRE

Civic? Just what does that connote in connection with the theatre? Civic Theatre! Flavor of politics, of sociology, of reformers and busy-bodies in the adjective; of stimulating pastime if not of art in the noun. Oil and water. Two bodies can not occupy —

But the paradox is more apparent than actual, more actual than inevitable. Where it has been actual, it has sprung from a misconception of the genre. The civic theatre in its inchoate, nebulous state has been the easy game of interested publicists, of amateur patriots. That the idea underlying it has survived these misguided and gratuitous meddlers, is testimony to its sound esthetic foundation, its potential service to the human emotions.

Hinted at in the last chapter as a passionately communal form of the theatre of "Let's pretend!" the civic theatre is almost as distant from dogmatic definition as the theatre of abstraction and its partners in revolt. Definition follows the fact, just as esthetic theory follows artistic creation. And the fact is we do not yet possess a civic theatre to define, although the idea, the foretaste, of one has been held tantalizingly within our grasp several times and as often snatched away. Percy MacKaye, who has had more than anyone else to do with directing the various American expeditions in search of this lost art of the theatre, can define out of his instructive experiences what the civic theatre *is not* — or at least what it *should* not be: " a vague maelstrom of fanfaring trumpets, bewildering lights, chaos of costumes, enigmatical actors, untangoing dancers, all helplessly entangled in frescos of civic reform; pageantry, in short."

Positively, MacKaye has ranged all the way, in an attempt at explicit interpretation, from the benignly sentimental " neighborliness " through such harmless and helpless generalities as " the efficient instrument of the recreative arts of a community," to this slightly more concrete but still indecisive summary: " The Civic Theatre idea, as a distinctive issue, implies the conscious awakening of a people to self-government in the activities of its leisure. To this end, organization of the arts of the theatre, participation by the people in these arts (not mere spectatorship), a new resulting technique, leadership by means of a permanent staff of artists (not merchants in art), elimination of private profit by endowment and public support, dedication in service to the whole community: these are chief among its essentials, and these imply a new and nobler scope for the art of the theatre itself."

This much is clear, then: the civic theatre does have both sociological and esthetic implications. But its sociology hasn't any ax to grind. And its esthetics aren't anything like anything since the festival of Dionysus in the bowl beneath the Acropolis. Its social implications are broad, humanitarian — by-product of a community's marshalled resources; not narrow, specific, propagandist. The conditions under which it must develop demand a form free, flexible, bold, dealing effectively with masses of people, with groups as characters — utterly unlike the intimate, meticulous, constrained theatre we know. The sweep of the prairie vs. the cozy door-yard garden. The Sistine ceiling vs. a miniature Dutch altar-piece. A novel of Dostoievsky vs. a tale by de Maupassant. A whitewash brush in place of an etcher's needle. The gesture of a boxer instead of the flash of an eye. Words, if retained at all, used as signals, pregnant with significance, rather than for subtle shades of meaning.

In the conclusion of the previous chapter, there was hint of the relation of this civic theatre to the theatre of " Let's pretend! " The link is logical, legitimate, but it must not be over-rated. Creative participation of the spectator with the performer, coöperation between audience and stage, is the spirit of both. But impromptu is the mood of " Let's pretend! " You go with an open mind, anticipatory, on tenterhooks — eye, ear and tongue on tip-toe, ready to take advantage of the first opportunity to get into the game. With the civic theatre, not merely the audience of a given night but the entire community is involved. Participation is not left to the inspiration of the moment but embraces both intensive and extensive preparation in advance. The comedians, the tragedians, the dancers, the violinists, the oboe players, the seamstresses, the carpenters, the electricians, the printers, the advertising agents, the efficiency experts, of an entire city and its suburban appendages, must be recruited, organized, set to work, each at the task for which his vocation or his avocation fits him. The community mobilized as in war, but for creation, not for destruction.

Ponder this if you would know why the civic theatre made more rapid growth in practice during the war than in all the years preceding. Cities found how simple, after all, it is to mobilize, to pool resources, to engender a spirit of coöperation more powerful than the combined impulses of individuals. They welcomed the heartening creative consequences of the civic theatre, no matter how crude, rudimentary, immature, as relief from the grim destructive chores of war on which they were likewise coöperating. The only pity is that this mighty driving force of the creative community was dissipated as suddenly and mysteriously as it came into being, simply through lack of sufficient able leaders to tell men and women what they had evolved, how precious it was and how it could be retained, nurtured and made to flower more richly than anyone has yet dreamed.

If one man or two or three could have told this story to a nation, Percy MacKaye, George Pierce Baker and Thomas Wood Stevens would have done it. But they were voices in a wilderness, drowned by financial panic and the revulsion to self-interest which followed in the wake of war. Each of these pioneers, however, has given himself to the job with whole-hearted and altruistic spirit but with equipment varyingly incomplete. Time and the opportunity to experiment, guaranteed by the generosity of ambitious communities, will be necessary to train these and other leaders so that they in turn may train their thousands of collaborators in the intelligent and effective practice of an art that is still in its infancy.

Of the three, MacKaye is best known, has tried his hand oftenest, has molded to his vision the largest numbers of participants, has most profoundly affected the communities in which he has worked, and has carried the Masque, the only articulate form yet developed by the civic theatre, farthest forward from its lineal progenitor, the English pageant. MacKaye considers, and rightly considers, his work as the continuation if not yet the fulfilment of the grandiose projects of his father, Steele MacKaye, typified by the Spectatorium, a vast amphitheatre for the exhibition of spectacular community drama which the panic of 1893 snatched from the roster of Chicago's World's Fair wonders. Imbued not only by the filial incentive to carry on that dream but also by the inspiration of Gordon Craig toward a new theatre, and admitting also his debt to the impulses and ideas of Reinhardt and his Theatre of the Five Thousand, MacKaye began as early as 1905, with the masque-prolog performed on the estate of Augustus Saint-Gaudens, to shift his ground from the conventional to the civic theatre.

Gloucester, Massachusetts, though, was the scene of MacKaye's first large-scaled production: "The Canterbury Pilgrims," August, 1909, with 1500 citizen participants. A year later, with John W. Alexander, he projected "A Masque of Labor" for Pittsburgh, but politics smothered it while it was still on paper. "Sanctuary" came next in 1913, the now-famous Bird Masque, an exquisite and apt example of the civic theatre as unobtrusive handmaiden to a more thoughtful humanity. In over a hundred performances before 200,000 spectators the length and breadth of the country, it has bred mercy in its trail.

With "Saint Louis," produced in May, 1914, to celebrate the city's one hundred and fiftieth birthday, MacKaye came of age as masque master and pioneer in the civic theatre. In Forest Park, on the hillside and by the lagoons where a decade earlier the Cascades had held a world's visitors in spell to a spectacle too vast to be comprised in the concept "theatre," MacKaye's path met that of Stevens in a joint production rivalling that previous scene, enlisting 7500 performers and playing to more than half a million spectators in five days. To Stevens fell the pageant by day, which he devised from historic sources and managed superbly. To MacKaye, the masque by night. Conceived as an allegory of world forces displacing the legendary Cahokia, symbol of the Mound Builders; making free, picturesque and plastic use of groups as characters, this masque through its original form cast Stevens' workmanlike but more conventional contribution into shadow.

"Saint Louis" insured MacKaye's next colossal project an eager hearing. It was "Caliban by the Yellow Sands," New York's and, later, Boston's communal commemoration of the tercentenary of Shakespeare's death — a masque of the art of the theatre, allegorical like its predecessor but interspersed with scene snatches from Shakespeare himself. Urban and Jones in New York, Jones alone in Boston, had by this time replaced Joseph Lindon Smith as MacKaye's designers; and with the coöperation of 2500 amateur and professional players, dancers and musicians in the City College Stadium, Manhattan, ten performances were given in May and June, 1916, to 135,000 people, while the following summer in the Harvard Stadium twice the number of performers were seen by twice the number of spectators.

Figures, figures, figures! While they hint vaguely at the impermeation of an entire populace with an idea, they bear no testimony to the pride and passion, the eagerness and enthusiasm, that ran through each of these communities like election news. In Boston, the participants in " Caliban " and the thousands of families in all parts of the city from which they volunteered had their own daily newspaper during rehearsals. In New York, particularly in St. Louis and Boston, the entire municipality awake, excited, transformed, as by nothing except a nip-and-tuck political campaign, a declaration of war, a proclamation of armistice and peace. The leaders themselves breed the contagion of all absorbing zest in the work in hand; MacKaye, Jones, Samuel Eliot, Jr., and Irving Pichel once saw dawn creep into the Harvard Stadium and wondered where the night had gone! By relay, then, this zest reaches the scattered families of the participants and the least seamstress fitting costumes for the chorus in a hall across the city. And finally, the man on the street.

It is this man on the street whom MacKaye has sought to capture. The figures show he has done so. And he has done so first by making his story simple and clear, by divesting art of pretentious obscurity; and secondly by keeping his social message above parties and classes.

In answer to those who have heckled him with the query as to where the citizens of today will find leisure to participate in his projects, he replies: "True, we can use leisure civically only when we have it. Revolution may or may not be necessary to get it. But meanwhile, let us use what leisure we have. Let us give people knowledge of how to use further leisure when they get it. Thereby we shall foster self-control in the struggle for further leisure. Herein lies the true social function of the civic theatre: not as a drug to lure men and women to forget their rights, but as a breath of fresh and exhilarating air to give them self-knowledge for facing manifestly necessary social, economic and industrial changes with better composure and less destructiveness."

The fruit of this broadly humanitarian policy is to be observed best, perhaps, in St. Louis. Nearly ten years have passed since MacKaye and Stevens persuaded an entire community to lay aside personal jealousies and petty bickerings and the retail killing of time for the invigorating pastime of using their leisure toward a common end. The spirit thus invoked resulted immediately in the adoption of a new charter

OUR CIVIC THEATRE

for the city and the authorization of a new bridge across the Mississippi as well as other civic betterments. In addition, the monetary surplus provided a fund out of which has grown a permanent outdoor stage and auditorium in Forest Park wherein the municipality gives a season of light opera at cost each summer. Modest blessings, these, measured by the proportions of MacKaye's dream of a civic theatre. But they are straws in the wind.

The boon still to be realized and reaped by the civic theatre is the permanent capitalization of the enthusiasm, the spirit of coöperation, engendered by one of these mammoth projects. "Such activities in every community," MacKaye insists, "should be constant and normal, not merely sporadic." He reports a "lost feeling" in Gloucester after the pageant was over. "Why has it got to end?" pleaded a little miss from the East Side who had sung alto in the chorus of "Caliban" up under the roof without so much as a glimpse of the production itself. Why, indeed? It was that question which MacKaye asked and covered with satisfactory answer that there must be no end, when he drew up the specifications of the proposed Masque of Cincinnati in 1920, a project which that year's panic nipped in the bud. And he will certainly demand, as all others embarking on similar journey should do, that permanence be written into the contract of any future project to which he lends a hand.

MacKaye has had his opponents who have resented the apparent ease with which he has held up his little finger and commanded a guaranty fund which would run an ordinary theatre for two or three seasons. By some of these he is considered to be the greatest stumbling block to the progress of the art of the theatre in America. To such as these, however, the theatre is a small and exclusive domain to be cherished for the few rather than opened to the creative participation of the many. Those who are in sympathy with the idea of a civic theatre, too, have been impatient of MacKaye's approximations. For they have been approximations, experiments, stumblings in the dark of a new *metier*. MacKaye and Jones, who has been twice associated with him, would be the first to admit that. On the eve of the premiere and only on the eve, has the comprehension dawned as to what it was all about. For them and their immediate assistants as well as for the community at large. And then it was too late. Something richer, more inspiring, than their original dream had come to the verge of being and then escaped. How to seize upon this something, make it articulate guide and lodestar from the beginning, is the problem of the master of the civic theatre for the solution of which vast sums and guaranty funds will continue to be justified.

Compared with MacKaye's dream of a civic theatre, Baker's and Stevens' conception is much more modest but valuable as far as it goes. Distinguished not only from the conventional theatre but also from the masque, the pageant form as these men have utilized it is derived by lineal descent from the early English examples of seven and eight centuries ago. Its purpose is the

PLYMOUTH COMMUNITY COMMEMORATES THE ADVENT OF
HER FOUNDERS

Field and Sea as Stage for the Civic Theatre in Professor George Pierce Baker's Production, "The Pilgrim Spirit"

reinterpretation of history by means of realistic spectacle. In its modern reincarnation, it has been most beholden to Louis N. Parker in England. Guided almost solely by its individual story, it has survived with a minimum of rule or technique, amounting often to little more than a procession of floats. But Parker with his training as a playwright and Baker and Stevens with their experience in teaching playwriting at Harvard and Carnegie are applying some of the elemental tests of the traditional indoor stage, with the result that such spectacles as Baker's "The Pilgrim Spirit" at Plymouth in 1921 and Stevens' "Missouri One Hundred Years Ago" in St. Louis the same year and his "The Pageant of Virginia" staged at Richmond the following summer, have clash and contrast and climax. The new pageant master lets the story tell itself, in the words which documented history has handed down in so far as that is possible, but he watches his pattern and his continuity after the manner of the dramatist.

Sometimes, as Baker found out at Plymouth, the exigency of the material ties the pageant master down to intimate and unimpressive scenes. The Pilgrims were not an imposing group after their first winter on Cole's Hill! The social and historic function of the pageant, clashing thus with the dramatic, must be assisted by the devising of contrastingly elaborate scenes, such as the Royal Progress of King James, motivated as the wall against which the Puritan petitioners broke their heads; the March of the Dutch Cities of Charity, marking the truce which gave them temporary haven in

Holland; and the finale, a conventionalized assembling of all the participants.

Both as masque and as pageant, the civic theatre needs experiment above all to bring out its hidden potentialities. Shall it abandon the spoken word as unsuitable medium for mass expression and for reaching an audience of five and six digits? Some think so. Others would retain the spoken word but deny it connected literary or narrative responsibility, restricting it to highly significant and climactic phrases. Words as searchlights, trumpet calls, newspaper headlines. Still others, keeping the word, would limit it to its tonal use as variant and adjunct to the music. Then there is light. Who will be the Belasco of the night sky? Pevcar of Boston bids for the post. Baker set him a definite task at Plymouth. With batteries of fifteen hundred watt lamps and projectors adjustible down to an arc of but seven degrees, he was able to surpass specifications, flood the entire field like day or cut out of the dark a small and sharply outlined rectangle of brilliance. But the full goal here, too, is dubious, distant, dependent on experiment.

One point is sure: Whether the spoken word be put to work or discharged, whether light keeps pace in growth with the other crafts, whether the esthetic of realism or of allegorical symbolism or of abstraction gains the upper hand or whether an eclectic pattern of several theories is found feasible in the open air, the civic theatre must remember from dawn till dawn that it is theatre first and civic afterward, that the theatre is an art, and that art is not a mere picnic.

Chapter XX

REVUE, VARIETY AND THE DANCE

Hors-d'oeuvre of the theatre. Revue: Follies, Passing Shows, Scandals, Snapshots, Brevities, Oddities, Vanities, Insanities, Nifties, Verbosities, Monstrosities, Grandiosities, Ecstasies. Musical Comedy, frisky maiden aunt of the Revue: *de luxe, intime.* Variety: two-a-day, three, continuous. The Dance: clog, buck-and-wing, cohan, ball-room, character, classic, the ballet.

Hors-d'oeuvre, these? If so, why defer them so late? Partly because they are all dependent on the same forces and factors as the theatre-at-large, and an understanding of these factors and forces automatically throws light on our lighter stage. Then, too, despite our amazing development of these genres in the last fifteen years, they are not yet really provocative enough to tease the appetite, to tempt the taster farther into the theatre. They may some day. That is their logical development. But today, they are oftener desserts — *tours de force* in French pastry; hasty pudding; mince pie; bitter-sweet bonbons; nuts!

Outside the works, whether first or last, these furbelows of the theatre are products of the same elements which give life to the play on the stage. There is the playwright in the guise of librettist, composer, choreograph. There is the producer frankly as producer, ballet-master. The producer even as institution. Witness B. F. Keith Vaudeville, organized, standardized, systematized, classified, catalogued. Or the Ziegfeld "Follies," sixteen years young, without a break, the Theatre Guild of the American girl glorified. Next, the actor, whether the actor resents it or not, as premier clown, prima donna, prima ballerina, down to the first chorister in the first row and even the last in the last. The designer, welcomed here when other latch strings were drawn in, is put up for the night, tolerated as a gay if somewhat mad vagrant. Many of these craftsmen accept employment both inside and outside the works, at the same or different times. The same playhouses, with few exceptions, are just as likely to serve whipped cream as roast. The same critics usually regard both domains as their privileged hunting grounds. And the same audience — or is it the same? To a large extent, surely, although Keith fans, "Follies" fans, Guild fans, are probably more clannish than the artists who minister to them.

Why, then, if the frontiers are so vague, the passport control so lax, should we consider this lighter stage of ours separately? Well, the public does, anyhow. It even locks brothers in lightness in water-tight compartments, hailing novelty, experiment, in the revue, while shying skittishly from it in vaudeville; spending vast sums on the dance in revue and variety and denying it endowment, support, attention, on its own as ballet. But there is more substantial reason for segregating our revue, variety and the dance as well as for grouping them together despite the internal boundaries erected by their clientele. That reason is the striking resemblance between this popular theatre of ours and the popular theatre of another age which the reformers have been dangling before our eyes as a new goal — the *commedia dell'arte*. What! Artistic rebirth from our clowns, our buffoons, our pagan panoramas, our revellers by night?

But there is nothing so strange in that. The popular theatre of one age, of one race, is likely to bear great resemblance to that of another. And if in one age, with one race — Renaissance Italy, to be exact — the popular theatre achieved distinction as the *commedia dell' arte*, there is no reason why it shouldn't do so again. The logical source of all true development is this popular theatre. Any other foundation is unnatural, precarious, ephemeral. Everything depends on the vitality possessed by this theatre of the people. Without this vitality, there is little hope for growth. With it, hope is pregnant, and the attempt to build on any other substructure is foolish, wasteful and wayward.

What evidences are there that this vitality is inherent in our popular theatre? Many, I think, and unmistakable. As in the theatre at large, New York and a few other cities are the only fair criteria. There the stones have been thrown in the lake, and the ripples take time to travel. A tenth rate company in a fifth rate tabloid musical comedy in Kokomo or a vulgar, inefficient vaudeville bill sandwiched in between motion pictures in a neighborhood theatre in Albany, would be a disheartening point of departure. In the metropolis, however, and in the few cities that still comprise " the road," only the blind and deaf could fail to see how far we have travelled in fifteen years and how strong is the urge behind our present pace.

In 1908, we imported from Vienna and London. Today, without ignoring Vienna's very occasional gems, without missing London's silence, we droll our own. We hold the door of the varieties and burlesque and the cabaret open to anyone who can rouse a smile, give him tether to find himself and then promote to fame in the revue a Jimmy Barton, a Bobby Clark, a Solly Ward, a Joe Cook. We reach out and commandeer the palette of an Urban, a Geddes, a Reynolds, or bid the commercial studios to copy them if we grudge the price of the genuine. Would Café Martin have dreamed fifteen years ago of paying Geddes the sum he asked for the *décors* of the Palais Royal? For material, we reach down to our own rhythms, wrestle undaunted and unashamed with the early terrors of jazz on tin pan and cow bell and finally tame it to the seductions of the saxophone. We cultivate our own sense of humor so intently, so assiduously, so without thought of what others will think, that Europe in the presence of "Yes, We Have No Bananas" cocks its ears at the discovery of an original mine of nonsense opened up across the sea. We scour Europe, we borrow, but we recreate, expand, enliven, vitalize, what we annex. The question, "What does it cost?" is seldom asked. When it is, the demands of rivalry nullify the answer. And the returns are so enormous that it doesn't really matter. Dare!

Plunge! Gamble! Youth and vitality know no odds. Nor poise, it is true. But there is time for that.

In all this, we are nearer than we realize to an art of comedy — a popular art, without long hair, flowing ties or other affectations, an art which need not disconcert the man on the street. Call it *commedia dell'arte*, if you like — a modern reincarnation of the improvisations which delighted the man on the street in old Milan, Venice, Vienna. How Thalia must be laughing in her sleeves at the way this modern art of comedy has developed unawares out of the unpretentious tunes, jests, and jigs in the resorts of the populace, while professors and theorists were trying in vain to conjure it to new life academically and properly from the musty records of the past! It has come naturally, spontaneously, unconsciously, the only way if it is to mean something to life rather than to a museum. To grow into that self-control, that delicately balanced knowledge of its own resources, which characterized the *commedia dell'arte*, it will have to accept the guidance of artists less naïve than those who have brought it thus far on its way. Otherwise, it will remain an awkward but engaging lummox, falling just short of satisfying contact with a civilization that prizes a house in order. Such leadership it need not fear, for it knows enough to protect its rights, and besides, its clientele will watch jealously the process of revision.

To realize just how near we are on our popular stage today to the spirit of the old Italian comedy, try a bit of detached analysis amid the gales of laughter that greet the impudent duologs — monologs being duologs with the audience as silent "feeder" — of Will Rogers; Al Jolson; Gallagher and Shean; Walter C. Kelly, the Virginia Judge; Chic Sale; Fannie Brice; Florence Moore; Frank Tinney and the orchestra conductor. Recall Fred Stone when David Montgomery was still living and listening. And Bert Savoy, "You don't know the half of it, dearie!" We didn't know or realize until it was too late. The process in every case consists of apparently more or less improvised jokes, plays on words, on ideas, situations. Rogers improvises most with his intimate *causerie* on the day's news; Jolson, sufficiently to be safely unpredictable; Tinney, least of all. Actually, however, even Rogers' game amounts to ringing new changes on a time-honored repertory. And strangely enough, Robert Edmond Jones, after exhaustive study of the records of *commedia dell'arte* in Italy, has come to the conclusion that genuine improvisation played a much smaller part in its technique than has been supposed, and that the participants were trained from childhood in a vast repertory of smart question and answer which they summoned from memory in endlessly changing permutation and combination.

It is the revue with its flexible structure that best epitomizes this spirit of a seemingly impromptu art of comedy. Compared to the revue, the old-fashioned musical plays, even Cohan's alert, ill-set and madly-danced versions, seem to be strict, narrow and confining channels for comedy, while vaudeville is its rough-and-tumble training school, beloved alike by those who prefer their edges untrimmed and by those scouts who find it a well-stocked preserve of ideas and talent in embryo. The borderland between both of these and the revue is often dim — in the direction of vaudeville when the revue doesn't sufficiently digest and unify its fund of raw material; in the direction of musical comedy when the latter provides generous leeway to its comedians to express their individual gifts. What, for instance, were the Princess cameos — "Nobody Home," "Very Good Eddie," "Oh, Boy!" "Oh, Lady, Lady!" and "Oh, My Dear"? Musical comedies or revues in miniature? If we had more of them today, we could tell better with our sharpened sense of values, but the clever young men and women who wrote and played them profitably in the tiny Princess Theatre are making too much money to revert to the engagingly simple toys of their novitiate.

The father of the American revue is Florenz Ziegfeld, Jr., Sandow, Anna Held, milk baths, Billie Burke. Under his exacting wand, the first "Follies" clambered out of its "Black Crook" chrysalis in 1907, fixing at once the outline and character of the revue as we were to practice it, although the significance of that fact did not dawn at once. Islands of comedy, satiric, ironic, making impudent gestures at current plays and popular foibles, and set in a sea of feminine faces, forms and more or less of costumes. Intriguing. Arresting. Sensuous rather than sensual, barring a misstep several times in the early years. Ziegfeld boldly summons to stop, look and listen. His lures are those of elemental color, sound and motion. With the Greeks of old, he

BRINGING DESIGN INTO THE REALM OF THE REVUE

From a Setting by Joseph Urban for the 1915 Edition of the Ziegfeld "Follies"

makes no attempt to deny the fascination of the human form. His exhibition of feminine beauty and the lines of his comedians have always been frank and unashamed but usually devoid of innuendo.

Ziegfeld's greatest lack has been a contemporary Aristophanes to tweak the noses of pretenders in art, letters, politics and life in terms provocative to the few but readily comprehensible to the man on the street. He might then have been a modern *Choregus,* lavishing on his protégé a production year after year to which only his own past achievements could be dangerous rival. But he has had to make his productions without a protégé. He has had an idea, but, barring the personal contributions of a few of his comedians like Bert Williams and Will Rogers, he has lacked ideas. Considering the fact that until he persuaded Urban to join him in 1915, he had no scenery worthy of the idea and the time, and that he never has had more than scattered tunes commensurate with his general scheme, his achievement is the more notable.

For ten years, Ziegfeld had no rivals but himself, barring a " Watch Your Step," in which the ambidextrous Charles Dillingham, graduate from the court of criticism, turned momentarily from drama, Hippodromes and traditional light opera, and excepting an incipient series of dangerously clever Cohan Revues, which the fickle George soon abandoned. Latterly, however, he has had his mettle tested by a swarm of insistent and variously able pretenders to his throne. John Murray Anderson with " The Greenwich Village Follies," five in a row, has conned the lesson best, repeated the formula with the least rote and the most originality. Superior to Ziegfeld as a master of pastel shades and the pleasantly grotesque, Anderson has also managed to instil into his productions the *insouciant* air of the gifted amateur, a talent nurtured by his Canadian birth and British training, enabling him, whether consciously or not, to carry on something of the deft and unobtrusive spirit of the late George Edwardes, of Gaiety fame. Like Edwardes, he recruits from non-professional ranks to achieve his ends; and like Edwardes, he molds his material with an almost feminine instinct for unobtrusively luxurious atmosphere.

Most formidable rival to Ziegfeld in the popular mind, of course, has been J. J. Shubert, lavish sheik bidding into being for his own pleasure and that of a faithful entourage the Winter Garden's "Passing Shows." Often heedless of niceties, of balance, of the limits of good taste in sensuous display, he has ministered profitably to the less exacting while distinctly furthering the art of comedy by encouragement of Jolson and Willie Howard. Younger and less experienced challengers to Ziegfeld are Irving Berlin and Hassard Short, hosts with Sam. H. Harris at the Music Box. Mechanism, the tricks of light and scenery achieved at whatever cost, are their household gods, but the art of comedy is likewise their concern, as it must be if the revue has hopes of making it a season. Hardly a year now passes without half a dozen new revues ambitious to make it a season and turn the corner into next with a fresh version, but thus far

George White's "Scandals" is the only other to lay the foundations of an annual series.

Weaving itself in and out of this pattern of our lighter stage, twin art with that of comedy, is the dance. No surer barometer of progress. The needle still points only to change, with fair weather beyond the horizon. But fifteen years ago, the indication was unmistakably and ominously — storm. Storm of lingering puritanic disapproval of the naked foot, the free figure, the use of the body to express joy and abandon — in short, of the dance as such. Devils danced; Dionysus. But not the devout. Cohan? But Cohan was an acrobat. That didn't matter. Men didn't dance. Men?

Against this stone wall of indifference, even of hostility, Isadora Duncan broke her youthful beauty, enthusiasm, spirit. Our wilful loss was her gain, forcing her out into a wider world — a back-handed service which she resented, while we, resenting her resentment, have built the wall yet higher for each of her increasingly pathetic homecomings. Our loss, her gain — hers and Russia's and Western Europe's and even our own by ironic indirection. Hailed in Moscow as a goddess from another earth, kindling, revitalizing the Russian Ballet, her spirit travelled westward again with Pavlova, Mordkin and Diagileff, conquered as it came and finally reached and stirred us by proxy, when the body which had housed it was aging and the mind which had driven it was turning bitter.

It is these visitors from Russia more than anyone else to whom the dance is indebted for partial restora-

THE REVUE IN UNOBTRUSIVELY LUXURIOUS MOOD

From a Setting by James Reynolds for the Perfume Ballet in John Murray Anderson's Production of "The Greenwich Village Follies of 1920"

tion of its heritage. To these and to the revue, which first felt the impact of the presence of the Russian dancers among us. Some of our revues have been a dizzying whirl of dancing, ranging all the way from the acrobatic to the classic steps. Men as well as women. And yet, with our revues studded with dancers, we still lack a native American ballet.

The ideal conditions for the growth of such a ballet, of course, would presuppose a tradition of the dance, a school or schools where children could be trained while still supple and amenable both physically and spiritually, and an audience at one and the same time critical and sympathetic. Lacking not one but all of these conditions, we shall have to be grateful when zealots like Margaret Severn, Ruth Page or Martha Lorber dare defy conditions, start training at an age when Russians would deem attainment impossible, and with courageous naïveté presume an audience which exists yet in ponderable numbers only when they merge their separate and distinct art in the melange which is the revue. They are, perhaps, pioneers of a tradition, stimulants to a school, creators of an audience.

CHAPTER XXI

AMERICA AS HOST TO FOREIGN DRAMA

"THERE were once, you know, the Greeks." With these suggestive words, Kenneth Macgowan concluded his best seller of the dramatic book stalls, "The Theatre of Tomorrow," referring to the heydey of Athens and implying the possibility of its reincarnation once more upon the earth.

There were once again the Greeks — other Greeks — and I wonder whether he did not have at least remotely in mind the likelihood of their reincarnation as well. I refer, of course, to the Greeks of that later Athens, Constantinople, who fled the downfall of their civilization before the Turk, swarmed westward into Italy and planted the seeds of which the epoch we know as the renaissance was the flower. And while we may look long and longingly for the counterparts of those earlier, more austere, more ecstatic, more naïve and more perfect Greeks, is it not possible that we are face to face in America today with the brothers in imagination, in flight and in power to inspire, of the godfathers of the golden Middle Ages?

Whether anything worthy of being called a second renaissance is going to happen to us or not, depends on us. The influx, the influence, the inspiration, are here. They have been coming unobtrusively for the last fifteen years, in ever greater numbers since the first year of the war. At first we thought they were using us as refuge to avoid the confusion of battle. But they stayed, just like those other Greeks of old. They stayed and more came. They stayed because they liked us and our opportunities for creative work and our comparatively prompt understanding of what they were trying to do, the " younger generation " to the contrary notwithstanding.

Some of them just came, particularly the pioneers. Increasingly, however, they have been brought, summoned for a distinct purpose. Today, we are using Europe as preceptor, not as the safe source of commercial gain after the manner of the old days of the Boucicault adaptations and the Frohman importations. Occasionally, the old spirit prevails, as in the reaching out for the secure plums of the French and British play markets. Sometimes, too, the motive is simply to fill a gap. But more and more, we pick from the old world's sample room exactly those specimens which seem most likely to provide further and richer stimulus to our own endeavors.

This newer spirit has been a long time getting itself recognized. It has not reached the pitch of today at a leap. The movement westward has not been a movement *en masse,* although it appears so at the present moment. It has been growing in impetus for years. Its motive has been growing in clarity. That both movement and motive are genuine is attested by the fact that we no longer complain as we used to — not even our actors, touchy souls — at the " Foreign Invasion." Neither do we bewail, camp-meeting fashion, as we did a dozen years ago, the lack of native effort on our stage.

HOST TO FOREIGN DRAMA

There isn't the same cause to bewail that lack, and yet the register of visitors is more crowded than ever before. The difference is that we realize why they are here and what they can do for us. Then, we knew not and knew not that we knew not. Today, we know not — at least not what we could and should — and know it. And we are willing to learn.

Consider, for instance, the first cabin immigrants of a single season. From England: Galsworthy's "Loyalties"; Shaw's "The Devil's Disciple"; Milne's "The Lucky One" and "The Romantic Age"; Clemence Dane's "Will Shakespeare"; Maugham's "East of Suez"; Pinero's "The Enchanted Cottage"; Sutro's "The Laughing Lady"; and Frederick Lonsdale's "Aren't We All," with the British Mr. Maude in person.

From France: Cécile Sorel, of the Comédie Française, supported by artists from that and other French stages in a comprehensive Gallic repertory; Géraldy's "To Love," sympathetically translated, staged and acted by Grace George; Bataille's "*La Tendresse*" and "The Love Child"; Claudel's "The Tidings Brought to Mary"; and Guitry's "Pasteur" and "The Comedian."

From Germany: Hauptmann's "Rose Bernd"; "Johannes Kreisler" by Bernauer and Meinhard; Kaiser's "From Morn to Midnight."

From Spain: "Malvaloca" by the Brothers Quintero.

From Italy: "The Plot Thickens" by Barzini and Fraccarroli; and Pirandello's "Six Characters in Search of an Author," mismated Pembertonian pearls.

From Czecho-Slovakia: " R. U. R." by one Capek; " The World We Live In " or " The Insect Comedy " by two.

From Norway: Ibsen's " Peer Gynt " — or rather, the ghost of it.

From Hungary: Molnar's " Fashions for Men."

From Russia: The Moscow Art Theatre — Stanislavsky, stalwart drum major, and one of the Tolstoys, Gorky, Tchehoff, Turgenieff and Dostoievsky in the parade; Balieff's Chauve-Souris, actually fosterson of the former, but apparently its god-father before American audiences; Andreieff's " Anathema " and " He Who Gets Slapped "; Gogol's " The Inspector General "; Sholom Ash's " The God of Vengeance "; and Fyodor Chaliapin, indentured to opera but ennobling and even shattering lyric bonds as the greatest living actor.

This international invasion may be sharply divided between those who arrive by proxy of adaptation and translation and those who come in their own person, speaking their own tongue. For the former, adaptation used to be favored, but the recent prevalence of translations is a happy omen.

Still, there are translations — and translations. Too often, the central purpose of the process is forgotten: to make clear the content and significance of the original, to convey this content and this purport in unmistakable idiomatic English, rather than to preserve a slavish " respect for the author's style." Not what words the author has used and what their literal English equivalents; but what ideas lie beneath those

THE ROBOTS RISE FOR THEIR RIGHTS

A Setting in the Theatre Guild's Production of Karel Capek's "R.U.R."
From a Design by Lee Simonson

words, how to express those ideas in eloquent English, how to approximate the general tone effect of the author's lines when spoken.

Here, then, is the crux of the matter: Any kind of translation, and especially translation for the theatre, should be done by those who have an intimate and native knowledge of the language into which the translation is to be made. The measuring-stick afforded by the most perfect scientific knowledge of English which a Russian or a Frenchman or a German could command, is far less effective than the keen intuition and the homely, idiomatic ease of expression of one brought up in our own tongue. The ideal translator will know both languages equally well, but, unlike the teacher who finds comparative deficiency in the tongue of his pupil a minor handicap, the translator will be able to do a finished and effective piece of work with a limited command of the original author's tongue or even, in case he has a collaborator in that tongue, with no knowledge of it at all.

There are three conceivable approaches to this task: the obtuse, inflexible way of the foreigner; the similarly laborious manner of the too literal-minded native; the sensitive course of one who adds fluent reinterpretation to the mere interchange of words. As an instance of the first of these courses, Andreieff's "He Who Gets Slapped" was a victim of Gregory Zilboorg's stiff and stilted English. Likewise, the overtones of Maeterlinck's vibrant, rhythmic French became mere monotonous and irritating repetitions of inconsequential phrases at the hands of Alexander

Teixeira de Mattos. Example of the second method is at hand in William Archer's invaluable and pioneer service as interpreter of Ibsen, for in Archer's broadly sympathetic mentality there is a Scotch inclination toward downright phrases which miss the aspect of the great Norwegian as a poet whose imagination revealed to him a social vision and who preserved to his last lines the poet's reverence for beauty of expression. More or less faithful and constant travellers down the third path have been Ludwig Lewisohn, who has carried over into simple, idiomatic and even colloquial English the spirit and atmosphere of Hauptmann; Benjamin Glazer, who ran down corresponding English idioms for the Hungarian slang and unlettered dialogue of " Liliom "; and Sidney Howard, whose version of Vildrac's " S. S. *Tenacity* " was the richest, subtlest and most sensitive translation from the French in many years.

It augurs well for the future of our imported drama that its reinterpretation is falling into the hands of such young men as Glazer and Howard. The profession of translation, however, is not necessarily limited to the younger generation. Nor is it a calling perforce separated from creative composition. Victor Hugo's translation of Shakespeare is one of the proudest possessions of French letters. It is not unreasonable, therefore, to hope that our own poets may be stirred to make for us genuinely poetic and genuinely American versions of the new poetic drama of Europe, and that our realists may perform a like service for Tchehoff and Wedekind and de Curel and their kindred overseas, while such men as Vachel Lindsay and Alfred Kreymborg might achieve something really exciting in transcriptions of the ultra-modernists of the Continent. Our literary and dramatic and artistic vision is broader than ever before, and it is inconceivable that out of our own virile and varied resources we shall not find those who will reclothe the dreams of the world in guise that we can comprehend.

Nevertheless, although the sympathetically translated play has considerably broadened our horizons, it is the foreign artists speaking their own tongue who have been the real modern Greeks to whom we are most beholden and whom we, as hosts, have welcomed in a mood no one would have dared predict a decade and a half ago.

Whenever I visit one of these foreign companies speaking its own tongue, I try to forget that the tongue is foreign. I try even to forget that such a thing as a tongue is concerned in the proceedings at all. And to the extent that I succeed in forgetting these surprisingly forgettable barriers, I am rewarded by a glimpse of drama pared to its essentials, by a fresh and vivid realization that the art of the theatre consists fundamentally in certain broad, simple, rhythmic elements of story appealing directly to the emotions through the sense of hearing and particularly through the sense of sight.

Of course, if all plays were like those legendary children of a past and peaceful generation, pleasantly visible in spotless bib-and-tucker but graciously inaudible, there would be no occasion for discussion of the problem. No stiles to climb to France, Germany, Italy, Spain, Scandinavia, Russia. No more than in music. But they are not. Speech has a seat at the theatre's table though not at its head.

As long as our theatre walked hand in hand with our politics and our other national pastimes in complacent isolation, there was small cause to exert ourselves further than to scrape an acquaintance with current Anglicisms in the libretti of Gilbert and the plays of Wilde and Pinero and Jones. French? We were content with the egregious "adaptation." *Double entente* innocuously halved and even quartered. Couches respectably transformed into tea-tables with a dispatch that would make a dealer in trick furniture turn green with envy. German? A thick and muddy and ponderous "translation." Russian? The insanely melodramatic "Siberia." Spanish and Italian? Not so much as a hint outside the opera.

If we craved dramatic caviar, we stole abroad, feasted our fill, and on our return reported rather charily our delight in Lavedan, Wedekind, d'Annunzio, Benavente, Tchehoff or Gorky in the original, for fear our complete sanity might be called in question.

All that, however, has changed. New York theatres harbor daily performances not only in the English and the American languages but also in Russian, Yiddish, French, German, Italian, Spanish, Greek and Negro, not to mention occasional productions in half a dozen other tongues, and the grand operatic Tower of Babel. And what is more, the clientele of these apparently exotic stages is not limited to those who are expert or even on bowing terms with their alien speech. One by one, like a gem of a restaurant buried in Broome Street, they are being dragged to light and "passed on" by such enterprising scouts as Carl Van Vechten and Stark Young. To his most enthusiastic admirers, Ben-Ami was as well-known while he was still at the Jewish Art Theatre as he is today. Wholly by his intermittent appearances along the Bowery in his native Sicilian, Giovanni Grasso has become the idol of a cult that girdles Manhattan.

Just what is it we take away from a play in a foreign tongue — from the Russians, for instance? The Moscow Art Theatre and Balieff's Chauve-Souris are still very much with us. And right here let us rule out of our inquiry all those who understand the foreign tongue — even those who know only a few words and phrases. A little knowledge in such a case is not only dangerous; it is disastrous. With the best will in the world, you let yourself lapse into a strained vigil for the words and phrases you recognize, to the utter neglect of far more important considerations. And when they come, they pop out at you like a jack-in-the-box with about as much significance or continuity as a printer's pi line.

What we take away from the theatre is measured, by the relentless rule of compensation, on what we take to the theatre.

Icicles in our pockets? The habitual coldness and boredom of the American at the play. " The Chauve-Souris? The Moscow Art Theatre? The Comédie Française? The Yiddish stages? Well, what of it?

All right, I suppose, but they don't hand me a thrill. Give me the Polo Grounds or the Yale Bowl or Tex Rickard's Arena."

Preconceptions of drama as a lackey to literature? A blank and devastating sense of having been deceived. "The plays these visitors present may be very good plays. But what is literature if you don't know the language? And what else is there to it besides the literature?"

Prejudice against all things alien, including speech? Prejudice fanned to hysteria. "Why can't these foreigners stay at home and starve? They're all Bolsheviks, anyhow."

A total lack of preparation of any kind? Irritating bewilderment. "What is it all about? What's the use of their opening their heads at all if you can't understand a word they say?"

An open-minded but casual curiosity? Attention arrested; curiosity whetted; desire for more adequate preparation in order to obtain sharper, more vivid reactions. "Well, this is something different! Why didn't you tell me about it before?"

A slight previous knowledge of the backgrounds of the production, of the narrative of the play? Surprise and keen satisfaction at the clarity with which the action may be followed. "Strange, but you don't really have to know a word of Russian, French or German. And who would have dreamed that the merest thread of the story tucked away in the program would light up so vividly under the spell of eloquent pantomime, significant tempo and the richly expressive use of the human voice, wholly apart from the actual words it utters?"

Thorough acquaintance in advance not only with the story but with the characters through reading the play in translation? An exciting and invigorating experience, stirring the emotions of the spectator and affording a new appreciation of the theatre as a place where one "sees."

What this seventh forehanded theatregoer says, what he takes away from the play in a foreign tongue, can not be compressed in a phrase. His experience is a stimulating and at the same time a restful vacation from jazz and fox-trots, from vitamines and furnaces fed on buckwheat diet, from six star newspapers and comic supplements, from stock tickers and bargain counters, from bootleggers and dry raids, from subways and taxis and limousines and commuters' trains, from income taxes and ticket speculators, from strikes and lockouts and all the confusing and exhausting welter of contemporary America.

Let him post himself properly in background and visit the immigrants in their lighter mood — Balieff's Chauve-Souris, for example — and he will be whisked away from these alarums and excursions to the mellow fragrance of forgotten folk tunes, to the intriguing beguilements of peasant pursuits and pastimes of other lands. Under the spell of color, melody and the dance, the foreignness of the tongue is an obstacle ignored. Something rich, human, universal, strides past that barrier as if it never existed.

The rewards of dalliance with serious dramatic companies — Stanislavsky's, for instance — are less obvious, more elusive, not quite so simple, so elemental, so in reach for the asking. But like anything requiring effort to attain, they are, to the extent that they must be mastered, the more generously remunerative. They are not the easy and soothing rewards of charming fantasy or rugged humor. Their range is in the realm of the imaginative, the esthetic, the spiritual. Here is drama pared of an obstructing " literature " down to an impassioned and colorful clash of human wills and desires. When ambition surges, it makes itself known not through cluttering words — feeble symbols at best, even in the hands of poetic genius — but through flaming eye, contracted muscles and hardened voice, emotional evidences that strike directly home to the feelings of the spectator. Fear, envy, revenge, heartsickening indecision — all these and more speak the same direct language to one who sees a play in its native tongue. Life eloquent in its own stuff without the need of words.

If it does nothing else, then, the experience of seeing a play in a foreign tongue emphasizes the visible nature of the theatre. What does the word " theatre " mean, after all? Gordon Craig has never tired of harking back to its etymological great-great-grandparent, the Greek $\theta \acute{\epsilon} \alpha \tau \rho o \nu$, a place for seeing shows, derived from $\theta \epsilon \acute{\alpha} o \mu \alpha \iota$, I see. And he adds in a note in " Towards a New Theatre ": " Not a word about it being a place for *hearing* 30,000 *words babbled* out in two hours."

Of course, the 30,000 words are " babbled " just the

same in a play in an alien tongue. But, somehow, they don't matter so much. You are thrown back on more fundamental and elemental aspects of the situation. You have to use your eyes, whether you will or no. And the experience is very likely to plant the seed of suspicion that we have been losing something in this latter-day talkative theatre of ours. Just because the Greeks looked on the theatre as a " place to *see* shows " is no final reason, of course, why we should not make use of it today as a place to hear them. And whether it is a reason or not, we are not likely all at once to discard a form out of which we have obtained a certain satisfaction. But side by side with our audible, " literary " theatre we are sitting in at the experimental recreation of the visible, theatrical theatre.

How ironical it would be — almost as much so as the birth of the modern theatre in the church which today curses it — if the Moscow Art Theatre should thus serve as encouraging god-father to the theatre where Sight and not Sound is the patron saint! Founded in reverent respect for the literary drama and preserving its faith in realism as the ablest esthetic means of interpreting that drama, it has held its ground doggedly against all the innovators like Meyerhold and Tairoff who would shift the emphasis from the ear to the eye. Perhaps if Stanislavsky and his charges had realized this ominous potentiality of their American visit, they would have thought twice before embarking on a tour which they must naturally have intended to serve as example and preceptor of their own cherished theories and practices.

Potential influence is one thing, actual another. But we can see the trace of the latter already. The impulse toward repertory, toward scouring the world for the best, toward institutional management, visible at the Theatre Guild, is not an essentially American intuition. Without the stimulus and example of the old world pointing to the values to be obtained by ranging great talents around an unobtrusive clearing house, the coterie bearing the insignia of Arthur Hopkins would have been unlikely if not impossible. Without hints from the same faraway source, the actors would never have dreamed of a coöperative theatre of their own like that of Equity.

How much of this influence would have registered articulately without a conscious motive to use our guests as example and spur, is apparent from the fortunes and residue of the pioneers who came unbidden and departed unappreciated in the years before the period of our survey. Duse, 1893, 1896 and 1902; Réjane, 1895 and 1905; Kommissarzhevskaya, 1908; Chaliapin, 1908. Bread upon the waters? No, rather a pebble dropped into a well, savings thrust into a Ponzi's pool.

The newer method, the newer motive, are visible in the recent ventures of Morris Gest. Equipped by birth in Russia with the heritage of the most vividly imaginative of modern nations, and trained by experience in America to stand up to a cold and practical world, he has been the erratic and plunging playboy among our producers. He has tasted the theatre from the sideshow, in which most of the Elder Showmen were schooled, to the spectacular extravaganzas, "Mecca" and "Aphrodite," which some of us liked and some of us decidedly didn't. But Gest liked them. They were his self-indulgence in passionate color, movement, story. He liked them and that was that! Besides, in his view, they enabled him to blazon his name as capital against a day of more ambitious need.

The Moscow Art Theatre brought that day, with Reinhardt to follow while the sun is still high. "From Bosco to Moscow," Ashton Stevens summarized the career of an Elder Showman who is still young. But the trip was not made by express train. There were stopovers and test runs in service to Hammerstein — object lessons in the wiles of publicity, in the riddles of crowd psychology, in the tricks of foreign artistic exchange. A disastrous blunder, too, in the first *Saison Russe*, 1911, attempted before its time. But when Gest deemed the time ripe for Stanislavsky, it was ripe — or he made it so, with his own ripened command of the producer's technique.

In a very real sense, Gest "produced" the Moscow Art Theatre. Stanislavsky and Nemirovitch-Dantchenko produced the plays: "Tsar Fyodor," "The Lower Depths" and the Tchehoff dramas. But Gest produced the theatre. He served as connecting link, interpreter, between the Russians and their American audience, instinctively understanding both better than either did the other, and assisting us for the first time, though surely not for the last, to enact the rôle of felicitous and efficient host to the theatre international.

Chapter XXII

THE ECONOMIC PROBLEMS OF OUR THEATRE

Our American Theatre. The theatre which the rest of the world will eventually accept as its refuge, clearing house, testing ground. Eventually. Why not now?

Partly because the rest of the world, with a few blunt, candid, plain-spoken exceptions, is still unwilling to admit that art and the theatre elsewhere are finished. Finished, at least in our time. Lingering faith among many Europeans fondly foresees the return of poise and material well-being out of which creative expression grows. But this faith is a mirage, a lost hope, and, like all lost causes, it is a long time dying.

There are other reasons for incredulity, however, reasons based on inescapable fact. At the heart of our awakening theatre are several ominous and disconcerting problems, on the solution of which must await our own self-assurance that we are ready to serve our native artists, not to mention fulfilling the function of international refuge and clearing house. Esthetic problems confront us, as we have seen, but time and experiment will clear up most of them. It is the economic problems of our theatre and their far-reaching implications which matter. For, like all economic problems, they are the most relentless, most obdurate.

The fact that these problems existed was avoided for a long time. Side-stepped. The skeleton locked in the closet and the key hidden. But misgivings arose. Some of the members of the family began to fear that others might use the key surreptitiously for their own advantage. Therefore the skeleton, or rather skeletons, were shamelessly dragged to the light and the family was organized into parties and cliques, each determined to make sure that the others would not get the better of it. Hence, the Producing Managers' Association. The International Theatrical Association. The Actors' Equity Association. The Actors' Fidelity League. The Dramatists' Guild. The Theatrical Press Representatives of America. The International Alliance of Theatrical Stage Employees and Moving Picture Machine Operators. The American Federation of Musicians. The International Alliance of Billposters and Billers. The Chorus Equity Association. The Brotherhood of Painters, Decorators and Paper Hangers, to which Jones, Geddes, Simonson and the rest of the scenic artists and designers have been firmly invited to belong. The International Brotherhood of Teamsters and Chauffeurs, without whose good will no scenery can be moved. These, up and down Broadway. Along Second Avenue in the Yiddish theatres, the ushers, door-tenders, scrubwomen and dressers are similarly regimented. Even if the play is " King Lear," " The Power of Darkness " or " The God of Vengeance," a chorus of eight with their dressers has to be engaged and paid. And understudies are supplied by rotation through the union office, with a fair chance of a bearded patriarch being sent to play Romeo, or a dumpy dowager, Juliet.

Matthew Arnold demanded an organized theatre. The theatre is organized!

The firm of Klaw and Erlanger, the once redoubtable Syndicate, set the pace and the fashion in organization over a quarter of a century ago. By 1908, Lee and J. J. Shubert had partially curbed organization by further organization. And so it has gone ever since — pyramid on pyramid. Ossa on Pelion. Two, three and four theatres sprang up to struggle and jostle one another where one had flourished in lonely peace and profit. And yet, somehow, the dramatic appetite of the public expanded to keep step with this apparently insane building program.

Mastered by the intricate real estate system of which in the beginning he was master, Lee Shubert has relinquished little by little the functions of a producer. For that rôle, his limited education ill prepared him, but a shrewd native executive ability enabled him to contrive an organism of wheels within wheels for the development, maintenance and operation of theatrical realty, until he is today the omnipotent traffic officer of the American stage, its commissioner of plant and structure, of ways and means, leaving largely to others the riskier pursuits of actual production, but controlling production indirectly through lease and rental, through sharing and staking and the other expedients of the theatrical game.

Under the Syndicate first but more intensively under the Shuberts, the " front of the house " has been transformed from a game of frontier poker to a business checked to the last cent by cost-accounting. Too great trust is still imposed in the necessity of a spy system, penalizing and humiliating the honest employees, but that is a hang-over from the old wild-cat days of the business side of the theatre, representatives of which are still extant within its ranks. Making the theatre business-like is no mean service. Waste, prodigality, duplication of effort, costly delays and indecision, entailing still more costly time-and-a-half for over-time — these have long been the chronic ailments of the theatre in America on its material side. Before the theatre can become free and eloquent as an art, it must be made sound financially. Efficiency in place of extravagance. Order in place of chaos. A program, a budget, for tomorrow, next year; rather than the whims of today, indulged by a loose purse and no ledger. In so far as he has carried our theatre appreciably along these paths, no matter what his motive, Lee Shubert has been a builder, a constructive force.

Real estate and the building of theatres as a by-product of warfare and competition in the organization and financial control of the theatre, are one thing. As a question of site, traffic-congestion, high ground rent and consequently exorbitant cost of production, they are another. From this angle, they present one of the most aggravating and insoluble of our theatre's economic problems. The case of New York is the most obvious, although the situation is repeated less urgently and on a smaller scale in other cities. The majority of the first-class playhouses in the metropolis are huddled within a half mile radius of that focal point of traffic. Four or five subway stations pour their tens of thousands of passengers every week-day night and half the afternoons into this tight and tangled web, and after the performance swallow them up again in even shorter time and more appalling confusion. And the end is not yet in sight.

A solution? Not that proposed by visitors to or from foreign capitals, envious or proud of their magnificent playhouses with four façades, vistas down imposing avenues, planted here, there and everywhere throughout the city. It is just as easy for a resident of Montparnasse to reach the Opéra as the Théâtre des Champs-Elysées. A dweller in Wilmersdorf recks not of the comparative distance to the Deutsches Theater or the Staatsoper. A denizen of Vienna's Inner City finds his way as readily to the Carl Theater as to the Josephstadt. Not so, New York. And never so. Manhattan is an island, long and narrow, with its theatre-going population mustered from its northern precincts and from suburbs in Jersey, on Long and Staten Islands, along four railroad arteries reaching into Westchester, the vast bulk of whom enter and deploy through two huge terminals, the Grand Central and the Pennsylvania. To expect any appreciable number of them to supplement their journey by devious additional routes to unfrequented corners of the mother island, is to dream idly. The full mile radius from Times Square may be filled out in time, but that is the logical limit.

If emulation of the Continent's policy of decentralization is out of the question, solution of the problem or an approximation of solution are still possible. The discomfort of congestion in going to and from the theatre is bound up with the entire issue of general transit which New York must disentangle sooner or later for the sake of its very existence. Transit relief, however, will not directly mitigate the burden of exorbitant ground rent, the overhead charge which is responsible not only for cramped stage room, lack of storage space essential to a genuine repertory system, and other restrictions to an experimental régime; but also — in part, at least — for the high cost of theatre-going. Turn back to Chapter XIII for Lee Simonson's most plausible program for alleviation of the former difficulties: Down to the cellar! Blast! If business can burrow, why not the theatre? Mechanism not as master but as servant.

We encounter a separate problem, however, when we consider high ground rent as contributory cause to a high scale of admission prices. It is a cause, but one of several and the one least likely to yield to modification. "Down to the cellar!" will affect merely the theatre's efficiency, not its cost of operation. The wiser course to follow, therefore, would seem to be to economize along other channels of the cost of production not so rigidly fixed by geography: the perfection of that business efficiency we have just been considering; the reduction of chance by the use of intelligence in addition to instinct — although the complete elimination of chance in the theatre is impossible; the provision for permanent companies, annual salaries, pensions, death and sick benefits — all inducing not only a better spirit throughout the theatre and an opportunity for the riper practice of its art, but also a monetary saving in view of the fact that the actor, thus protected from the current uncertainties and hardships of his calling, might be persuaded to forego the fantastic salaries which many of his craft demand today and receive — when they are at work.

Barring a Sunday supplement curiosity in these salaries and their capricious recipients, the public bothers its head about the economics of the theatre only at the point of direct contact: the theatre ticket and the price of it. Speculators, agencies, buy-outs, cut-rates, two-for-one, ten per cent war tax, passes. The tale is as old as the theatre itself. Everyone is eager to get into the theatre for nothing — unless entrance is too easy. Pittsburgh suspected Carnegie's "All seats free!" at first until Stevens proved he was giving away something of value in return for an intelligent and critical audience for his students. As old as the theatre; and as likely to persist. At least, as long as the theatre continues stubbornly to disregard or resist the economic law of supply and demand.

The attempted nullification of that law and the retributive way in which it strikes back at those who respect it so lightly, distinguish the theatre from any other business or profession. Within a range quite incommensurate with the varying costs of production and the widely differing markets, prices of admission remain static. Using the top of the scale as dimension, we find the producer asking the public to pay $2 to $4 for a glimpse of that on which he has spent anywhere from $6000 to a quarter of a million; $2 to $4, whether nobody cares a fig for his wares or all the world is clamoring for standing room.

Manifestly, this comparatively inflexible price of theatre tickets is wrong, an attempt to defy logic and nature. It is easier, however, to insist and prove that theatre values are not spanned by a ratio of two to one, than it is to suggest remedies. Calculation of those values according to costs? No, for value is often out of all proportion, just as in all the arts. According to public demand, regardless of cost? No, for the laxity or intensity of that demand may never be predicted with certainty, until after the premiere. And if the price scale originally announced is thereafter reduced, there is suspicion; increased, resentment.

Riddle: Why are theatre tickets like water? Answer: Because they tend to reach their own level. Regardless of the normal equality at which they emerge from the various box offices, heedless of the obstacles which seem to stand in the way of a frank recognition of the law of supply and demand, they often find ways, underground ways, circuitous ways, ways brazenly and shamelessly direct and visible, to the pocket of the actual consumer at somewhere near their true value according to that law. Sometimes with the connivance of the producer, sometimes not. Again and again, whenever public indignation rises high enough over the working of that law (in reality, over the inequality of its working), there have been attempts to curb it by other laws, man-made laws, city ordinances and acts of the legislature. But always in vain. The tickets for the play the public desires to see are bought up, bid up, held at a premium in the shoe shop and the millinery store next door; those for the play it disdains are a drug on the market, losing caste and finally reaching second-hand stores, bargain sales — Leblang and the cut-rates. In vain, too, the managers propose a single central agency, run by themselves. Blackballed. And impossible without unanimity.

In sum, then: Can economic law be flouted, controlled by an artificial balance wheel? Partially, but never wholly. Can speculators be driven from the street? The majority, if the Producing Managers' Association really wishes to, if its members without exception agree and abide by their agreement to sell only through their own box offices and the reputable agencies which charge a small fee for service and for carrying their customers' accounts. Can any course curb the cut-rate — the cut-throat, insidious borer into the theatre's economic vitals, lending fictitious life to plays usually worthless, encouraging more of them, vitiating public taste and sense of value? Yes, any course — on which the Producing Managers coincide.

The same coöperation, too, is all that is necessary to keep permanently laid the ghost of censorship which periodically walks after a "Rubicon," an "Artists and Models." Censorship is not in itself an economic problem, but, once fastened like a leech upon the theatre, it might become one of the most corrupt of them all.

Coöperation! Think of all that depends, among the managers alone, on the rediscovery, understanding and use of that rarest of all contemporary processes! And then consider what it might accomplish in solution of the constantly recurring differences between any two or among all of the super-organized factions of our theatre! In particular, of the ominous impasse between the Producing Managers' Association and the Actors' Equity Association. Both of these parties to a controversy unresolved by the strike of 1919 are confident of the justice of their cause. The spirit of neither is what it should be. Akin to the mood of self-interest and suspicion abroad in the world today, and losing sight of the forest of a larger good for the trees of material and ephemeral satisfactions, this spirit is the inheritance of injustices committed and endured by both parties through a number of years. The wraiths of this past rise up today, as they did between England and Ireland, to thwart any simple, direct solution of the problem.

It is not from any lazy faith that there is no use borrowing trouble before it comes, that I refrain from detailed analysis of the case of each side. There is such a thing as talking about the inevitability of war until there *is* war. It is much more important to hold in the mind's foreground the necessity for a peaceful and unselfish solution of the problem if our American theatre is to advance toward repertory, the permanent company, adequate rehearsals and the score of other vistas which the last fifteen years have revealed to us. No matter with what clean hands and scroll of grievances the actors should enter such a struggle, no matter how justifiable the managers might be in refusing further concessions, nothing but immediate and irreparable harm could result for the theatre, if the issue is joined. For the loser, creative energies wasted for years on plans for revenge. For the victor, nothing but defeat in the long run and indefinite postponement of a goal just in sight!

APPENDICES

I

IMPORTANT PRODUCTIONS ON THE AMERICAN STAGE, 1908-1923 *

Vera Kommissarzhevskaya, in repertory, including " A Doll's House," by Henrik Ibsen; " Children of the Sun," by Maxim Gorky; " The Girl Without a Dowry," by Alexander Ostrovsky; " The Fires of St. John " and " The Battle of the Butterflies," by Hermann Sudermann; and *" Le Misanthrope,"* by Molière; at Daly's Theatre, New York, Spring of 1908

" The Devil," by Franz Molnar, produced at the Belasco Theatre (now the Republic), New York, August 18, 1908, by David Belasco, with George Arliss

" Salvation Nell," by Edward Sheldon, produced at the Hackett Theatre, New York, November 17, 1908, by Harrison Grey Fiske, with Minnie Maddern Fiske

" What Every Woman Knows," by James M. Barrie, produced at the Empire Theatre, New York, December 23, 1908, by Charles Frohman, with Maude Adams

---

* The basis of choice has been excellence of workmanship or experimental significance on the part of any one or more than one of the theatre's component crafts. The list is not complete; it aims merely to be representative — or expressionistic! — The Author.

"The Easiest Way," by Eugene Walter, produced at the Stuyvesant Theatre (now the Belasco), New York, January 19, 1909, by David Belasco, with Frances Starr. Revived at the Lyceum Theatre, New York, September 6, 1921, by Mr. Belasco, with Miss Starr

"The Climax," by Edward Locke, produced at Weber's Theatre, New York, April 12, 1909, by Joseph M. Weber. Revived at the Comedy Theatre, New York, January 16, 1919, by Lee and J. J. Shubert, with Eleanor Painter

"Joan of Arc," by Friedrich von Schiller, produced at the Stadium of Harvard University, June 22, 1909, by Maude Adams

"The Canterbury Pilgrims," by Percy MacKaye, produced as the Gloucester Pageant at Gloucester, Massachusetts, August 3, 1909, by Eric Pape, with 1,500 citizens

"The Fortune Hunter," by Winchell Smith, produced at the Gaiety Theatre, New York, September 4, 1909, by Cohan and Harris, with John Barrymore

"The Melting Pot," by Israel Zangwill, produced at the Comedy Theatre, New York, September 6, 1909, by George C. Tyler, for Liebler and Company, with Walker Whiteside

"Strife," by John Galsworthy, produced at the New Theatre (now the Century), New York, November 17, 1909, by Winthrop Ames

"The Nigger," by Edward Sheldon, produced at the New Theatre (now the Century), New York, December 4, 1909, by Winthrop Ames

APPENDIX I

"The Chocolate Soldier," by Oscar Straus, produced at the Lyric Theater, New York, December 13, 1909, by F. C. Whitney. Revived at the Century Theatre, New York, December 12, 1921, by Lee and J. J. Shubert

"The School for Scandal," by Richard Brinsley Sheridan, produced at the New Theatre (now the Century), New York, December 16, 1909, by Winthrop Ames

"The City," by Clyde Fitch, produced at the Lyric Theatre, New York, December 21, 1909, by Lee and J. J. Shubert

"Mid-Channel," by Arthur Wing Pinero, produced at the Empire Theatre, New York, January 31, 1910, by Charles Frohman, with Ethel Barrymore

"A Man's World," by Rachel Crothers, produced at the Comedy Theatre, New York, February 8, 1910, by Lee and J. J. Shubert, with Mary Mannering

The Russian Ballet, presented at the Metropolitan Opera House, New York, March 4, 1910, with Anna Pavlova and Mihail Mordkin

"Sister Beatrice," by Maurice Maeterlinck, produced at the New Theatre (now the Century), New York, March 14, 1910, by George Foster Platt, with Edith Wynne Matthison

"Pillars of Society," by Henrik Ibsen, produced at the Lyceum Theatre, New York, March 28, 1910, by Harrison Grey Fiske, with **Minnie Maddern Fiske and Holbrook Blinn**

"A Winter's Tale," by William Shakespeare, produced at the New Theatre (now the Century), New York, March 28, 1910, by Louis Calvert; on a Shakespearean stage designed by E. Hamilton Bell

"Hannele," by Gerhart Hauptmann, produced at the Lyceum Theatre, New York, April 11, 1910, by Harrison Grey Fiske, with Minnie Maddern Fiske and Holbrook Blinn

"Little Eyolf," by Henrik Ibsen, produced at Nazimova's Theatre (now the Thirty-Ninth Street), April 18, 1910, by Lee and J. J. Shubert, with Alla Nazimova.

"Her Husband's Wife," by A. E. Thomas, produced at the Garrick Theatre, May 9, 1910, by Klaw and Erlanger, with Henry Miller. Revived at the Lyceum Theatre, New York, January 8, 1917, by Henry Miller, with Marie Tempest

"The Blue Bird," by Maurice Maeterlinck, produced at the New Theatre (now the Century), New York, October 1, 1910, by Winthrop Ames

"The Concert," by Hermann Bahr, produced at the Belasco Theatre, New York, October 4, 1910, by David Belasco, with Leo Ditrichstein

"The Merry Wives of Windsor," by William Shakespeare, produced at the New Theatre (now the Century), New York, November 7, 1910, by Winthrop Ames

"The Thunderbolt," by Arthur Wing Pinero, produced at the New Theatre (now the Century), New York, November 12, 1910, by Winthrop Ames

APPENDIX I

"Nobody's Widow," by Avery Hopwood, produced at the Hudson Theatre, New York, November 15, 1910, by David Belasco, with Blanche Bates

"The Faun," by Edward Knoblauch (now Knoblock), produced at Daly's Theatre, New York, January 16, 1911, by William Faversham, with William Faversham

"The Scarecrow," by Percy MacKaye, produced at the Garrick Theatre, New York, January 17, 1911, by Henry B. Harris, with Frank Reicher

"Chantecler," by Edmond Rostand, produced at the Knickerbocker Theatre, New York, January 23, 1911, by Charles Frohman, with Maude Adams; designer, John W. Alexander

"The Boss," by Edward Sheldon, produced at the Astor Theatre, New York, January 30, 1911, by William A. Brady, with Holbrook Blinn and Emily Stevens

"Mrs. Bumpstead-Leigh," by Harry James Smith, produced at the Lyceum Theatre, New York, April 3, 1911, by Harrison Grey Fiske, with Minnie Maddern Fiske

"*Saison Russe,*" Russian Ballet, presented at the Winter Garden, New York, June 14, 1911, by F. Ray Comstock and Morris Gest, with Gertrude Hoffman, Lydia Lopokova, Alexander Volinin, Alexei and Fyodor Kosloff, and others; designer, Leon Bakst

"Disraeli," by Louis N. Parker, produced at Wallack's Theatre, New York, September 18, 1911, by

George C. Tyler, for Liebler and Company, with George Arliss

"The Thief," by Henry Bernstein, produced at Daly's Theatre, New York, October 16, 1911, by Liebler and Company, with Mme. Simone

"The Return of Peter Grimm," by David Belasco, produced at the Belasco Theatre, New York, October 17, 1911, by David Belasco, with David Warfield. Revived at the Belasco Theatre, New York, September 21, 1921, by Mr. Belasco, with Mr. Warfield

"The Garden of Allah," by Robert Hichens and Mary Anderson, produced at the Century Theatre, New York, October 21, 1911, by George C. Tyler, for Liebler and Company, with Mary Mannering

"The Playboy of the Western World," by John Millington Synge, produced at the Maxine Elliott Theatre, New York, November 27, 1911, by the Irish Players

"Kindling," by Charles Kenyon, produced at Daly's Theatre, New York, December 5, 1911, by E. J. Bowes, with Margaret Illington

"Kismet," by Edward Knoblauch (now Knoblock), produced at the Knickerbocker Theatre, New York, December 25, 1911, by Harrison Grey Fiske, with Otis Skinner

"Sumurûn," by Friedrich Freksa and Victor Hollaender, produced at the Casino Theatre, New York, January 16, 1912, by Richard Ordynski, after the production of Professor Max Reinhardt, for Winthrop Ames

APPENDIX I

"The Pigeon," by John Galsworthy, produced at the Little Theatre, New York, March 12, 1912, by Winthrop Ames. Revived at the Greenwich Village Theatre, New York, February 2, 1922, by Edward Goodman

"The 'Mind-the-Paint' Girl," by Arthur Wing Pinero, produced at the Lyceum Theatre, New York, September 9, 1912, by Charles Frohman, with Billie Burke

"Within the Law," by Bayard Veiller, produced at the Eltinge Theatre, New York, September 11, 1912, by Selwyn and Company, with Jane Cowl

"Fanny's First Play," by George Bernard Shaw, produced at the Comedy Theatre, New York, September 16, 1912, by Lee and J. J. Shubert

"Milestones," by Arnold Bennett and Edward Knoblauch (now Knoblock), produced at the Liberty Theatre, New York, September 17, 1912, by Joseph Brooks

"Broadway Jones," by George M. Cohan, produced at Cohan's Theatre, New York, September 23, 1912, by Cohan and Harris, with George M. Cohan

"The Affairs of Anatol," by Arthur Schnitzler, produced at the Little Theatre, New York, October 14, 1912, by Winthrop Ames, with John Barrymore

"The Yellow Jacket," by J. Harry Benrimo and George C. Hazelton, produced at the Fulton Theatre, New York, November 4, 1912, by Henry B. Harris and Edgar Selwyn

"Hindle Wakes," by Stanley Houghton, produced at the Maxine Elliott Theatre, New York, December 9, 1912, by William A. Brady. Revived as " Fanny Hawthorne " at the Vanderbilt Theatre, New York, May 11, 1922, by the Vanderbilt Producing Company

"Years of Discretion," by Frederic and Fanny Hatton, produced at the Belasco Theatre, New York, December 25, 1912, by David Belasco, with Herbert Kelcey and Effie Shannon

"The Poor Little Rich Girl," by Eleanor Gates, produced at the Hudson Theatre, New York, January 21, 1913, by Arthur Hopkins, with Viola Dana

"Romance," by Edward Sheldon, produced at the Maxine Elliott Theatre, New York, February 10, 1913, by Lee and J. J. Shubert, with Doris Keane. Revived at the Playhouse, New York, February 28, 1921, by Lee Shubert, with Miss Keane

"The Trojan Women," by Euripides, produced at the Little Theatre, Chicago, February, 1913, by Maurice Browne

"The Switchboard," by Edgar Wallace; "Fear," by H. R. Lenormand and Jean d'Auguzan; "Fancy Free," by Stanley Houghton; and "Any Night," by Edward Ellis, a bill of one-act-plays produced at the Princess Theatre, New York, March 14, 1913, by F. Ray Comstock and Morris Gest, with Holbrook Blinn

"Damaged Goods," by Eugene Brieux, produced at the Fulton Theatre, New York, March 14, 1913,

APPENDIX I

by Richard Bennett, with Richard Bennett and Wilton Lackaye

"Believe Me, Xantippe," by Frederick Ballard, produced at the Thirty-Ninth Street Theatre, August 19, 1913, by William A. Brady, with John Barrymore

"Where Ignorance Is Bliss," by Franz Molnar, produced at the Lyceum Theatre, New York, September 3, 1913, by Harrison Grey Fiske

"Sanctuary," a Bird Masque, by Percy MacKaye, produced at Meriden, New Hampshire, September 12, 1913, by Joseph Lindon Smith, Ernest Harold Baynes, and the Author

"Seven Keys to Baldpate," by George M. Cohan and Earl Derr Biggers, produced at the Astor Theatre, New York, September 22, 1913, by Cohan and Harris, with George M. Cohan

"Prunella, or Love in a Garden," by Laurence Housman and Granville Barker, produced at the Little Theatre, New York, October 27, 1913, by Winthrop Ames, with Marguerite Clark and Ernest Glendinning

"The Philanderer," by George Bernard Shaw, produced at the Little Theatre, New York, December 30, 1913, by Winthrop Ames

"The Legend of Leonora," by James M. Barrie, produced at the Empire Theatre, New York, January 5, 1914, by Charles Frohman, with Maude Adams

"Lady Windermere's Fan," by Oscar Wilde, produced at the Hudson Theatre, New York, March 30, 1914, by George Foster Platt and Margaret

Anglin, with Margaret Anglin and Sarah Cowell LeMoyne

"Saint Louis, a Civic Masque," by Percy MacKaye, produced on Art Hill, Forest Park, St. Louis, Missouri, May 28, 1914, by Joseph Lindon Smith and the Author, with 7,500 citizens. Preceded by "The Pageant of Saint Louis," by Thomas Wood Stevens

"On Trial," by Elmer L. Reizenstein (now Rice), produced at the Candler Theatre (now the Sam H. Harris), New York, August 19, 1914, by Arthur Hopkins and Cohan and Harris

"The Phantom Rival," by Franz Molnar, produced at the Belasco Theatre, New York, October 6, 1914, by David Belasco, with Leo Ditrichstein

"Pygmalion," by George Bernard Shaw, produced at the Liberty Theatre, New York, October 12, 1914, by Liebler and Co., with Mrs. Patrick Campbell

"A Pair of Silk Stockings," by Cyril Harcourt, produced at the Little Theatre, New York, October 20, 1914, by Winthrop Ames

"Chin-Chin," by Anne Caldwell, R. H. Burnside and Ivan Caryll, produced at the Globe Theatre, New York, October 20, 1914, by Charles B. Dillingham, with Fred Stone and David Montgomery

"Watch Your Step," by Irving Berlin and Harry B. Smith, produced at the New Amsterdam Theatre, New York, December 8, 1914, by Charles B. Dillingham, with Vernon and Irene Castle and Frank Tinney; designers, Robert McQuinn and Helen Dryden

APPENDIX I

"The Show Shop," by James Forbes, produced at the Hudson Theatre, New York, December 31, 1914, by Selwyn and Company, with Douglas Fairbanks and George Sidney

"Children of Earth," by Alice Brown, produced at the Booth Theatre, New York, January 12, 1915, by Winthrop Ames, with Herbert Kelcey and Effie Shannon·

"Marie-Odile," by Edward Knoblauch (now Knoblock), produced at the Belasco Theatre, New York, January 26, 1915, by David Belasco, with Frances Starr

"Androcles and the Lion," by George Bernard Shaw, produced at Wallack's Theatre, New York, January 27, 1915, by Granville Barker, with O. P. Heggie; preceded by "The Man Who Married a Dumb Wife," by Anatole France, with scenery by Robert Edmond Jones

"Jephthah's Daughter," dance drama, music by Lilia Mackay-Cantell, produced at the Neighborhood Playhouse, New York, February 12, 1915, by the Festival Dancers as the first bill of the Playhouse

"A Midsummer Night's Dream," by William Shakespeare, produced at Wallack's Theatre, New York, February 16, 1915, by Granville Barker

"Interior," by Maurice Maeterlinck; "Licensed," by Basil Lawrence (Lawrence Langner); "Eugenically Speaking," by Edward Goodman; and "Another Interior," a pantomime arranged by Ralph Roeder — four one-act-plays produced at the Bandbox Theatre, New York, February 19, 1915, by the Washington Square Players as their first bill

"The Glittering Gate," by Lord Dunsany, produced at the Neighborhood Playhouse, New York, March 6, 1915, by the Neighborhood Players

"The Doctor's Dilemma," by George Bernard Shaw, produced at Wallack's Theatre, New York, March 26, 1915, by Granville Barker

"John Gabriel Borkman," by Henrik Ibsen, produced at the Forty-Eighth Street Theatre, New York, April 13, 1915, by Emanuel Reicher

"Nobody Home," by Guy Bolton and Jerome Kern, produced at the Princess Theatre, New York, April 20, 1915, by F. Ray Comstock and Morris Gest

"Constancy," by Neith Boyce; and "Suppressed Desires," by George Cram Cook and Susan Glaspell, produced at the Wharf Theatre, Provincetown, Massachusetts, in the summer of 1915, by the Provincetown Players as their first bill

The Stratford-upon-Avon Players, in Shakespearean Repertory, with Frank H. Benson and Murray Carrington, appearing in many cities outside New York during the season of 1915–1916

"The Boomerang," by Winchell Smith and Victor Mapes, produced at the Belasco Theatre, New York, August 10, 1915, by David Belasco, with Arthur Byron, Wallace Eddinger and Martha Hedman

"The New York Idea," by Langdon Mitchell, revived at the Playhouse, New York, September 28, 1915, by William A. Brady, with Grace George

APPENDIX I 299

"The Unchastened Woman," by Louis K. Anspacher, produced at the Thirty-Ninth Street Theatre, New York, October 9, 1915, by Oliver Morosco, with Emily Stevens

"Major Barbara," by George Bernard Shaw, produced at the Playhouse, New York, December 9, 1915, by William A. Brady, with Grace George

"The Weavers," by Gerhart Hauptmann, produced at the Garden Theatre, New York, December 14, 1915, by Emanuel Reicher, for the Modern Stage Society

"The Devil's Garden," by William B. Maxwell and Edith Ellis, produced at the Harris Theatre, New York, December 28, 1915, by Arthur Hopkins

Diagileff *Ballet Russe*, presented, with extended repertory, at the Century Theatre, New York, January 16, 1916, by the Metropolitan Opera Company; designers, Leon Bakst, Alexander Benois, Alexander Golovin, etc.

"Erstwhile Susan," by Helen R. Martin and Marian de Forest, produced at the Gaiety Theatre, New York, January 18, 1916, by Corey, Williams and Riter, with Minnie Maddern Fiske

"The Cohan Revue, 1916," by George M. Cohan, produced at the Astor Theatre, New York, February 9, 1916, by George M. Cohan

"The Magical City," by Zoë Akins, produced at the Bandbox Theatre, New York, March 20, 1916, by the Washington Square Players

"Justice," by John Galsworthy, produced at the Candler Theatre (now the Sam H. Harris), New York,

April 3, 1916, by John D. Williams, with John Barrymore

"A Night at an Inn," by Lord Dunsany, produced at the Neighborhood Playhouse, New York, April 22, 1916, by the Neighborhood Players

"The Tempest," by William Shakespeare, produced at the Century Theatre, New York, April 24, 1916, by John Corbin and Louis Calvert, for the Drama Society

"Caliban, By the Yellow Sands," by Percy MacKaye, produced at the Stadium of the College of the City of New York, May 25, 1916, by the Author, Joseph Urban, Robert Edmond Jones, Richard Ordynski, Garnet Holme, Cecil Sharpe, Hazel MacKaye and Irving Pichel for the New York City Shakespeare Tercentenary Celebration Committee, with Isadora Duncan, John Drew, Edith Wynne Matthison, etc., and 2,500 citizens; designers, Joseph Urban and Robert Edmond Jones. Reproduced at the Harvard Stadium, Cambridge, Massachusetts, July 2, 1917, by the Author, Frederick Stanhope, Robert Edmond Jones, Irving Pichel, Samuel A. Eliot, Jr., Virginia Tanner, Percy Burrell and Hazel MacKaye, with 5,000 citizens

"Good Gracious, Annabelle," by Clare Kummer, produced at the Republic Theatre, New York, October 31, 1916, by Arthur Hopkins; designer, Robert Edmond Jones

"Bound East for Cardiff," by Eugene O'Neill; "The Game," by Louise Bryant; and "King Arthur's

APPENDIX I

Socks," by Floyd Dell — three one-act-plays produced at the Provincetown Playhouse, New York, in the autumn of 1916, by the Provincetown Players as their first bill in New York City

"Trifles," by Susan Glaspell; and "Bushido," from the Japanese of Takeda Izumo, two of a bill of four short plays produced at the Comedy Theatre, New York, November 13, 1916, by the Washington Square Players

"The Inca of Perusalem," by George Bernard Shaw; "The Queen's Enemies," by Lord Dunsany, and "Great Catherine," by George Bernard Shaw — three short plays produced November 14, 1916, at the Neighborhood Playhouse by Gertrude Kingston

"The Gods of the Mountain," by Lord Dunsany; "Six Who Pass While the Lentils Boil," and "Nevertheless" by Stuart Walker — three short plays produced in the Portmanteau Theatre at the Thirty-Ninth Street Theatre, New York, November 27, 1916, by Stuart Walker

"A Kiss for Cinderella," by James M. Barrie, produced at the Empire Theatre, New York, December 25, 1916, by Charles Frohman, Inc., with Maude Adams

"A Successful Calamity," by Clare Kummer, produced at the Booth Theatre, New York, February 5, 1917, by Arthur Hopkins, with William Gillette; designer, Robert Edmond Jones

"The Great Divide," by William Vaughn Moody, revived at the Lyceum Theatre, New York, February 7, 1917, by Henry Miller, with Henry Miller

"The Kairn of Koridwen," dance drama, music by Charles T. Griffes, produced at the Neighborhood Playhouse, New York, February 10, 1917, by the Festival Dancers

"Nju," by Ossip Dymow, produced at the Bandbox Theatre, New York, March 22, 1917, by Joseph Urban and Richard Ordynski; designer, Joseph Urban

"The Rider of Dreams," "Granny Maumee," and "Simon the Cyrenian," three short plays by Ridgeley Torrence, produced at the Garden Theatre, New York, April 5, 1917, by Emily Hapgood; designer, Robert Edmond Jones

"The Deluge," by Henning Berger, produced at the Hudson Theatre, New York, August 20, 1917, by Arthur Hopkins, with Pauline Lord. Revived at the Plymouth Theatre, New York, January 27, 1922, by Mr. Hopkins

"Chu Chin Chow," by Oscar Asche and Frederick Norton, produced at the Manhattan Opera House, New York, October 22, 1917, by F. Ray Comstock and Morris Gest

"Madame Sand," by Philip Moeller, produced at the Criterion Theatre, New York, November 19, 1917, by Arthur Hopkins for Klaw and Erlanger, with Minnie Maddern Fiske

Théâtre du Vieux Colombier, of Paris (Jacques Copeau, director), opening a two-year engagement at the Garrick Theatre, New York, December 3, 1917, with "Les Fourberies de Scapin," by Molière

"Why Marry?" by Jesse Lynch Williams, produced at the Astor Theatre, New York, December 25, 1917, by Selwyn and Co., with Nat C. Goodwin

"Josephine," by Hermann Bahr, adapted by Frank E. Washburn-Freund, produced at the Knickerbocker Theatre, New York, January 28, 1918, by The Josephine Company, Inc., with Arnold Daly and Virginia Harned; designer, Rollo Peters

"The Copperhead," by Augustus Thomas, produced at the Shubert Theatre, New York, February 18, 1918, by John D. Williams, with Lionel Barrymore

"The Wild Duck," by Henrik Ibsen, produced at the Plymouth Theatre, New York, March 11, 1918, by Arthur Hopkins, with Alla Nazimova; designer, Robert Edmond Jones

"A Very Good Young Man," by Martin Brown, produced at the Plymouth Theatre, New York, August 19, 1918, by Arthur Hopkins, with Wallace Eddinger

"Lightnin'," by Winchell Smith and Frank Bacon, produced at the Gaiety Theatre, New York, August 26, 1918, by John Golden, with Frank Bacon

"Redemption," by Count Lyoff Tolstoy, produced at the Plymouth Theatre, New York, October 3, 1918, by Arthur Hopkins, with John Barrymore; designer, Robert Edmond Jones

"Be Calm, Camilla," by Clare Kummer, produced at

the Booth Theatre, New York, October 31, 1918, by Arthur Hopkins; designer, Robert Edmond Jones

"Dear Brutus," by James M. Barrie, produced at the Empire Theatre, New York, December 23, 1918, by Charles Frohman, Inc., with William Gillette

"Molière," by Philip Moeller, produced at the Liberty Theatre, New York, March 17, 1919, by Henry Miller, with Henry Miller, Blanche Bates, Holbrook Blinn and Estelle Winwood

"Bernice," by Susan Glaspell, produced at the Provincetown Playhouse, New York, March 29, 1919, by the Provincetown Players

"The Jest," by Sem Benelli, adapted by Edward Sheldon, produced at the Plymouth Theatre, New York, April 9, 1919, by Arthur Hopkins, with John and Lionel Barrymore; designer, Robert Edmond Jones

"Papa," by Zoë Akins, produced at the Little Theatre, New York, April 10, 1919, by F. C. Whitney

"The Bonds of Interest," by Jacinto Benavente, translated by John Garrett Underhill, first production of the Theatre Guild at the Garrick Theatre, New York, April 14, 1919

"John Ferguson," by St. John Ervine, produced at the Garrick Theatre, New York, May 12, 1919, by the Theatre Guild, with Augustin Duncan, Dudley Digges and Rollo Peters

"Clarence," by Booth Tarkington, produced at the Hudson Theatre, New York, September 20, 1919, by George C. Tyler

APPENDIX I

"Declassée," by Zoë Akins, produced at the Empire Theatre, New York, October 6, 1919, by Charles Frohman, Inc., with Ethel Barrymore

"The Lost Leader," by Lennox Robinson, produced at the Greenwich Village Theatre, New York, November 12, 1919, by William Harris, Jr., with Frank Conroy

"Abraham Lincoln," by John Drinkwater, produced at the Cort Theatre, New York, December 15, 1919, by Lester Lonergan for William Harris, Jr.

"The Famous Mrs. Fair," by James Forbes, produced at Henry Miller's Theatre, New York, December 22, 1919, by Henry Miller, with Henry Miller and Blanche Bates

"Night Lodging," by Maxim Gorky, produced at the Plymouth Theatre, New York, December 22, 1919, by Arthur Hopkins

"Mama's Affair," by Rachel Barton Butler, produced at the Little Theatre, New York, January 19, 1920, by Oliver Morosco, with Effie Shannon

"The Beautiful Sabine Women," by Leonid Andreieff, produced at the Neighborhood Playhouse, New York, February 2, 1920, by the Neighborhood Players

"Beyond the Horizon," by Eugene O'Neill, produced at the Morosco Theatre, New York, February 3, matinee, 1920, by John D. Williams, with Richard Bennett; designer, Homer Saint-Gaudens

"The Letter of the Law," by Eugene Brieux, produced at the Criterion Theatre, New York, February

23, 1920, by John D. Williams, with Lionel Barrymore

"Jane Clegg," by St. John Ervine, produced at the Garrick Theatre, New York, February 23, 1920, by Emanuel Reicher for the Theatre Guild, with Margaret Wycherly; designer, Lee Simonson

"Richard III," by William Shakespeare, produced at the Plymouth Theatre, New York, March 6, 1920, by Arthur Hopkins, with John Barrymore; designer, Robert Edmond Jones

"What's in a Name?" by John Murray Anderson and Milton Ager, produced at the Maxine Elliott Theatre, New York, March 19, 1920, by John Murray Anderson; designers, Robert Locker and James Reynolds

"*La Boutique Fantasque,*" music by Rossini, produced at the Neighborhood Playhouse, New York, May 8, 1920, by the Festival Dancers

"Enter Madame," by Gilda Varesi and Dolly Byrne, produced at the Garrick Theatre, New York, August 16, 1920, by Brock Pemberton, with Gilda Varesi; designer, Robert Edmond Jones

"The Bad Man," by Porter Emerson Browne, produced at the Comedy Theatre, New York, August 30, 1920, by Lester Lonergan for William Harris, Jr., with Holbrook Blinn; designer, Livingston Platt

"Greenwich Village Follies of 1920," by John Murray Anderson and A. Baldwin Sloane, produced at the Greenwich Village Theatre, New York, August 30, 1920, by John Murray Anderson for

APPENDIX I

the Bohemians, Inc., with Margaret Severn; designers, Robert Locker and James Reynolds

"The Mob," by John Galsworthy, produced at the Neighborhood Playhouse, New York, October 9, 1920, by the Neighborhood Players

"The First Year," by Frank Craven, produced at the Little Theatre, New York, October 20, 1920, by Winchell Smith, for John Golden, with Frank Craven

"The Skin Game," by John Galsworthy, produced at the Bijou Theatre, New York, October 20, 1920, by Basil Dean, for William A. Brady

"The Emperor Jones," by Eugene O'Neill, produced at the Provincetown Theatre, New York, November 1, 1920, by the Provincetown Players, with Charles S. Gilpin; designer, Cleon Throckmorton

"Heartbreak House," by George Bernard Shaw, produced at the Garrick Theatre, New York, November 10, 1920, by Dudley Digges, for the Theatre Guild; designer, Lee Simonson

"Samson and Delilah," by Sven Lange, produced at the Greenwich Village Theatre, New York, November 17, 1920, by Arthur Hopkins, with Jacob Ben-Ami and Pauline Lord; designer, Robert Edmond Jones

"Mixed Marriage," by St. John Ervine, produced at the Bramhall Playhouse, New York, December 14, 1920, by Augustin Duncan; designer, Rollo Peters

"Sally," by Guy Bolton and Jerome Kern, produced at the New Amsterdam Theatre, New York, December 21, 1920, by F. Ziegfeld, Jr., with Marilyn Miller and Leon Erroll; designer, Joseph Urban

"Deburau," by Sacha Guitry, adapted by Granville Barker, produced at the Belasco Theatre, December 23, 1920, by David Belasco; designer, Ernest Gros

"Diff'rent," by Eugene O'Neill, produced at the Provincetown Playhouse, New York, December 27, 1920, by the Provincetown Players; designer, Cleon Throckmorton

"Miss Lulu Bett," by Zona Gale, produced at the Belmont Theatre, New York, December 27, 1920, by Brock Pemberton, with Carroll McComas

"The Beggar's Opera," by John Gay, Nigel Playfair's London production presented at the Greenwich Village Theatre, New York, December 29, 1920, by Arthur Hopkins; designer, C. Lovat Fraser

"Erminie," by Harry Paulton and E. Jacobowski, revisions by Marc Connelly, revived at the Park Theatre, New York, January 3, 1921, by George C. Tyler, with Francis Wilson and De Wolf Hopper; designer, Norman-Bel Geddes

"Macbeth," by William Shakespeare, produced at the Apollo Theatre, New York, February 17, 1921, by Arthur Hopkins, with Lionel Barrymore and Julia Arthur; designer, Robert Edmond Jones

"Mr. Pim Passes By," by A. A. Milne, produced at the Garrick Theatre, New York, February 28, 1921, by Philip Moeller, for the Theatre Guild; designer, Lee Simonson

APPENDIX I

"The Hero," by Gilbert Emery, produced at the Longacre Theatre, New York, Monday afternoon, March 14, 1921, by Sam Forrest for Sam H. Harris, with Robert Ames. Revived at the Belmont Theatre, New York, September 5, 1921

"Inheritors," by Susan Glaspell, produced at the Provincetown Theatre, New York, March 21, 1921, by the Provincetown Players; designer, Cleon Throckmorton

"The Trial of Joan of Arc," by Emile Moreau, produced at the Century Theatre, New York, April 3, 1921, by Margaret Anglin and Maurice Browne, with Miss Anglin; designer, Ernest de Weerth

"Liliom," by Franz Molnar, produced at the Garrick Theatre, New York, April 20, 1921, by Frank Reicher for the Theatre Guild, with Joseph Schildkraut; designer, Lee Simonson

"Shuffle Along," by Miller and Lyles, produced at the Sixty-Third Street Theatre, New York, May 23, 1921, by Walter Brooks, for the Nikko Producing Company, Inc.

"The Pilgrim Spirit," by George Pierce Baker, produced at Plymouth, Massachusetts, July 20, 1921, by Professor Baker; designer, Rollo Peters

"The Detour," by Owen Davis, produced at the Astor Theatre, New York, August 23, 1921, by Augustin Duncan for Lee and J. J. Shubert, with Augustin Duncan and Effie Shannon

"Daddy's Gone a-Hunting," by Zoë Akins, produced at the Plymouth Theatre, New York, August 31,

1921, by Arthur Hopkins, with Marjorie Rambeau; designer, Robert Edmond Jones

"Swords," by Sidney Howard, produced at the National Theatre, New York, September 1, 1921, by Brock Pemberton, with Clare Eames; designer, Robert Edmond Jones

"The Circle," by W. Somerset Maugham, produced at the Selwyn Theatre, New York, September 12, 1921, by Clifford Brooke for the Selwyns, with Mrs. Leslie Carter and John Drew

"The White-Headed Boy," by Lennox Robinson, produced at Henry Miller's Theatre, New York, September 15, 1921, by J. B. Fagan for Charles Dillingham, with Arthur Sinclair and Maire O'Neill

"The Music Box Revue, 1921," by Irving Berlin, produced at the Music Box, New York, September 22, 1921, by Hassard Short for Sam H. Harris and Irving Berlin.

"Blossom Time," by A. M. Willner, H. Reichert and Dorothy Donnelly, music arranged from Franz Schubert, produced at the Ambassador Theatre, New York, September 29, 1921, by Lee and J. J. Shubert

"Bombo," by Harold Atteridge and Sigmund Romberg, produced at Jolson's Fifty-Ninth Street Theatre, New York, October 6, 1921, by J. C. Huffman for Lee and J. J. Shubert, with Al Jolson

"Ambush," by Arthur Richman, produced at the Garrick Theatre, New York, October 10, 1921, by Robert Milton for the Theatre Guild

APPENDIX I

"A Bill of Divorcement," by Clemence Dane, produced at the George M. Cohan Theatre, New York, October 10, 1921, by Basil Dean for Charles B. Dillingham, with Allan Pollock and Katherine Cornell

"The Claw," by Henry Bernstein, produced at the Broadhurst Theatre, New York, October 17, 1921, by Arthur Hopkins, with Lionel Barrymore; designer, Robert Edmond Jones

"Anna Christie," by Eugene O'Neill, produced at the Vanderbilt Theatre, New York, November 2, 1921, by Arthur Hopkins, with Pauline Lord and George Marion; designer, Robert Edmond Jones

"The Straw," by Eugene O'Neill, produced at the Greenwich Village Theatre, New York, November 10, 1921, by George C. Tyler, with Margalo Gilmore and Otto Kruger

"Kiki," by André Picard and David Belasco, produced at the Belasco Theatre, New York, November 29, 1921, by David Belasco, with Lenore Ulric

"The Dover Road," by A. A. Milne, produced at the Bijou Theatre, New York, December 23, 1921, by Guthrie McClintic

"Captain Applejack," by Walter Hackett, produced at the Cort Theatre, New York, December 30, 1921, by the author for Sam H. Harris, with Wallace Eddinger

"S. S. *Tenacity*," by Charles Vildrac, translated by Sidney Howard, produced at the Belmont Theatre, New York, January 2, 1922, by Augustin Duncan; designer, Robert Edmond Jones

Balieff's Chauve-Souris (*Letutchaya Muish* or the Bat Theatre of Moscow), presented at the Forty-Ninth Street Theatre, New York, February 3, 1922, and moved to the Century Roof Theatre, June 5, 1922, by F. Ray Comstock and Morris Gest, with Nikita Balieff; designers, Sergei Sudeykin and Nikolai Remisoff

"Back to Methuselah," by George Bernard Shaw, five parts produced in three evenings at the Garrick Theatre, New York, February 26, March 5 and March 12, 1922, by Alice Lewisohn, Agnes Morgan and Frank Reicher for the Theatre Guild; designer, Lee Simonson

"The Hairy Ape," by Eugene O'Neill, produced at the Provincetown Playhouse, New York, March 9, 1922, by the Provincetown Players, assisted by Arthur Hopkins, with Louis Wolheim; designers, Robert Edmond Jones and Cleon Throckmorton

"The Truth About Blayds," by A. A. Milne, produced at the Booth Theatre, New York, March 14, 1922, by Winthrop Ames, with O. P. Heggie; designer, Norman-Bel Geddes

"*Salut au Monde*," by Walt Whitman, set to music by Charles T. Griffes, produced at the Neighborhood Playhouse, New York, April 22, 1922, by the Neighborhood Players; designer, Esther Peck

"From Morn to Midnight," by Georg Kaiser, translated by Ashley Dukes, produced at the Garrick

Theatre, New York, May 21, 1922, by Frank Reicher for the Theatre Guild; designer, Lee Simonson

"Loyalties," by John Galsworthy, produced at the Gaiety Theatre, New York, September 27, 1922, by Basil Dean for Charles B. Dillingham

"R. U. R.," by Karel Capek, translated by Paul Selver and Nigel. Playfair, produced at the Garrick Theatre, New York, October 9, 1922, by Philip Moeller for the Theatre Guild; designer, Lee Simonson

"To Love," by Paul Géraldy, translated by Grace George, produced at the Bijou Theatre, New York, October 17, 1922, by Grace George, with Grace George, Norman Trevor and Robert Warwick

"Six Characters in Search of an Author," by Luigi Pirandello, translated by Edward Storer, produced at the Princess Theatre, New York, October 30, 1922, by Brock Pemberton

"The World We Live In" ("The Insect Comedy"), by Josef and Karel Capek, adapted by Owen Davis, produced at Jolson's Fifty-Ninth Street Theatre, New York, October 31, 1922, by John Cromwell for William A. Brady; designer, Lee Simonson

"Rain," by John Colton and Clemence Randolph, founded on a story by W. Somerset Maugham, produced at the Maxine Elliott Theatre, New York, November 7, 1922, by John D. Williams for Sam H. Harris, with Jeanne Eagels

"Hamlet," by William Shakespeare, produced at the Sam H. Harris Theatre, New York, November 16, 1922, by Arthur Hopkins, with John Barrymore and Rosalind Fuller; designer, Robert Edmond Jones

"The Merchant of Venice," by William Shakespeare, produced at the Belasco Theatre, New York, December 21, 1922, by David Belasco, with David Warfield

"Why Not?" by Jesse Lynch Williams, produced at the Forty-Eighth Street Theatre, New York, December 25, 1922, by the Equity Players, Inc.

"Will Shakespeare," by Clemence Dane, produced at the National Theatre, New York, January 1, 1923, by Winthrop Ames; designer, Norman-Bel Geddes

The Moscow Art Theatre, Constantin Stanislavsky and Vladimir Nemirovitch-Dantchenko, Directors, presented at Jolson's Fifty-Ninth Street Theatre, New York, by F. Ray Comstock and Morris Gest in the following repertory, with dates of premieres: "Tsar Fyodor Ivanovitch," by Count Alexei Tolstoy, January 8, 1923; "The Lower Depths," by Maxim Gorky, January 15, 1923; "The Cherry Orchard," by Anton Tchehoff, January 22, 1923; "The Three Sisters," by Anton Tchehoff, January 29, 1923; "The Brothers Karamazoff" (three scenes), by Fyodor Dostoievsky, and "The Lady from the Provinces," by Ivan Turgenieff, February 26, 1923

APPENDIX I

"Romeo and Juliet," by William Shakespeare, produced at Henry Miller's Theatre, New York, January 24, 1923, by Frank Reicher for the Selwyns, with Jane Cowl; designer, Rollo Peters

"Icebound," by Owen Davis, produced at the Sam H. Harris Theatre, New York, February 10, 1923, by Sam Forrest for Sam H. Harris

"You and I," by Philip Barry, produced at the Belmont Theatre, New York, February 19, 1923, by Robert Milton for Richard G. Herndon, with Lucile Watson and H. B. Warner

"The Devil's Disciple," by George Bernard Shaw, produced at the Garrick Theatre, New York, April 23, 1923, by Philip Moeller for the Theatre Guild; designer, Lee Simonson

II

THE PULITZER DRAMA PRIZE AWARDS

1917. No award
    Jury: AUGUSTUS THOMAS, *Chairman*
                 RICHARD BURTON
                 HAMLIN GARLAND

1918. Prize awarded to "Why Marry," by Jesse Lynch Williams, produced at the Astor Theatre, December 25, 1917, by Selwyn and Co.
    Jury: AUGUSTUS THOMAS, *Chairman*
                 RICHARD BURTON
                 HAMLIN GARLAND

1919. No award
    Jury: HAMLIN GARLAND, *Chairman*
                 RICHARD BURTON
                 CLAYTON HAMILTON

1920. Prize awarded to "Beyond the Horizon," by Eugene O'Neill, produced at the Little Theatre, February 3, 1920, by John D. Williams
    Jury: HAMLIN GARLAND, *Chairman*
                 RICHARD BURTON
                 WALTER PRICHARD EATON

1921. Prize awarded to "Miss Lulu Bett," by Zona Gale, produced at the Belmont Theatre,

APPENDIX II

       December 27, 1920, by Brock Pemberton
    Jury: HAMLIN GARLAND, *Chairman*
             RICHARD BURTON
             WILLIAM LYON PHELPS

1922. Prize awarded to " Anna Christie," by Eugene O'Neill, produced at the Vanderbilt Theatre, November 2, 1921, by Arthur Hopkins
    Jury: WILLIAM LYON PHELPS, *Chairman*
             HAMLIN GARLAND
             JESSE LYNCH WILLIAMS

1923. Prize awarded to " Icebound," by Owen Davis, produced at the Sam H. Harris Theatre, February 10, 1923, by Sam H. Harris
    Jury: WILLIAM LYON PHELPS, *Chairman*
             CLAYTON HAMILTON
             OWEN JOHNSON

III

THE HARVARD PRIZE PLAY AWARDS

1911. "The End of the Bridge," by Florence Lincoln, produced at the Castle Square Theatre, Boston. Prize of $500 awarded by John Craig

1912. "The Product of the Mill," by Elizabeth McFadden, produced at the Castle Square Theatre, Boston. Prize of $500 awarded by John Craig

1913. "Believe Me, Xantippe," by Frederick Ballard, produced by William A. Brady by arrangement with John Craig at the Thirty-Ninth Street Theatre, New York. Prize of $500 awarded by John Craig

1915. "Common Clay," by Cleves Kinkead, produced by John Craig at the Castle Square Theatre, Boston. Prize of $500 awarded by John Craig

1916. "Between the Lines," by Charlotte Chorpenning, produced at the Castle Square Theatre, Boston. Prize of $500 awarded by John Craig

1917. "The Year of the Tiger," by Kenneth Andrews, produced at the Castle Square Theatre, Boston. Prize of $500 awarded by John Craig

APPENDIX III 319

1919. "Mama's Affair," by Rachel Barton Butler, produced by Oliver Morosco, at the Fulton Theatre, New York. Prize of $500 awarded by Oliver Morosco
1920. "The Copy," by Thomas P. Robinson, not yet produced. Prize of $500 awarded by Oliver Morosco
1922. "You and I," by Philip Barry, produced by Richard G. Herndon, at the Belmont Theatre, New York. Prize of $500 awarded by Richard G. Herndon
1923. "The Dud," by Dorothy Heyward, not yet produced. Prize of $500 awarded by Richard G. Herndon

IV

A COMPLETE LIST OF THE PLAYS OF EUGENE O'NEILL

(*Dates Indicate Year of Composition*)

1913

" A Wife for Life," one act; destroyed

" The Web," one act; published 1914, with four succeeding plays

" Thirst," one act; produced 1916, by the Provincetown Players

1914

" Recklessness," one act

" Warnings," one act

" Fog," one act; produced 1917, by the Provincetown Players

" Bread and Butter," four acts; destroyed

" Servitude," three acts; destroyed

" Bound East for Cardiff," one act; produced 1916, by the Provincetown Players

" Abortion," one act; produced 1916, by the Provincetown Players

1915

" A Knock at the Door," one act, comedy; destroyed

" The Sniper," one act; produced 1917, by the Provincetown Players; destroyed

APPENDIX IV

"The Personal Equation," four acts; destroyed
"Belshazzar," a biblical play in six scenes; destroyed

1916

"Before Breakfast," one act; produced 1916–1917, by the Provincetown Players
"The Movie Man," one act, comedy; destroyed
"Now I Ask You," three acts, farce-comedy; destroyed
"Atrocity," one act, pantomime; destroyed
"'Ile," one act; produced 1917, by the Provincetown Players
"In the Zone," one act; produced 1917, by the Washington Square Players
"The Long Voyage Home," one act; produced 1917, by the Provincetown Players
"The Moon of the Caribbees," one act; produced 1918, by the Provincetown Players
"The G. A. M.," one act, farce-comedy; destroyed

1918

"Till We Meet," one act; destroyed
"The Rope," one act; produced 1918, by the Provincetown Players
"Beyond the Horizon," three acts, six scenes; produced 1920, by John D. Williams
"The Dreamy Kid," one act; produced 1919, by the Provincetown Players
"Shell-Shock," one act; destroyed
"Where the Cross is Made," one act; produced 1918, by the Provincetown Players

APPENDIX IV

"The Straw," three acts, five scenes; produced 1921, by George C. Tyler

1919

"Honor Among the Bradleys," one act; destroyed

"Chris," three acts, six scenes; produced 1920, outside New York; destroyed

"The Trumpet," one act, comedy; destroyed

"Exorcism," one act, comedy; produced 1920, by the Provincetown Players

1920

"Gold," four acts; produced 1921, by John D. Williams

"Anna Christie," four acts; produced 1921, by Arthur Hopkins

"The Emperor Jones," eight scenes; produced 1920, by the Provincetown Players

"Diff'rent," two acts; produced 1920, by the Provincetown Players

1921

"The First Man," four acts; produced 1922, by Augustin Duncan and the Neighborhood Playhouse

"The Fountain," eleven scenes; to be produced 1923, by Arthur Hopkins

"The Hairy Ape," eight scenes; produced 1922, by the Provincetown Players

1923

"Welded," three acts; unproduced

"Marco Polo," uncompleted

"All God's Children Got Wings"; unproduced

APPENDIX V

"The Red Cloak," a marionette pantomime by Josephine A. Meyer and Lawrence Langner

Fourth Bill, March 20, 1916

"The Magical City," by Zoë Akins
"Children," by Guy Bolton and Tom Carlton
"Pierre Patelin," translated from the French by Maurice Rélonde
"The Age of Reason," by Cecil Dorrian

Fifth Bill, May 22, 1916

"The Sea-Gull," by Anton Tchehoff, translated from the Russian by Marian Fell

At the Comedy Theatre

PRELIMINARY SEASON, JUNE 5, 1916

"The Honorable Lover," by Roberto Bracco
"Helena's Husband," by Philip Moeller
"The Clod," by Lewis Beach
"Pierre Patelin"

FIRST SEASON

Review Bill, Aug. 30, 1916

"Literature," by Arthur Schnitzler
"Eugenically Speaking," by Edward Goodman
"A Miracle of St. Anthony," by Maurice Maeterlinck
"A Bear," by Anton Tchehoff

First Bill, October 2, 1916

"The Sugar House," by Alice Brown

"Lover's Luck," by Georges de Porto-Riche
"The Merry Death," by Nikolai Yevreynoff
"Sisters of Susanna," by Philip Moeller

Second Bill, November 13, 1916

"Trifles," by Susan Glaspell
"Another Way Out," by Lawrence Langner
"Bushido," from the Japanese of Izumo
"Altruism," adapted from the German of Karl Ettlinger, by Benjamin F. Glazer

Third Bill, January 14, 1917

"The Life of Man," by Leonid Andreieff, translated from the Russian by Clarence L. Meader and Fred Newton Scott

Fourth Bill, February 5, 1917

"The Death of Tintagiles," by Maurice Maeterlinck, translated from the French by Philip Moeller
"The Last Straw," by Bosworth Crocker
"The Hero of Santa Maria," by Kenneth Sawyer Goodman and Ben Hecht
"A Private Account," by Georges Courteline, translated from the French by Edward Goodman and Beatrice de Holthoir

Fifth Bill, March 21, 1917

"Plots and Playwrights," by Edward Massey
"The Poor Fool," by Hermann Bahr, translated from the German by Mrs. Frank E. Washburn-Freund
"Sganarelle," by Molière, translated from the French by Philip Moeller

V

THE RECORD OF THE WASHINGTON SQUARE PLAYERS

At the Bandbox Theatre, East 57th Street

FIRST SEASON

First Bill, February 19, 1915

"Interior," by Maurice Maeterlinck

"Licensed," by Basil Lawrence

"Eugenically Speaking," by Edward Goodman

"Another Interior," a pantomime arranged by Ralph Roeder

Second Bill, March 26, 1915

"Love of One's Neighbor," by Leonid Andreieff

"Two Blind Beggars and One Less Blind," by Philip Moeller

"Moondown," by John Reed

"The Shepherd in the Distance," a pantomime in black and white, by Holland Hudson

"My Lady's Honor," by Murdock Pemberton (added a week later)

Third Bill, May 7, 1915

"The Miracle of St. Anthony," by Maurice Maeterlinck, translated from the French by Ralph Roeder

"Forbidden Fruit," an adaptation by George Jay
    Smith from a theme by Octave Feuillet
"In April," by Rose Pastor Stokes
"Saviors," by Edward Goodman

Collective Bill, May 24, 1915

"A Bear," by Anton Tchehoff
"Interior," by Maurice Maeterlinck
"Eugenically Speaking," by Edward Goodman
"The Shepherd in the Distance," by Holland Hudson

SECOND SEASON

First Bill, October 4, 1915

"Helena's Husband," by Philip Moeller
"Fire and Water," by Hervey White
"Night of Snow," by Roberto Bracco, translated from
    the Italian by Ralph Roeder
"The Antick," by Percy MacKaye

Second Bill, November 8, 1915

"Literature," by Arthur Schnitzler
"Overtones," by Alice Gerstenberg
"The Honorable Lover," by Roberto Bracco
"Whims," by Alfred de Musset

Third Bill, January 10, 1916

"The Tenor," by Frank Wedekind, translated from
    the German by André Tridon
"The Clod," by Lewis Beach
"The Roadhouse in Arden," by Philip Moeller

Sixth Bill, May 7, 1917

"Ghosts," by Henrik Ibsen, with Mary Shaw

Seventh Bill, May 28, 1917

"Pariah," by August Strindberg
"Another Way Out," by Lawrence Langner
"Plots and Playwrights," by Edward Massey

SECOND SEASON

Extra Bill, September 17, 1917

"The Family Exit," by Lawrence Langner

First Bill, October 31, 1917

"In the Zone," by Eugene O'Neill
"The Avenue," by Fenimore Merrill
"Blind Alleys," by Grace Latimer Wright
"His Widow's Husband," by Jacinto Benavente, translated from the Spanish by John Garrett Underhill

Second Bill, December 3, 1917

"The Critic's Comedy," by Samuel Kaplan
"Neighbors," by Zona Gale
"The Girl in the Coffin," by Theodore Dreiser
"Yum Chapab," pantomime founded on Maya legends, by Beatrice de Holthoir and L. Garcia Pimentel

Third Bill, January 23, 1918

"Habit," by Frank Dare

"Suppressed Desires," by George Cram Cook and Susan Glaspell

"The Sandbar Queen," by George Cronyn

"Pokey," by Philip Moeller

Fourth Bill, February 20, 1918

"Youth," by Miles Malleson

Fifth Bill, March 11, 1918

"Mrs. Warren's Profession," by George Bernard Shaw

Sixth Bill, April 22, 1918

"The Home of the Free," by Elmer L. Reizenstein (now Rice)

"Lonesome-Like," by Harold Brighouse

"Salome," by Oscar Wilde

Seventh Bill, May 13, 1918

"Close the Book," by Susan Glaspell

"The Rope," by Eugene O'Neill

"Lonesome-Like," by Harold Brighouse

"The Home of the Free," by Elmer L. Reizenstein (now Rice)

VI

THE RECORD OF THE THEATRE GUILD

(All Productions Were Made at the Garrick Theatre, and, With the Exceptions Noted, the Entire Engagement was Played There)

Season of 1919, Spring

"The Bonds of Interest," by Jacinto Benavente, produced April 14, 1919; 31 performances

"John Ferguson," by St. John Ervine, produced May 12, 1919; 131 performances at the Garrick and Fulton Theatres

Season of 1919–1920

"The Faithful," by John Masefield, produced October 13, 1919; 48 performances

"The Rise of Silas Lapham," by William Dean Howells, produced November 25, 1919; 47 performances

"The Power of Darkness," by Lyoff Tolstoy, produced January 19, 1920; 40 performances

"Jane Clegg," by St. John Ervine, produced February 23, 1920; 177 performances

"The Dance of Death," by August Strindberg, produced May 9, 1920; 2 special performances for subscribers

APPENDIX VI

Season of 1920–1921

"The Treasure," by David Pinski, produced October 4, 1920; 36 performances

"Heartbreak House," by George Bernard Shaw, produced November 10, 1920; 129 performances

"John Hawthorne," by D. Liebovitz, produced January 23, 1921; 6 matinees only

"Mr. Pim Passes By," by A. A. Milne, produced February 28, 1921; 232 performances at the Garrick and Henry Miller Theatres

"Liliom," by Franz Molnar, produced April 20, 1921; 311 performances at the Garrick and Fulton Theatres

"John Ferguson," by St. John Ervine, revived May 23, 1921; 25 performances

"The Cloister," by Emil Verhaeren, produced June 5, 1921; 2 special performances for subscribers

Season of 1921–1922

"Ambush," by Arthur Richman, produced October 10, 1921; 57 performances at the Garrick and Belmont Theatres

"The Wife With a Smile," by Denys Amiel and André Obey, and "*Boubouroche*," by Georges Courteline, produced November 28, 1921; 40 performances

"He Who Gets Slapped," by Leonid Andreieff, produced January 9, 1922; 154 performances at the Garrick and Fulton Theatres

"Back to Methuselah," by George Bernard Shaw, produced February 27, 1922; 75 performances

APPENDIX VI 331

"What the Public Wants," by Arnold Bennett, produced May 1, 1922; 24 performances

"From Morn to Midnight," by Georg Kaiser, produced May 21, 1922; 56 performances at the Garrick and Frazee Theatres

Season of 1922-1923

"R. U. R.," by Karel Capek, produced October 9, 1922; 182 performances at the Garrick and Frazee Theatres

"The Lucky One," by A. A. Milne, produced November 20, 1922; 32 performances

"The Tidings Brought to Mary," by Paul Claudel, produced December 25, 1922; 32 performances

"Peer Gynt," by Henrik Ibsen, produced February 5, 1923; 122 performances at the Garrick and Shubert Theatres

"The Adding Machine," by Elmer Rice, produced March 18, 1923; 72 performances at the Garrick and Comedy Theatres

"The Devil's Disciple," by George Bernard Shaw, produced April 23, 1923; 191 performances

VII

THE RECORD OF THE PROVINCETOWN PLAYERS

At the Wharf Theatre, Provincetown, Mass.

SUMMER SEASON, 1915

First Bill

"Constancy," by Neith Boyce
"Suppressed Desires," by George Cram Cook and Susan Glaspell

Second Bill

"Change Your Style," by George Cram Cook
"Contemporaries," by Wilbur Daniel Steele

SUMMER SEASON, 1916

First Bill

"Freedom," by John Reed
"Winter's Night," by Neith Boyce
"Suppressed Desires," by George Cram Cook and Susan Glaspell

Second Bill

"The Game," by Louise Bryant
"Bound East for Cardiff," by Eugene O'Neill
"Not Smart," by Wilbur Daniel Steele

APPENDIX VII

Third Bill

" The Eternal Quadrangle," by John Reed
" Constancy," by Neith Boyce
" Trifles," by Susan Glaspell

Fourth Bill

" Contemporaries," by Wilbur Daniel Steele
" Change Your Style," by George Cram Cook
" Thirst," by Eugene O'Neill

Review Bill

" The Game "
" Bound East for Cardiff "
" Suppressed Desires "

At the Playwright's Theatre, Macdougal Street, New York

SEASON OF 1916–1917

First Bill

" Bound East for Cardiff," by Eugene O'Neill
" The Game," by Louise Bryant
" King Arthur's Socks," by Floyd Dell

Second Bill

" Freedom," by John Reed
" Enemies," by Neith Boyce and Hutchins Hapgood
" Suppressed Desires," by George Cram Cook and Susan Glaspell

Third Bill

"Before Breakfast," by Eugene O'Neill
"Lima Beans," by Alfred Kreymborg
"The Two Sons," by Neith Boyce

Fourth Bill

"Joined Together," by Bror Nordfeldt
"The Obituary," by Saxe Commins
"Sauce for the Emperor," by John Mosher

Fifth Bill

"Bored," by John Mosher
"A Long Time Ago," by Floyd Dell
"Fog," by Eugene O'Neill

Sixth Bill

"Pan," by Kenneth MacNichol
"Winter's Night," by Neith Boyce
"The Dollar," by David Pinski

Seventh Bill

"Ivan's Homecoming," by Irwin Granich
"Barbarians," by Rita Wellman
"The Sniper," by Eugene O'Neill

Eighth Bill

"The Prodigal Son," by Harry Kemp
"Cocaine," by Pendleton King
"The People," by Susan Glaspell

Review Bill

"Barbarians"
"The People"
"Cocaine"
"Suppressed Desires"

APPENDIX VII

SEASON OF 1917–1918

First Bill

"The Long Voyage Home," by Eugene O'Neill
"Close The Book," by Susan Glaspell
"Night," by James Oppenheim

Second Bill

"Knot-Holes," by Maxwell Bodenheim
"'Ile," by Eugene O'Neill
"The Gentle Furniture Shop," by Maxwell Bodenheim
"Funiculi-Funicula," by Rita Wellman

Third Bill

"Down the Airshaft," by Irwin Granich
"The Angel Intrudes," by Floyd Dell
"The Outside," by Susan Glaspell

Fourth Bill

"The Slave with Two Faces," by Mary Caroline Davies
"About Six," by Grace Potter
"Sweet and Twenty," by Floyd Dell

Fifth Bill

"The Athenian Women," by George Cram Cook

Sixth Bill

"The Devil's Glow," by Alice Woods
"The Rib-Person," by Rita Wellman
"Contemporaries," by Wilbur Daniel Steele

APPENDIX VII

Seventh Bill

"The Hermit and His Messiah," by F. B. Kugelman
"The Rope," by Eugene O'Neill
"Woman's Honor," by Susan Glaspell

SEASON OF 1918–1919

First Bill

"The Princess Marries the Page," by Edna St. Vincent Millay
"Where the Cross is Made," by Eugene O'Neill
"Gee-Rusalem," by Florence Kiper Frank

Second Bill

"The Moon of the Caribbees," by Eugene O'Neill
"The Rescue," by Rita Smith
"Tickless Time," by Susan Glaspell and George Cram Cook

Third Bill

"From Portland to Dover," by Otto K. Liveright
"50-50," by Robert Parker
"The Widow's Veil," by Alice L. Rostetter
"The String of the Samisen," by Rita Wellman

Fourth Bill

"The Baby Carriage," by Bosworth Crocker
"The Squealer," by Mary Barber
"Not Smart," by Wilbur Daniel Steele

Fifth Bill

"The Peace That Passeth Understanding," by John Reed
"Bernice," by Susan Glaspell

APPENDIX VII

First Review Bill

" The Widow's Veil "
" Night "
" Bound East for Cardiff "
" Woman's Honor "

Second Review Bill

" The Rope "
" The Angel Intrudes "
" Cocaine "
" Tickless Time "

SEASON OF 1919–1920

First Bill

" The Dreamy Kid," by Eugene O'Neill
" The Philosopher of Butterbiggens," by Harold Chapin
" Three from the Earth," by Djuna Barnes
" Getting Unmarried," by Winthrop Parkhurst

Second Bill

" Brothers," by Lewis Beach
" Aria da Capo," by Edna St. Vincent Millay
" Not Smart," by Wilbur Daniel Steele

Third Bill

" The Eldest," by Edna Ferber
" An Irish Triangle," by Djuna Barnes
" Money," by Irwin Granich

APPENDIX VII

Fourth Bill

" Vote the New Moon," by Alfred Kreymborg
" Three Travelers Watch a Sunrise," by Wallace Stephens
" Pie," by Lawrence Langner

Fifth Bill

" Last Masks," by Arthur Schnitzler
" Kurzy of the Sea," by Djuna Barnes
" Exorcism," by Eugene O'Neill

Review Bill

" Where the Cross Is Made "
" Aria da Capo "
" Sweet and Twenty "

SEASON OF 1920–1921

First Bill

" Matinata," by Lawrence Langner
" The Emperor Jones," by Eugene O'Neill

Second Bill

" What d'You Want," by Lawrence Vail
" Diff'rent," by Eugene O'Neill

Third Bill

" The Spring," by George Cram Cook

Fourth Bill

" Love," by Evelyn Scott

APPENDIX VII

Fifth Bill

" Inheritors," by Susan Glaspell

Review Bill

" Trifles," by Susan Glaspell
" Grotesques," by Cloyd Head
" The Moon of the Caribbees," by Eugene O'Neill

SEASON OF 1921–1922

First Bill

" The Verge," by Susan Glaspell

Second Bill

" The Hand of the Potter," by Theodore Dreiser

Third Bill

" A Little Act of Justice," by Norman C. Lindau
" Footsteps," by Donald Corley
" The Stick-Up," by Pierre Loving

Fourth Bill

" Mr. Faust," by Arthur Davison Ficke, presented by the Ellen Van Volkenburg-Maurice Browne Repertory Company as guest artists

Fifth Bill

" The Hairy Ape," by Eugene O'Neill

Sixth Bill

" Chains of Dew," by Susan Glaspell

VIII

THE RECORD OF THE NEIGHBORHOOD PLAYHOUSE

(Exclusive of Revivals and of Performances by Visiting Companies)

SEASON OF FEBRUARY TO JUNE, 1915

* * "Jephthah's Daughter," dance drama, music by Lilia Mackay-Cantell
* * "Tethered Sheep," by Robert Gilbert Welsh
* * "The Glittering Gate," by Lord Dunsany
* * "The Maker of Dreams," by Oliphant Down
* "Captain Brassbound's Conversion," by George Bernard Shaw
* * "The Waldies," by J. G. Hamlen
* * "Womenkind," by Wilfrid Wilson Gibson

SEASON OF 1915–1916

* * "Wild Birds," by Violet Pearn
* * "Festival of Thanksgiving"
* "Petrushka," ballet by Igor Stravinsky
* * "The Subjection of Kezia," by Mrs. Havelock Ellis
* * "A Marriage Proposal," by Anton Tchehoff
* * "With the Current," by Sholom Ash

* First time in New York

APPENDIX VIII

* " The Price of Coal," by Harold Brighouse
* " A Night at an Inn," by Lord Dunsany

SEASON OF 1916-1917

* " Great Catherine," by George Bernard Shaw
* " The Inca of Perusalem," by George Bernard Shaw
* " The Queen's Enemies," by Lord Dunsany
* " The Married Woman," by C. B. Fernald
* " The Kairn of Koridwen," dance drama, music by Charles T. Griffes
* " Black 'ell," by Miles Malleson
* " A Sunny Morning," by the Quinteros, English version by Anna S. MacDonald
" The People," by Susan Glaspell
* " *La Boîte à Joujoux*," ballet by Claude Debussy

SEASON OF 1917-1918

" Pippa Passes," by Robert Browning
* " Tamura," a Japanese Noh (Fenellosa-Pound version)
* " Fortunato," by the Quinteros, English version by Anna S. MacDonald
* " Free," by Mme. Rachilde
* " Festival of Pentecost "

SEASON OF 1918-1919

* " Festival of Tabernacles,"
* " Guibour," English version by Anna S. MacDonald

* First time in New York.

* "The Eternal Megalosaurus," by Justina Lewis
* "The Noose," by Tracy Mygatt
* "Everybody's Husband," by Gilbert Cannan
* *Ma Mère l'Oye,* ballet by Maurice Ravel

SEASON OF 1919–1920

* "Mary Broome," by Allan Monkhouse
* "The Beautiful Sabine Women," by Leonid Andreieff
* *La Boutique Fantasque,* ballet, music by Rossini
* "The Fair," by Violet Pearn

SEASON OF 1920–1921

* "The Mob," by John Galsworthy
* "The Whispering Well," by F. H. Rose
"The Great Adventure," by Arnold Bennett
* "Innocent and Annabel," by Harold Chapin
* "The Harlequinade," by Granville Barker and Dion Clayton Calthrop
* "The Royal Fandango," ballet by Gustavo Morales

SEASON OF 1921–1922

* "The Madras House," by Granville Barker
"The Royal Fandango," by Gustavo Morales
* "The Midweek Interludes" (Thomas Wilfred's Color Organ or Clavilux, etc.)
* "The First Man," by Eugene O'Neill

* First time in New York.

* " The Green Ring," by Zinaida Hippius
* " *Salut au Monde,*" from the poem by Walt Whitman, music by Charles T. Griffes
* " The Makers of Light," by Frederick Lansing Day
* " The Grand Street Follies," a revue of the Neighborhood Season

* First time in New York.

IX

LIST OF LITTLE, EXPERIMENTAL AND COMMUNITY THEATRES IN THE UNITED STATES *

ALABAMA

Birmingham. Drama League Players
Mobile. Little Theatre
Selma. Drama League Players

ARKANSAS

Little Rock. Little Theatre

CALIFORNIA

Anaheim. Community Players
Berkeley. Campus Little Theatre
          English Club Players, University of California
          Greek Theatre
          Mask and Daggers
          Theatre of Allied Arts
Glendale. Community Theatre Service Players

* This list of Little Theatres has been compiled from various sources and, owing to the ephemeral nature of many of these groups and their frequent change of name, there are probably a number of omissions and duplications as well as names of organizations no longer active. Corrections in the list will be appreciated for inclusion in succeeding editions. — The Author.

APPENDIX IX

Hollywood. Community Theatre
　　　　　　Patio Playhouse
Los Angeles. Egan Little Theatre
　　　　　　Literary Theatre
　　　　　　Touchstone Theatre, University of Southern California
Monrovia. Foothill Players
Mt. Tamalpais. Mountain Play Association
Oakland. Boulevard Little Theatre
Pasadena. Community Playhouse Association
　　　　　　Summer Art Colony
Pomona. Genesha Park Players
Redlands. Community Players
Sacramento. Little Theatre
San Diego. Players
　　　　　　Two Masque Players, San Diego State College
San Francisco. Burlington Dramatic Club
　　　　　　Green Theatre, University of California
　　　　　　Harlequin Players
　　　　　　Little Theatre
　　　　　　Maitland Players
　　　　　　Pacific Players
　　　　　　Players Club
　　　　　　Sequoia Little Theatre Players
　　　　　　Stage Guild
San Jose. DeMolay Players
　　　　　　Pacific Players
Santa Ana. Players
Santa Barbara. Community Arts Association

San Mateo. Community League
Sausalito. Players
Vasalia. Dramatic Club
Whittier. Community Players

COLORADO

Boulder. Little Theatre
Colorado Springs. Drama League
Denver. Bungalow Theatre
        Little Theatre

CONNECTICUT

Bethel. Community Theatre
Bridgeport. Little Theatre League
        Players
Bristol. Community Players
Greenwich. Fairfield Players
Hartford. Hartford Players
Madison. Community Playhouse
        Playhouse
Meriden. Little Theatre Guild
New Haven. The Craftsman, Yale College
New London. Community Players
Stamford. Masquers

DELAWARE

Wilmington. Drama League

DISTRICT OF COLUMBIA

Washington. The Arts Club
        Little Theatre
        Ram's Head Players

Lafayette. Lafayette Parish
Richmond. Union Mission, Earlham College
West Hammond. Community Players

IOWA

Ames. Dramatic Association, Iowa State College
Bloomfield. Little Theatre Association
Blue Grass. Community Players
Burlington. Little Theatre
Cedar Rapids. Little Theatre, Coe College
    Little Theatre
Davenport. Tri-City Arts League
Des Moines. Little Theatre Association
    Little Theatre Society, Drake University
Dubuque. Dramatic Club, Columbia College
    Dramatic Arts Guild
Fort Dodge. Dramatic League
Grinnell. Little Theatre Association
Iowa City. Little Theatre Association
    Little Theatre Circuit
    Players, University of Iowa
Mason. Little Theatre Association
Mystic. Dramatic Club
Newton. Little Theatre Association
Sioux City. Little Theatre Association
Waterloo. Federation of Women's Clubs

KANSAS

Lawrence. Little Theatre, University of Kansas

KENTUCKY

Barbourville. National Theatre
Lexington. Community Theatre
Louisville. Campus Players
    Dramatic Club of Nazareth College
    Little Theatre Guild
    Normal School Dramatic Club
    Players
    Players, University of Louisville
    Players Club

LOUISIANA

Baton Rouge. Little Theatre Guild
Lafayette. Community Service of Lafayette Parish
    Little Theatre Guild
Lincoln Heights. Players
Morgan City. Teche Players
New Iberia. Little Theatre
New Orleans. Dramatic Club, Tulane University
    Dramatic Class of the New Orleans Conservatory of Music and Dramatic Art
    Dramatic Society, Young Women's Hebrew Association
    Jerusalem Temple
    Le Petit Théâtre du Vieux Carré
    Little Theatre

MAINE

Bangor. Little Theatre
Hollis. Quillcote Theatre

APPENDIX IX

        Stanley Hall Little Theatre
        Studio Players
Montevideo. Citizens' Opera House
Owatonna. Dramatic Students, High School

MISSOURI

Boonville. Kemper Dramatic Club, Kemper Military School
Columbia. Children's Theatre of Christian College
        The Masquers, State University of Missouri
Kansas City. Community Players
        Drama Players
        Little Theatre
Kirkville. Dramatic Class of Northeast State Teachers' College
Marysville. American Legion Auxiliary Dramatic Club
St. Louis. Artists' Guild
Springfield. Little Theatre

MONTANA

Bozeman — Theatre Arts Club
Missoula. University Masquers
Red Lodge. Mask and Frolic Club

NEBRASKA

Fremont. Wynn Players
Kearney. Dramatic League
Omaha. Children's Theatre
        Little Theatre

NEW HAMPSHIRE

Hanover. Dartmouth Players
Peterboro. Outdoor Players

NEW JERSEY

Hightstown. Players
Jersey City. Little Theatre League
    Thespians
Montclair. Players' Playhouse
Newark. Catholic Young Women's Club
    Little Theatre Guild
    Neighborhood Players
    The Thalians, Barringer High School
Orange. Drama Guild of the Oranges
    The Masquers
Princeton. Triangle Club, Princeton University
Summit. Players Association
Trenton. Guild Players

NEW MEXICO

Santa Fé. Community Players

NEW YORK

Albany. The Bohemians
    Mackaye Players
    St. Patrick's Players
Alfred. Wee Playhouse
Astoria (L. I.). Precious Blood Players
Auburn. Amateur Dramatic Club

Green Ring Players, West 14th Street

Greenwich House Dramatic Society, 27 Barrow Street

Guild Players, University Settlement

Hunter College
Dramatic Association
The Pipers

Inter-Theatre Arts, 65 East 56th Street

Labor Guild, 15th Street

Lenox Hill Players, 511 East 69th Street

Lenox Hill Theatre Players, 52 East 78th Street

The Lipstick Players, Grand Concourse

Little Theatre Circuit Players, 1493 Broadway

Little Theatre Club, Hotel Majestic

Marionette Theatre Studio, 27 West 8th Street

Morningside Players

The New Group, 229 West 51st Street

New York University, Dr. Sommerville's Drama Class
Varsity Dramatic Society

Lillian Owen's Marionettes

People's Players, 7 East 15th Street
Players Assembly, Belmont Theatre
Players' League, 450 Madison Avenue
Playwrights' Club, Hotel McAlpin
Salamander Players, 12 East 59th Street
Stockbridge Stocks, 335 West 145th Street
Strolling Players, 1121 West Farms Road
Stuyvesant Players, 152 West 55th Street
Temple Players
Three Arts Club, Dramatic Department, 340 West 85th Street
Town Drama Guild, Belmont Avenue at 180th Street
The Triangle, 7th Avenue at 11th Street
Union of the East and West Dramatic Society, 67 West 44th Street
University Guild Players, 99 Claremont Avenue
Wigs and Cues, Barnard College

Nyack. Players
Pelham Manor. Manor Club
Phoenicia. Woodland School Dramatic Club
Plainfield. Plainfield Theatre
Port Edward. High School Club

FLORIDA

Barton. Women's Club
Jacksonville. Brentwood Players
　　　　　　　Community Players
Palatka. Community Service
Tampa. Community Players

GEORGIA

Atlanta. Drama League
　　　　Little Theatre Guild
　　　　Players Club
Savannah. Varsity Dramatic Society
　　　　　Village Players

ILLINOIS

Berwyn. Community Service Drama Council
Burlington. Drama League
Carthage. College Dramatic Club
Chicago. The Arts Club
　　　　The Boys' Dramatic Club
　　　　Brownson Players
　　　　Children's Theatre
　　　　Civic Club Theatre Association
　　　　Coach House Players
　　　　College Players
　　　　Community Players
　　　　Dill Pickle Club
　　　　Graeme Players
　　　　Hull House Players
　　　　Players Club, Chicago Hebrew Institute

        Playmongers
        Sinai Center Players
        Studio Players

Decatur. Dramatic Club, James Milliken University
        Little Theatre

East Moline. Community League

Evanston. Campus Players, Northwestern University
        Community Theatre Association

Joliet. The Growlers, Joliet Junior College

Lake Forest. Playhouse

Peoria. Mask and Gavel Club, Bradley College
        Paramount Players
        Players

River Forest. Rosary College Dramatic Club

Rockford. College Dramatic Society

Springfield. Community Players

Streator. Senior Dramatic Club, High School

Urbana. Players Club

Willmette. North Shore Players

Winnetka. Community Playhouse

INDIANA

Anderson. Little Theatre

Evansville. Drama League

Gary. Musical Academy

Indianapolis. Drama Department, City of Indianapolis
        Dramatic Club
        Little Theatre Society of Indiana
        Players Club
        Pythian Dramatic Club

Oberlin. Dramatic Association, Oberlin College
Oxford. Ernst Theatre
Plain City. Knights of Pythias Dramatic Club
Portsmouth. Little Theatre
Urban. Community Players
Warren. Dramatic Players, East Junior High School
Yellow Springs. Dramatic Association of Antioch College

OKLAHOMA

Norman. Little Theatre Group, University City Center
Oklahoma City. Little Theatre Players
Tulsa. Little Theatre Players

OREGON

Grass Valley. Little Theatre
Marshfield. Little Theatre Club
Portland. Drama Department, High School Teachers' Union
Silverton. Playmakers

PENNSYLVANIA

Brookfield. Little Theatre
Butler. Community Playhouse
Erie. Community Playhouse
    Little Theatre
Germantown. Philadelphia Belfry Club of Germantown Academy
Lincoln. Players
Philadelphia. Dramatic Association, Adelphia College

APPENDIX IX

                Plays and Players
                Theatre Guild
                Three Arts Club
                University of Pennsylvania, Philomathean Society
                University Dramatic Club

Pittsburgh. Department of Drama in the College of Fine Arts, Carnegie Institute of Technology
                Duquesne Players
                Guild Players
                Pitt Players, University of Pittsburgh
                Temple Players

Rose Valley. Players
Sewickley. Guild Players
State College. Penn State Players
Titusville. Little Theatre

RHODE ISLAND

Pawtucket. Community Theatre
Providence. Players

SOUTH CAROLINA

Columbia. Stage Society
North Charleston. Community Players

SOUTH DAKOTA

Mitchell. Dramatic Society, College of Mitchell
Sioux Falls. Dramatic League

Ogunquit. Village Studio Guild
Portland. Maitland Playhouse

MARYLAND

Baltimore. All University Dramatic Club
　　　　　Children's Theatre
　　　　　Everybody's Theatre
　　　　　The Homewood Playshop, Johns Hopkins University
　　　　　Neighborhood Players
　　　　　Stagecraft Studios
　　　　　Vagabond Players
Cumberland. Carroll Players
Frostburg. Dramatic Class, State Normal School
Towson. Craft Club of Maryland State Normal School

MASSACHUSETTS

Boston. Children's Theatre
　　　　Elizabeth Peabody Playhouse
　　　　Experimental Theatre Guild
Brockton. Community Service
Cambridge. Harvard Dramatic Club
　　　　　　47 Workshop
Deerfield. Dramatic Society of Deerfield Academy
East Gloucester. Playhouse
　　　　　　　　Playhouse in the Moors
Jamaica Plain. Footlight Club
Lawrence. Community Players
Medford. Pen, Paint and Pretzels Dramatic Society of Tufts College

Methuen. St. John's Dramatic Society
Northampton. Dramatic Association, Smith College
McCallum Theatre
Players
Theatre Workshop, Smith College
Plymouth. Plymouth Theatre
South Hadley. English 26 Playshop, Mt. Holyoke College
Springfield. Blue Triangle Players
Wellesley. Dramatic Society, Wellesley College
Williamstown. Dramatic Club, Williams College
Winthrop. Community Theatre

MICHIGAN

Detroit. Circle Theatre and Vaudeville House
Dramatic Club of Temple Beth El
Detroit Community Theatre, Ltd.
Flint. Community Dramatic League
Jackson. Dramatic Council of Community Service
Peterburg. Little Theatre
Pontiac. Little Theatre
Saginaw. Little Theatre
Ypsilanti. Players' Playhouse

MINNESOTA

Duluth. Children Players
Little Theatre
Minneapolis. Catholic Women's League
Playbox Theatre, University of Minnesota
Portal Playhouse

TENNESSEE

Memphis. Little Theatre Players

TEXAS

Austin. Community Players
Little Theatre
Dallas. Little Theatre
Fort Worth. Little Theatre
Georgetown. Mask and Wig Club, Southwestern University
Houston. Greenmask Players
Little Theatre
Rice Dramatic Society
Huntsville. Dramatic Club
Paris. Little Theatre Players
San Antonio. Little Theatre
Wichita Falls. Community Theatre
Studio Players

VIRGINIA

Hollins. Hollins Theatre, Hollins College
Lynchburg. Little Theatre League
Norfolk. Arts Players
Richmond. Little Theatre
Richmond Hill Players
Taylorstown. Little Theatre

WASHINGTON

Aberdeen. Community Theatre
Centralia. Civic Dramatic Club

Hoquiam. Community Players
Seattle. East-West Players, University of Washington
　　　　　Repertory Theatre
　　　　　Theatre Guild
Tacoma. Drama League

WEST VIRGINIA

Charleston. Sunset Theatre
Huntington. Neighborhood Players

WISCONSIN

Appleton. Dramatic Society, Lawrence College
Madison. Players, University of Wisconsin
Milwaukee. Wisconsin Players

X

THE LEADING COMMISSIONS OF ROBERT EDMOND JONES

(New York Productions Except When Noted)

"The Man Who Married a Dumb Wife," produced 1915, by Granville Barker

"The Devil's Garden," produced 1915, by Arthur Hopkins

"The Happy Ending," produced 1916, by Arthur Hopkins

"Caliban" (New York, with Urban), produced 1916, by Percy MacKaye

"Till Eulenspiegel," produced 1916, by Vaslaff Nizhinsky and the Diagileff *Ballet Russe*

"Good Gracious, Annabelle," produced 1916, by Arthur Hopkins

"A Successful Calamity," produced 1917, by Arthur Hopkins

"Granny Maumee," "The Rider of Dreams" and "Simon the Cyrenian," produced 1917, by Emily Hapgood

"Caliban" (Boston), produced 1917, by Percy MacKaye

"The Wild Duck," produced 1918, by Arthur Hopkins

"Be Calm, Camilla," produced 1918, by Arthur Hopkins

"Guibour," produced 1918, by Yvette Guilbert and the Neighborhood Playhouse

"Redemption," produced 1918, by Arthur Hopkins

"The Gentile Wife," produced 1918, by Arthur Hopkins

"The Jest," produced 1919, by Arthur Hopkins

"The Birthday of the Infanta," produced 1920, by the Chicago Opera Company

"George Washington," produced 1920, by Walter Hampden

"Samson and Delilah," produced 1920, by Arthur Hopkins

"Richard the Third," produced 1920, by Arthur Hopkins

"Daddy's Gone a-Hunting," produced 1921, by Arthur Hopkins

"Swords," produced 1921, by Brock Pemberton

"The Claw," produced 1921, by Arthur Hopkins

"The Mountain Man," produced 1921, by Charles Wagner

"Anna Christie," produced 1921, by Arthur Hopkins

"Macbeth," produced 1921, by Arthur Hopkins

"S. S. *Tenacity,*" produced 1922, by Augustin Duncan

"Voltaire," produced 1922, by Arthur Hopkins

"The Hairy Ape" (With Cleon Throckmorton), produced 1922, by the Provincetown Players

"Rose Bernd," produced 1922, by Arthur Hopkins

"Hamlet," produced 1922, by Arthur Hopkins

"Romeo and Juliet," produced 1922, by Arthur Hopkins

"The Laughing Lady," produced 1923, by Arthur Hopkins

XII

THE LEADING COMMISSIONS OF NORMAN-BEL GEDDES

(New York Productions Except When Noted)

"Nju" (Los Angeles), produced 1916, by Aline Barnsdall

"Papa" (Los Angeles), produced 1916, by Aline Barnsdall

"La Nave" (Chicago), produced 1919, by the Chicago Opera Company

"Boudour" (Chicago), produced 1919, by the Chicago Opera Company

"Cleopatra's Night," produced 1920, by the Metropolitan Opera Company

"Erminie," produced 1920, by George C. Tyler

"The Truth about Blayds," produced 1921, by Winthrop Ames

"The Rivals," produced 1922, by the Players' Club

"Will Shakespeare," produced 1923, by Winthrop Ames

"The School for Scandal," produced 1923, by the Players' Club

XI

THE LEADING COMMISSIONS OF LEE SIMONSON

(All Productions in New York)

"Overtones," produced 1915, by the Washington Square Players

"Pierre Patelin," produced 1916, by the Washington Square Players

"The Magical City," produced 1916, by the Washington Square Players

"The Miracle of St. Anthony," produced 1916, by the Washington Square Players

"The Faithful," produced 1919, by Augustin Duncan for the Theatre Guild

"The Rise of Silas Lapham," produced 1919, by Philip Moeller, for the Theatre Guild

"The Power of Darkness," produced 1920, by Emanuel Reicher for the Theatre Guild

"The Cat Bird," produced 1920, by Arthur Hopkins

"Jane Clegg," produced 1920, by Emanuel Reicher for the Theatre Guild

"Martinique," produced 1920, by Walter Hast and Laurence Eyre

"The Dance of Death," produced 1920, by Emanuel Reicher for the Theatre Guild

"The Treasure," produced 1920, by Emanuel Reicher for the Theatre Guild

"Heartbreak House," produced 1920, by Dudley Digges for the Theatre Guild

"Mr. Pim Passes By," produced 1921, by Philip Moeller for the Theatre Guild

"Liliom," produced 1921, by Frank Reicher for the Theatre Guild

"Don Juan," produced 1921, by Frank Reicher

"He Who Gets Slapped," produced 1922, by Robert Milton for the Theatre Guild

"Back to Methuselah," produced 1922, by Alice Lewisohn, Agnes Morgan and Frank Reicher for the Theatre Guild

"From Morn to Midnight," produced 1922, by Frank Reicher for the Theatre Guild

"R. U. R.," produced 1922, by Philip Moeller for the Theatre Guild

"The World We Live In" ("The Insect Comedy"), produced 1922, by William A. Brady

"The Lucky One," produced 1922, by Fyodor Kommissarzhevsky for the Theatre Guild

"The Tidings Brought to Mary," produced 1922, by Fyodor Kommissarzhevsky for the Theatre Guild

"Peer Gynt," produced 1923, by Fyodor Kommissarzhevsky for the Theatre Guild

"The Adding Machine," produced 1923, by Fyodor Kommissarzhevsky for the Theatre Guild

"As You Like It," produced 1923, by Robert Milton for the National Theatre

"The Devil's Disciple," produced 1923, by Philip Moeller for the Theatre Guild

INDEX*

"Abortion," 320.
"About Six," 335.
"Abraham Lincoln," 98, 305.
Abstraction, 157, 158, 195, 207, 209, 213, 245.
Acting, 54, 102. *See also* Actors.
Actors, 3, 6, 10, 76, 90, 99, 109-110, 121, 124, 136-148, 150, 260. *See also* Acting.
Actors' Equity Association, 5-6, 10, 54, 148-149, 189, 276, 284-285.
Actors' Fidelity League, 276.
Adams, Franklin P., 227.
Adams, Maude, 2, 6-7, 49, 141, 153, 287-288, 291, 295, 301.
"Adding Machine, The," 25, 212, 331, 368.
Ade, George, 14, 16.
Admission prices, 280-283.
"Affairs of Anatol, The," 61, 293.
"Age of Reason, The," 325.
Ager, Milton, 306.
Agricultural College of North Dakota, 127.
Akins, Zoë, 2, 20-21, 79, 81, 166, 200, 299, 304-305, 309, 325.
Alexander, John W., 7, 152, 237, 291.
"All God's Children Got Wings," 322.
Allen, Viola, 29.
"Altruism," 326.

"Ambush," 20, 83, 188, 200-201, 310, 330.
America as Host to Foreign Drama, 64, 259-274.
American Federation of Musicians, 276.
American Magazine, 86.
Ames, Robert, 147, 309.
Ames, Winthrop, 2, 4, 16, 55, 61-63, 84, 127, 130, 165, 169, 288-290, 292-293, 295-297, 312, 314, 369.
Amiel, Denys, 330.
"Anathema," 262.
Anderson, John Murray, 4, 64, 214, 254, 257, 306.
Anderson, Mary, 292.
Anderson, Sherwood, 25.
Andreieff, Leonid, 80, 83, 110, 119, 262, 264, 305, 323, 326, 330, 342.
Andrews, Kenneth, 318.
"Androcles and the Lion," 297.
"Angel Intrudes, The," 335, 337.
Anglin, Margaret, 126, 142, 167, 295-296, 309.
Anisfeld, Boris Izmailovitch, 167.
"Anna Christie," 3-4, 28, 31, 34-35, 40, 142, 145, 157, 188, 197, 204, 311, 317, 322, 366.
"Another Interior," 78, 297, 323.
"Another Way Out," 326, 327.
Anspacher, Louis K., 16, 299.
"Antick, The," 324.

* (The Little Theatres listed in Appendix IX are not included in this index, in as much as they are there arranged alphabetically by states and cities. — The Author).

INDEX

Antoine, André, 196.
"Any Night," 294.
"Aphrodite," 274.
Appia, Adolf, 130.
Archer, William, 102, 265.
Architectural League, 172.
Architectural Record, The, 175.
Architecture, Theatrical. *See* PLAYHOUSE.
"Aren't We All?" 261.
"Argumentation," 128.
"Aria da Capo," 21, 98, 337–338.
Aristophanes, 214.
Arliss, George, 3, 140, 287, 292.
Arnold, Matthew, 189, 277.
Arthur, Helen, 105.
Arthur, Julia, 308.
"Artists and Models," 283.
Arvold, Alfred G., 127.
"As a Man Thinks," 14.
"As You Like It," 368.
Asche, Oscar, 302.
Ash, Sholom, 262, 340.
"Athenian Women, The," 335.
"Atrocity," 321.
Atteridge, Harold, 310.
Audience. *See* THEATRE AUDIENCE.
Austrian Theatre, 45.
"Avenue, The," 327.
"Awakening of Spring, The," 34.

"BABBIT," 20.
"Baby Carriage, The," 336.
"Back to Methuselah," 83, 85, 160, 312, 330, 368.
Bacon, Frank, 303.
"Bad Man, The," 18, 142, 306.
Bahr, Hermann, 290, 303, 326.
Baiko, Onoye, 130.
Baker, Professor George Pierce, 5, 29, 106, 125, 127–131, 243–244, 309.

Bakst, Leon, 154, 291, 299.
Balieff, Nikita Fyodorovitch, 55, 220, 222–228, 230–232, 312.
Balieff's Chauve-Souris, 220, 222–226, 228, 230–231, 262, 268, 270, 312.
Ballantine, E. J., 99, 110.
Ballard, Frederick, 16, 128, 295, 318.
"Barbarians," 334.
Barber, Mary, 336.
Barker, Harley Granville, 9, 12, 152, 154, 295, 297–298, 308, 342, 365.
Barnes, Djuna, 91, 337–338.
Barnhart, Harry, 232.
Barnsdall, Aline, 163, 369.
Barnum, Phineas T., 47, 191.
Baron, Henry, 63.
Barratt, Watson, 167.
Barrie, James M., 287, 295, 301, 304.
Barry, Philip, 20–21, 315, 319.
Barrymore, Ethel, 3, 6, 49, 59, 141, 289, 305.
Barrymore, John, 3, 6, 59, 141, 155, 288, 293, 295, 300, 303–304, 306, 314.
Barrymore, Lionel, 59, 141, 303–304, 306, 308, 311.
Barton, Jimmy, 249.
Barzini, Luigi, 261.
Bassermann, Albert, 140.
Bataille, Henry, 261.
Bates, Blanche, 142, 291, 304–305.
"Battle of the Butterflies, The," 287.
Baynes, Ernest Harold, 295.
"Be Calm, Camilla," 18, 303, 366.
Beach, Lewis, 20, 79, 81, 324–325, 337.

Batavia. Crosby Players
Brooklyn. Acme Players
Clark Street Players
Institute Players
New York Art Theatre
Ovington Players, Bay Ridge High School
Repertory Theatre
Buffalo. The Buffalo Players, Inc.
Chrysalis Players
Dramatic Society of Canisius College
D'Youville Players
Thumb Box Players
Douglaston (L. I.). Players
Elmira. Community Theatre on Wheels
Elmhurst (L. I.). Jackson Heights Players
Flushing (L. I.). League Players
Forest Hills (L. I.). Gardens Players
Glens Falls. College Players
Mask and Gown Club
Players Club
Great Neck (L. I.). Players
Gouverneur. Players
Hudson Falls. St. Mary's Dramatic Club
Huntington (L. I.). Neighborhood Players
Ithaca. Dramatic Club, Cornell University
Jamaica (L. I.). Community Players
Repertory Theatre
Kew Gardens (L. I.). Players
Mt. Vernon. El Zada Players
Nassau (L. I.). Dramatic League

APPENDIX IX

New Brighton (S. I.). Amateur Comedy Club Players

New York City. George Grey Barnard's Cloister of St. Guillem, Fort Washington Ave. and 190th St.

Cellar Players, 436 West 27th Street

Children's Hour Theatre, Room 422, Putnam Building

Children's Theatre of Heckscher Foundation, Fifth Avenue at 105th Street

Circle Players

Civic Club Drama Group, 14 West 12th Street

Columbia University Players

Cooper Players of Cooper Union Institute, 8th Street

Cubby-Hole Players, 1493 Broadway

The Curtain, 260 Riverside Drive

Cutler Comedy Club of Cutler School, 785 Madison Avenue

Dramatic Society of Washington Square College

East West Players, 60 Northern Avenue

Federation Players, 115 East 116th Street

Free Theatre (Butler Davenport), 138 East 27th Street

APPENDIX IX

Poughkeepsie. Community Theatre
                 Goodfellowship Club, Vassar College
Richmond Hill (L. I.). South Dramatic Society of Long Island
Rochester. Kiwanis Club
           Little Theatre
           Prince Street Players
Rockville Center (L. I.). Fortnightly Community Players
St. George (S. I.). Wayside Players
Saratoga. Dramatic Club, Skidmore College
         Women's Civic Club
Scarborough. Beechwood Players
Scarsdale. Wayside Players
Schenectady. The Harlequinaders
            The Mountebanks
Seneca Falls. Dramatic Club
Syracuse. Little Theatre
Tottenville (S. I.). Unity Dramatic Society
Troy. The Box and Candle Dramatic Club of Russell Sage College
     Dramatic Society of Emma Willard School
     High School Dramatic Club
     Ilium Dramatic Club
     The Masque Players
Utica. American Legion Players
Warner. Players
Watervliet. St. Bridget's Dramatic Club
West Point. Dramatic Society, United States Military Academy

White Plains. Fenimore Country Club
              Fireside Players
Yonkers. Workshop Theatre

NORTH CAROLINA

Chapel Hill. Carolina Playmakers
Durham. Community Theatre
Raleigh. Community Players
         Playmakers, University of North Carolina

NORTH DAKOTA

Fargo. Little Country Theatre
University. Dakota Playmakers

OHIO

Akron. Civic Drama Association, Akron Players
Cincinnati. Art Theatre
            Community Dramatic Institute
            Dramatic Department of Cincinnati Community Service
            Little Playhouse
            Workshop Theatre of Rockdale Center
Cleveland. Chronicle House
           Drama Workshop of Five Arts League
           Playhouse
           Shaker Village Players
           Thimble Theatre
Fostoria. Association of Amateur Producers
Granville. Masquers, Denison University
Hamilton. Drama League
Miamisburg. Town Players

INDEX

"Bear, A," 324-325.
"Beautiful Sabine Women, The," 110, 305, 342.
"Before Breakfast," 321, 334.
"Beggar's Opera, The," 191, 308.
Belasco, David, 2, 5-6, 9, 14, 48, 52-55, 65, 84, 115, 152, 156, 167, 196, 198-199, 217, 245, 287-292, 294, 296-298, 308, 311, 314.
"Believe Me, Xanthippe," 16, 295, 318.
Bell, Clive, 186.
Bell, E. Hamilton, 290.
Belmont Theatre Prize, 129.
"Belshazzar," 321.
Ben-Ami, Jacob, 6, 59, 110, 146, 268, 307.
Benavente, Jacinto, 81, 267, 304, 327, 329.
Benchley, Robert C., 25, 184, 227.
Benda, Wladislaw T., 167, 214, 227.
Benelli, Sem, 304.
Bennett, Arnold, 16, 293, 331, 342.
Bennett, James O'Donnell, 181, 185.
Bennett, Richard, 33, 295, 305.
Benois, Alexander Nikolaievitch, 299.
Benrimo, J. Harry, 4, 15-17, 293.
Benson, Frank H., 297.
Berger, Henning, 301.
Bergman, Robert, 168.
Berlin, Deutsches Theater, 154, 218, 279; Kammerspiele, 118; Staatsoper, 279.
Berlin, Irving, 4, 64, 255, 296, 310.
Bernauer, Rudolph, 261.

"Bernice," 25, 89, 304, 336.
Bernstein, Henry, 292, 311.
"Between the Lines," 318.
"Beyond the Horizon," 28, 31, 33-34, 66, 188, 197, 204, 305, 316, 321.
Biggers, Earl Derr, 22, 295.
"Bill of Divorcement, A," 311.
Billboard, The, 117.
"Bingo Farm," 227.
Binney, Constance, 227.
"Bird of Paradise, The," 18.
"Birthday of the Infanta, The," 157, 366.
"Black Crook, The," 3, 48, 252.
"Black 'ell," 341.
Blackmer, Sidney, 147.
"Blind Alleys," 327.
Blinn, Holbrook, 142, **289-291**, 294, 304, 306.
Block, Ralph, 185.
Blok, Alexander, 11, 207.
"Blossom Time," 310.
"Blue Bird, The," 290.
Bodenheim, Maxwell, 91, 335.
Bohemians, Inc., 307.
"Boîte à Joujoux, La," 110, 341.
Bolton, Guy, 23, 298, 307, 325.
"Bombo," 310.
"Bonds of Interest, The," 81, 304, 329.
Boni, Albert, 78.
"Boomerang, The," 298.
Booth, Edwin, 187, 195.
Booth, William, 222.
"Bored," 334.
"Boss, The," 21, 291.
Boston, Castle Square Theatre, 61, 129, 318; Opera Company, 153; Toy Theatre, 117.
Boston Evening Transcript, x, 9, 184.

"*Boubouroche,*" 330.
Boucicault, Dion, 195.
"Boudour," 369.
"Bound East for Cardiff," 33, 96, 300, 320, 333–334, 337.
"*Boutique Fantasque, La,*" 306, 342.
Bowes, E. J., 292.
Boyce, Neith, 94, 298, 332–334.
Bracco, Robert, 324–325.
Brady, Alice, 145.
Brady, William A., 50–51, 145, 160, 166, 291, 294–295, 298–299, 307, 313, 318, 368.
Bragdon, Claude, 168, 175.
Brahm, Otto, 196.
"Bread and Butter," 320.
Brice, Fannie, 229, 251.
Brieux, Eugene, 294, 305.
Brighouse, Harold, 327, 341.
"Broadway Jones," 4, 293.
Brooke, Clifford, 310.
Brooklyn Daily Eagle, 183.
Brooks, Joseph, 293.
Brooks, Walter, 309.
Brotherhood of Painters, Decorators and Paper Hangers, 276.
"Brothers," 337.
"Brothers Karamazoff, The," 314.
Broun, Heywood, 182, 227.
Brown, Alice, 16, 297, 325.
Brown, Martin, 23, 303.
Browne, Maurice, 9, 65, 113, 116–117, 167, 216, 294, 309, 339.
Browne, Porter Emerson, 18, 306.
Browning, Robert, 341.
Bryant, Louise, 300, 332, 333.
Buchanan, Thompson, 18.
Burke, Billie, 144, 252, 293.
Burlesque, 249.

Burnside, R. H., 296.
Burrell, Percy, 300.
Burton, Richard, 316–317.
"Bushido," 80, 301, 326.
Butler, Rachel Barton, 305, 318.
Butler, Sheppard, 183.
Byrne, Dolly, 306.
Byron, Arthur, 298.

CADMAN, CHARLES WAKEFIELD, 163.
Caldwell, Anne, 296.
"Caliban by the Yellow Sands," 4, 238–239, 241, 300, 365.
Calthrop, Dion Clayton, 342.
Calvert, Louis, 290, 300.
Campbell, Mrs. Patrick, 296.
Cannan, Gilbert, 342.
"Canterbury Pilgrims, The," 237, 288.
Capek, Josef, 50, 51, 191, 262, 313.
Capek, Karel, 50, 51, 83, 191, 262–263, 313, 331.
"Captain Applejack," 311.
"Captain Brassbound's Conversion," 340.
"Captain Jinks," 81.
Carlton, Tom, 325.
Carlyle, Thomas, 154.
Carnegie Institute of Technology, Pittsburgh, Dramatic Department of, 6, 64–65, 126–127, 131–133, 244, 281.
Carpenter, John Alden, 227.
Carrington, Murray, 298.
Carroll, Albert, 110.
Carroll, Earl, 63.
Carter, Mrs. Leslie, 140, 310.
Carter, Lincoln J., 198.
Caryll, Ivan, 296.
Castle, Irene, 296.
Castle, Vernon, 296.

INDEX

"Cat Bird, The," 367.
Cawthorn, Joseph, 227.
Censorship, 283–284.
Century Magazine, The, x, 89.
"Chains of Dew," 339.
Chaliapin, Fyodor Ivanovitch, 3, 262, 273.
"Change Your Style," 95, 332, 333.
"Chantecler," 3, 7, 153, 291.
Chapin, Harold, 337, 342.
Chatterton, Ruth, 146.
Cheney, Sheldon, 9, 173, 184, 208.
"Cherry Orchard, The," 314.
Chevalier, Albert, 229.
Chicago, Apollo Theater, 8, 170; Art Institute, 173; Chicago Theatre Society, 72; Hull House Players, 117, 127; Little Theatre, 113, 116, 167, 294; World's Columbian Exposition, 237.
Chicago Daily Journal, 184.
Chicago Daily News, 184.
Chicago Evening Post, 184.
Chicago Herald and Examiner, 184.
Chicago Opera Company, 166, 366, 369.
Chicago Record-Herald, 181.
Chicago Tribune, 183.
"Children," 325.
"Children of Earth," 16, 297.
"Children of the Ghetto," 48.
"Children of the Sun," 287.
"Chin-Chin," 296.
Chinese Theatre, 15, 174.
"Chocolate Soldier, The," 289.
Chorpenning, Charlotte, 318.
Chorus Equity Association, 276.
"Chorus Lady, The," 63.
"Chris," 322.

"Christian, The," 48.
Christy, Howard Chandler, 15.
"Chu Chin Chow," 302.
"Circle, The," 310.
Circus as Theatre, 208.
"City, The," 289.
Civic Theatre, 2, 4, 208–209, 232–245.
Claire, Ina, 145.
"Clarence," 16, 304.
Clark, Bobby, 249.
Clark, Margaret, 295.
Claudel, Paul, 261, 331.
Clavilux, 215, 216.
"Claw, The," 157, 311, 366.
"Cleopatra's Night," 369.
"Climax, The," 16, 288.
"Clod, The," 79, 324–325.
"Cloister, The," 330.
"Close the Book," 97, 327, 335.
"Clothes," 16.
Coburn, Charles Douvelle, 147.
"Cocaine," 334, 337.
Coghlan, Charles, 48.
Cohan, George M., 2, 4, 22, 42, 49, 125, 251, 288, 293, 295, 299.
Cohan, Jere, 49.
Cohan and Harris, 288, 293, 295–296.
"Cohan Revue 1916, The," 254, 299.
Cohan Revues, 254.
"Colleen Bawn, The," 48.
Collins, Charles, 183.
Color Organ, 110, 215–216.
Colton, John, 313.
Columbia University, 127.
"Comedian, The," 261.
Commedia dell'Arte, 11, 141, 207, 217–218, 231, 248, 250–251.
Commins, Saxe, 334.

"Common Clay," 318.
Comstock, F. Ray, 64, 291, 294, 298, 302, 312, 314.
"Concert, The," 290.
Connelly, Marc, 22–23, 227, 308.
Conrad, Joseph, 29, 40.
Conroy, Frank, 80, 110, 305.
"Constancy," 94–95, 298, 332.
"Contemporaries," 95, 332–333, 335.
"Continental Stagecraft," ix.
Cook, George Cram, 18, 91–92, 94–95, 98–101, 298, 328, 332–333, 335, 338.
Cook, Joe, 249.
Copeau, Jacques, 45, 81, 302.
"Copperhead, The," 303.
"Copy, The," 319.
Corbin, John, 182, 300.
Corey, Williams and Riter, 299.
Corley, Donald, 339.
Cornell Katherine, 80, 109–110, 145, 311.
Cosmopolitan, 84.
"Country Boy, The," 49.
Courteline, Georges, 326, 330.
Cowl, Jane, 6, 141–143, 293, 315.
Cox, Elinor, 80.
Craig, Edward Gordon, 9, 11, 44, 129–130, 152, 160, 214, 237, 271.
Craig, James, 183.
Craig, John, 318.
Craven, Frank, 22–23, 142, 200, 307.
Criticism, Dramatic, 3, 8, 177–186, 192.
Critics, Dramatic. *See* CRITICISM, DRAMATIC.
"Critic's Comedy, The," 327.
Croce, Benedetto, 178, 205, 218.
Crocker, Bosworth, 80, 91, 326, 336.

Cromwell, John, 313.
Cronyn, George, 327.
Crosman, Henrietta, 144.
Crothers, Rachel, 19–20, 289.
Czecho-Slovakian Drama, 262.

"DADDY'S GONE A-HUNTING," 22, 200, 309, 366.
Dahler, Warren, 110, 168.
Dale, Alan, 182.
Daly, Arnold, 84, 303.
Daly, Augustin, 47, 67, 195.
"Damaged Goods," 294.
Dana, Viola, 294.
Dance, 64, 246–247, 256, 258.
"Dance of Death, The," 329, 367.
Dane, Clemence, 165, 261, 311, 314.
d'Annunzio, Gabriele, 267.
Dante, 152, 166, 208.
Dare, Frank, 327.
"Darling of the Gods, The," 54, 142, 152.
Darnton, Charles, 183.
d'Auguzan, Jean, 294.
Davies, Mary Caroline, 335.
Davis, Owen, 2, 4, 14, 20, 50, 200–201, 309, 313, 315, 317.
Day, Frederick Lansing, 343.
Dean, Basil, 307, 311, 313.
"Dear Brutus," 304.
"Death of Tintagiles, The," 133, 326.
"Deburau," 308.
Debussy, Claude, 110, 341.
"Déclassée," 22, 305.
de Curel, François, 265.
de Forest, Marian, 299.
de Holthoir, Beatrice 326–327.
Dell, Floyd, 91, 301, 333–335.
"Deluge, The," 302.

INDEX

"De Massa Run, ha! ha!" 227.
de Maupassant, Guy, 235.
De Mille, William, 18, 49.
de Musset, Alfred, 324.
de Porto-Riche, Georges, 326.
Designers. *See* STAGE DESIGNERS.
"Detour, The," 14, 200, 309.
"Devil, The," 3, 287.
"Devil's Disciple, The," 83, 261, 315, 331, 368.
"Devil's Garden, The," 59, 299, 365.
"Devil's Glow, The," 335.
de Weerth, Ernest, 110, 167, 309.
Diagileff *Ballet Russe,* 152, 365.
Diagileff, Sergei, 256.
Dial, The, 185.
Dickinson, Thomas H., 126.
"Diff'rent," 28, 31, 34, 98, 188, 197, 308, 322, 338.
Digges, Dudley, 81, 147, 304, 307, 368.
Dillingham, Charles B., 4, 64, 254, 296, 310–311, 313.
Dinehart, Allan, 147.
"Disraeli," 291.
Ditrichstein, Leo, 140, 290, 296.
"Doctor's Dilemma, The," 298.
"Dollar, The," 334.
"Doll's House, A," 287.
"Don Juan," 368.
Donnelly, Dorothy, 310.
Dorrian, Cecil, 325.
Dostoievsky, Fyodor Mihailovitch, 235, 262, 314.
"Dover Road, The," 311.
Down, Oliphant, 340.
"Down the Airshaft," 335.
Drama, The, 9, 117.
Drama League of America, 189–190.
Dramatic Criticism. *See* CRITICISM, DRAMATIC.
Dramatic Critics. *See* CRITICISM, DRAMATIC.
"Dramatic Technique," 128.
Dramatists' Guild, 276.
Draper, Ruth, 227.
Drawing and Design, x.
"Dreamy Kid, The," 321, 337.
Dreiser, Theodore, 18, 208, 327, 339.
Drew, John, 140, 300, 310.
Drinkwater, John, 63, 305.
Dryden, Helen, 296.
"Dud, The," 319.
Dukes, Ashley, 312.
"Dulcy," 23.
Duncan, Augustin, 5, 64, 81, 147, 304, 307, 309, 312, 322, 366–367.
Duncan, Isadora, 147, 256, 300.
Dunsany, Lord, 77, 94, 110, 298, 300–301, 340–341.
Duse, Eleonora, 3, 136.
Dwight, Timothy, 124.
Dymow, Ossip, 166, 302.

EAGELS, JEANNE, 145, 313.
Eames, Clare, 145–310.
"Easiest Way, The," 2, 15, 28, 53, 142, 196–198, 200–202, 204, 288.
"East of Suez," 261.
Eaton, Walter Prichard, 86, 181, 184, 203, 316.
Economic Problems of Theatre, 64, 275–285.
Eddinger, Wallace, 147, 298, 303, 310–311.
Edwardes, George, 255.
"Egoist, The," 24.
"Eldest, The," 337.
Eldridge, Florence, 146.

INDEX

Eliot, Samuel A., Jr., 9, 77, 117, 126, 239, 300.
Ellis, Charles, 100, 110.
Ellis, Edith, 299.
Ellis, Edward, 294.
Ellis, Mrs. Havelock, 340.
Emery, Gilbert, 20, 309.
"Emperor Jones, The," 25, 31, 34, 36–37, 40–41, 92–93, 98, 147, 197, 307, 322, 338.
"Enchanted Cottage, The," 261.
"End of the Bridge, The," 16, 18, 318.
"Enemies," 333.
English, 47, 128, 129.
English Drama, 261, 267.
English Theatre, 11, 229.
"Enter Madame," 18, 63, 306.
Equity Theatre, *See* NEW YORK EQUITY THEATRE.
Erlanger, A. L., 64, 189, 277, 290, 302.
"Erminie," 164, 166, 308, 369.
Errol, Leon, 227, 308.
"Erstwhile Susan," 141, 299.
Ervine, St. John, 82, 84, 86, 304, 306–307, 329–330.
Esthetic Creation, 178.
"Eternal Megalosaurus, The," 342.
"Eternal Quadrangle, The," 333.
Ettlinger, Karl, 326.
"Eugenically Speaking," 78, 297, 323–325.
Euripides, 116, 294.
"Everybody's Husband," 342.
"Everywoman," 207.
"Exorcism," 322, 338.
"Experience," 207.
Expressionism, 18, 25, 37, 83, 158, 195, 208, 216.
Eyre, Lawrence, 367.

FAGAN, J. B., 310.
"Faint Perfume," 24.
"Fair, The," 342.
"Fair and Warmer," 50.
Fairbanks, Douglas, 297.
"Faithful, The," 160, 329, 367.
"Family Exit, The," 327.
"Famous Mrs. Fair, The," 23, 305.
"Fancy Free," 294.
Fang, Mei Lan, 130.
"Fanny's First Play," 293.
"Fashions for Men," 262.
"Father, The," 34.
"Faun, The," 16, 291.
Faversham, William, 291.
"Fear," 294.
Fell, Marian, 325.
Fenellosa, Ernest, 341.
Ferber, Edna, 337.
Ferguson, Elsie, 145.
Fernald, C. B., 341.
"Festival of Pentecost," 341.
"Festival of Thanksgiving," 340.
Festival of the Tabernacles, 107, 341.
Feuillet, Octave, 324.
Ficke, Arthur Davison, 339.
"50–50," 336.
"Fire and Water," 324.
"Fires of St. John, The," 287.
"First Fifty Years, The," 25.
"First Man, The," 64, 322, 342.
"First Year, The," 23, 307.
Fiske, Harrison Grey, 50, 287, 289–292, 295.
Fiske, Minnie Maddern, 3, 6, 53, 84, 102, 141, 145, 287, 289–291, 299, 302.
Fitch, Clyde, 14, 289.
Fitzgerald, M. Eleanor, 100.
"Florist's Shop, The," 118.
"Fog," 36, 320, 334.

Fontanne, Lynn, 146.
"Fool, The," 15, 50, 207.
"Fool There Was, A," 18.
"Footsteps," 339.
Forbes, James, 23, 297, 305.
"Forbidden Fruit," 324.
Foreign Artists of the Theatre, 3, 4, 8, 259–274.
Foreign Drama, 64, 259–274.
Forrest, Sam, 65, 309, 315.
"Fortunato," 341.
"Fortune Hunter, The," 288.
"Forty-Niners, The," 227.
47 Workshop, 129.
"Fountain, The," 28, 31, 36, 38, 40, 322.
Four Cohans, 22.
Fourberies de Scapin, Les, 303.
Fraccaroli, Arnaldo, 261.
France, Anatole, 154, 297.
Frank, Florence Kiper, 336.
Frank, Waldo, 80.
Fraser, C. Lovat, 308.
"Free," 341.
"Freedom," 332–333.
Freeman, Helen, 81.
Freeman, The, x.
French Drama, 261, 267.
French Theatre, 12, 45, 229.
Freksa, Friedrich, 292.
Frohman, Charles, 47, 62–64, 260, 287, 289, 291, 293, 295, 304.
Frohman, Charles, Inc., 301, 305.
Frohman, Daniel, 47.
Frohman, Gustave, 47.
"From Morn to Midnight," 83, 160, 261, 312, 331, 368.
"From Portland to Dover," 366.
Frost, Robert, 25.
Fuller, Rosalind, 155, 227, 314.
"Funiculi-Funicula," 335.

"G. A. M., The," 321.
Gale, Zona, 24, 126, 200, 308, 316, 327.
Gallagher and Shean, 251.
Galsworthy, John, 12, 62, 102–103, 109–110, 134, 261, 288, 293, 299, 307, 313, 342.
"Game, The," 300, 332–333.
"Garden of Allah, The," 48, 292.
"Garden of Paradise, The," 48, 153.
Garland, Hamlin, 316–317.
Gates, Eleanor, 57, 294.
Gaul, George, 147.
Gay, John, 308.
Geddes, Norman-Bel, 3, 6, 49, 55, 130, 152–153, 162–165, 173, 175–176, 208, 214, 227, 249, 276, 308, 312, 314, 369.
"Gee-Rusalem," 336.
Gémier, Firmin, 45.
"Gentile Wife, The," 18, 366.
"Gentle Furniture Shop, The," 335.
George, Grace, 50, 142, 261, 298–299, 313.
"George Washington," 366.
Géraldy, Paul, 191, 193, 261, 313.
German Drama, 261, 267.
German Theatre, 11, 45, 140, 229.
Gerstenberg, Alice, 79, 324.
Gest, Morris, 2, 4, 55, 64, 84, 154, 166, 176, 193, 273–274, 291, 294, 298, 302, 312, 314.
"Getting Unmarried," 337.
"Ghosts," 327.
Gibson, Wilfred Wilson, 116, 340.
Gilbert, William Schwenk, 267.
Gillette, William, 49, 140, 301, 304.
Gilmore, Margalo, 145, 311.
Gilpin, Charles S., 98, 147, 307.

380 INDEX

"Girl of the Golden West, The," 53–54, 142, 152, 198.
"Girl in the Coffin, The," 327.
"Girl without a Dowry, The," 287.
Glaspell, Susan, 25, 79, 81, 91–92, 94, 96–101, 109, 298, 301, 304, 309, 326, 328, 332–336, 339, 341.
Glazer, Benjamin F., 265, 326.
Glendinning, Ernest, 295.
Glinka, Mihail Ivanovitch, 228.
"Glittering Gate, The," 77, 94, 298, 340.
Gloucester, Massachusetts, Pageant, 237, 241, 288.
"God of Vengeance, The," 262, 276.
"Gods of the Mountain, The," 301.
Gogol, Nikolai Vassilievitch, 263.
"Gold," 33, 36, 322.
Golden, John, 50, 303, 307.
Goldsmith, Oliver, 24.
Golovin, Alexander, 299.
"Good Gracious, Annabelle," 18, 59, 300, 365.
Goodman, Edward, 77–78, 81, 293, 297, 323–326.
Goodman, Jules Eckert, 14.
Goodman, Kenneth Sawyer, 326.
Goodwin, Nat C., 303.
Gorky, Maxim, 53, 92, 206, 262, 267, 287, 305, 314.
"Governor's Lady, The," 198.
"Grand Street Follies, The," 343.
Granich, Irwin, 334–335, 337.
"Granny Maumee," 302, 365.
Granville-Barker, Harley. *See* BARKER, HARLEY GRANVILLE.
Grasso, Giovanni, 268.
"Great Adventure, The," 342.

"Great Catherine," 110, 301, 341.
"Great Divide, The," 28, 301.
Greek drama, 116, 169.
Greek Theatre, 11, 125, 234, 252, 259, 271–272.
"Green Ring, The," 343.
"Greenwich Village Follies, The," 214, 254–255, 257, 306.
Gregory, Lady Augusta, 11.
Gribble, Harry Wagstaff, 24.
Griffes, Charles T., 110–111, 302, 312, 341, 343.
Griswold, Grace, 79.
Gros, Ernest, 167, 308.
"Grotesques," 339.
Ground-rent, 66, 174, 278, 281.
Guest, Edgar, 15.
"Guibour," 341, 366.
Guilbert, Yvette, 105, 110, 229, 336.
Guitry, Lucien, 140.
Guitry, Sacha, 261, 308.

"HABIT," 327.
Hackett, Francis, 185.
Hackett, Walter, 311.
"Hairy Ape, The," 4, 28, 31, 36–41, 59, 83, 92, 157, 168, 178, 188, 197, 312, 322, 339, 366.
Hale, Louise Closser, 144.
Hall, O. L., 184.
Hamilton, Clayton, 185, 316, 317.
Hamlen, J. G., 340.
"Hamlet," 6, 59, 155, 157, 192, 314, 366.
Hammerschlag, Arthur, 132.
Hammerstein, Oscar, 2, 274.
Hammond, Percy, 182–183.
Hampden, Walter, 127, 147, 366.
"Hand of the Potter, The," 339.
Hanlon Brothers, 48.

INDEX

"Hannele," 290.
Hapgood, Emily, 302, 365.
Hapgood, Hutchins, 333.
"Happy Ending, The," 365.
Harcourt, Cyril, 296.
"Harlequinade, The," 342.
Harned, Virginia, 303.
Harris, Henry B., 63, 291, 293.
Harris, Sam H., 4, 49, 255, 288, 309-310, 311, 313, 315, 317.
Harris, William, Jr., 4, 55, 63, 305-306.
Harris, William, Jr., 4, 55, 63.
Harvard Dramatic Club, 154.
Harvard Prize Plays, 16.
Harvard Prize Play Awards, 63, 129, 318-319.
Harvard Stadium, 239, 288, 300.
Harvard University, 5-6, 21, 29, 61, 125-131, 134, 154, 159, 244.
Hasenclever, Walter, 11.
Hast, Walter, 367.
Hatton, Fanny, 294.
Hatton, Frederic, 185, 294.
Hauptmann, Gerhart, 11, 53, 261, 265, 291, 299.
"Fanny Hawthorne," 294.
Hayes, Helen, 145.
"Hazel Kirke," 48.
Hazelton, George C., 4, 15-17, 293.
Head, Cloyd, 339.
Hearst, William Randolph, 182.
"Heartbreak House," 82-83, 160, 307, 330, 368.
Hecht, Ben, 24, 81, 326.
Hedman, Martha, 146, 298.
Heggie, O. P., 146, 297, 312.
Helburn, Theresa, 82, 86.
Held, Anna, 252.
"Helena's Husband," 79, 324-325.
Heming, Violet, 145.

Herbert, Henry, 81, 147.
"Her Husband's Wife," 16, 290.
"Hermit and His Messiah, The," 336.
Herndon, Richard, G., 4, 63, 129, 315, 319.
Herne, James A., 14.
"Hero of Santa Maria, The," 326.
"Hero, The," 20, 309.
"He Who Gets Slapped," 83, 163, 262, 264, 330, 368.
Hewlett, Russell, 132.
Heyward, Dorothy, 319.
Hichens, Robert, 292.
"Hindle Wakes," 294.
Hippius, Zinaida, 343.
Hiroshige, 158.
"His Widow's Husband," 327.
Hitchcock, Raymond, 228.
Hoffman, Aaron, 14-15.
Hoffman, Gertrude, 291.
Hokusai, 158.
Hollaender, Victor, 292.
Holme, Garnet, 300.
"Home of the Free, The," 328.
"Honor Among the Bradleys," 322.
"Honorable Lover, The," 324-325.
Hooker, Brian, 227.
Hopkins, Arthur, 2, 4, 9, 55, 57-61, 63, 84, 100, 130, 152, 154-156, 163, 169, 179, 188, 193, 209-213, 224, 273, 294, 296, 299-312, 314, 317, 322, 365-367.
Hopper, De Wolf, 308.
Hopwood, Avery, 14, 16, 50, 291.
Houghton, Stanley, 12, 294.
Houseman, Laurence, 295.
Howard, Bronson, 14.
Howard, Leslie, 147.

Howard, Sidney, 20, 21, 265, 310–311.
Howard, Willie, 255.
Howells, William Dean, 329.
"How's Your Second Act?" 56, 58.
Hoyt, Charles H., 14, 23.
Hudson, Holland, 78, 323–324.
Huffaker, Lucy, 78.
Huffman, J. C., 310.
Hugo, Victor, 265.
Hull, Henry, 147.
Hume, Sam, 9, 65, 126.
"Humoresque," 188.
Huneker, James, 3.
Hungarian Drama, 262.
Hunter, Glenn, 80, 147.
Hurlbut, William C., 15.

IBSEN, HENRIK, 11, 53, 84, 116, 191, 196, 262, 287, 289, 291, 298, 303, 327, 331.
"Icebound," 4, 14, 200, 315, 317.
"Idle Inn, The," 156.
"'Ile," 33, 97, 321, 335.
Illington, Margaret, 292.
Impressionism, 194.
"In April," 324.
"In the Zone," 33, 320, 327.
"Inca of Perusalem, The," 110, 301, 341.
"Inchin' Along like a Poor Inchworm," 227.
Independent, The, 185.
Indianapolis, Little Theatre, 117, 126, 208.
"Inheritors," 25, 98, 309, 338.
"Innocent and Annabel," 342.
"Insect Comedy, The," *See* "THE WORLD WE LIVE IN."
"Inspector General, The," 262.
Institutional Theatre, 2, 5, 66–74, 113, 117, 135, 273, 285.

"Interior," 297, 323–324.
International Alliance of Billposters and Billers, 276.
International Alliance of Theatrical Stage Employees and Moving Picture Machine Operators, 276.
International Brotherhood of Teamsters and Chauffeurs, 276.
International Theatrical Association, 276.
"Inwhich," 163.
Irish Players, 147, 292.
Irish Theatre, 11.
"Irish Triangle, An," 337.
Irving, Sir Henry, 195.
Isaacs, Edith J. R., 9.
Italian Drama, 261, 267.
"Ivan's Homecoming," 334.
Izumo, Takeda, 80, 301, 326.

JACOBOWSKI, E., 308.
James, William, 203.
"Jane Clegg," 82, 160, 306, 329, 367.
Janis, Elsie, 229.
Japanese Theatre, 174.
Javanese Theatre, 174.
"Jephthah's Daughter," 297, 340.
Jessner, Leopold, 45.
"Jest, The," 59, 304, 366.
"Joan of Arc," 288.
"Johannes Kreisler," 50, 261.
"John Ferguson," 64, 82, 147, 304, 329–330.
"John Gabriel Borkman," 298.
"John Hawthorne," 330.
Johnson, C. Raymond, 167.
Johnson, Owen, 317.
"Joined Together," 334.
Jolson, Al, 6, 228–229, 251, 255, 310.
Jones, Henry Arthur, 267.

INDEX

Jones, Robert Edmond, 3, 6, 9, 39, 55, 59, 77–78, 81, 94–95, 100, 110, 127, 151, 153–156, 158–160, 162–164, 168, 179, 193, 209–215, 227, 239, 242, 251, 276, 297, 300–304, 306–308, 310–312, 314, 365–366.
Jonson, Ben, 134.
"Josephine," 303.
Josephine Company, Inc., The, 303.
"Justice," 62, 299.

KAHN, OTTO H., 81, 166.
"Kairn of Koridwen, The," 302, 341.
Kaiser, Georg, 11, 83, 191, 261, 312, 331.
Kalich, Bertha, 56.
Kane, Whitford, 134, 147.
Kaplan, Samuel, 327.
Kaufman, George S., 22–23, 227.
Keane, Doris, 142, 294.
Keith, B. F., Vaudeville, 247.
Kelcey, Herbert, 294, 297.
Kelly, George, 24.
Kelly, Walter C., 251.
Kemp, Harry, 91, 334.
Kemper, Collin, 50.
"Kempy," 24.
Kennedy, Madge, 146.
Kenton, Edna, 100.
Kenyon, Charles, 16, 292.
Kern, Jerome, 298, 307.
"Kiki," 311.
"Kindling," 16, 292.
"King Arthur's Socks," 300–301, 333.
King, Dennis, 147.
"King Lear," 166, 276.
King, Pendleton, 334.
Kingston, Gertrude, 105, 301.

Kinkead, Cleves, 15, 128, 318.
"Kismet," 16, 292.
"Kiss for Cinderella, A," 301.
Klauber, Adolph, 65, 98, 185.
Klaw and Erlanger, 64, 189, 277, 290, 302.
Klaw, Marc, 64, 189, 277, 290, 302.
"Kleschna, Leah," 18.
Knoblauch, Edward. *See* KNOBLOCK, EDWARD.
Knoblock, Edward, 16, 128, 291–293, 297.
"Knock at the Door, A," 320.
"Knot-Holes," 335.
Kommissarzhevsky, Fyodor, 75, 368.
Kommissarzhevskaya, Vera, 3, 8, 273, 287.
Kosloff, Alexei, 291.
Kosloff, Fyodor, 291.
"Krazy Kat," 227.
Kremer, Theodore, 50.
Kreymborg, Alfred, 25, 91, 227, 266, 334, 338.
Kruger, Otto, 147, 317.
Kugelman, F. B., 336.
Kummer, Clare, 18, 300–301, 303.
"Kurzy of the Sea," 338.

LACKAYE, WILTON, 295.
Lady Frederick," 3.
"Lady from the Provinces, The," 314.
"Lady Windermere's Fan," 142, 295.
Lange, Sven, 307.
Langner, Lawrence, 78, 81–82, 297, 323–325, 327, 338.
Lardner, Ring, 25.
"Last Masks," 338.
"Last Straw, The," 80, 326.
Lauder, Harry, 229.

INDEX

"Laughing Gas," 208.
"Laughing Lady, The," 261, 366.
Lawrence, Basil. *See* LANGNER, LAWRENCE.
Lawrence, D. H., 166.
Lawrence, Margaret, 146.
Lawson, John Howard, 25, 191, 212.
Leacock, Stephen, 229.
Leblang, Joseph, 283.
Le Gallienne, Eva, 145.
"Legend of Leonora, The," 295.
Leiber, Fritz, 147.
Le Moyne, Sarah Cowell, 105, 296.
Lenihan, Winifred, 145.
Lenormand, H. R., 294.
Leslie, Amy, 184.
"Letter of the Law, The," 305.
Lewis, Justina, 342.
Lewis, Sinclair, 20.
Lewisohn, Alice, 75, 105–106, 108, 312, 368.
Lewisohn, Irene, 75, 105–106, 108.
Lewisohn Ludwig, 184, 265.
"Licensed," 78, 297, 323.
Liebler and Company, 48, 288, 292, 296.
Liebovitz, D., 330.
Life, 183, 185.
"Life of Man, The," 119, 326.
Light, James, 98–99, 101.
"Light of St. Agnes, The," 56.
Light opera, 254.
"Lightnin'," 303.
"Liliom," 83, 146, 160–161, 265, 309, 330, 368.
"Lima Beans," 334.
Lincoln, Florence, 16, 318.
Lindau, Norman C., 339.
Lindsay, Vachel, 25, 222, 229, 266.
"Lion and the Mouse, The," 63.
Lippmann, Walter, 81.

Liszt, Franz, 162.
"Literature," 324–325.
"Little Act of Justice, A," 339.
Little Country Theatre, 127.
"Little Eyolf," 290.
"Little Minister, The," 81.
"Little Nellie Kelly," 49.
Little Theatre Tournament, 115, 122.
Little Theatres, 2, 5, 55, 79, 113–122, 344–364.
Littmann, Professor Max, 172.
Liveright, Otto K., 336.
Locke, Edward, 16, 288.
Locker, Robert, 168, 306–307.
London, Gaiety Theatre, 255.
Lonergan, Lester, 305–306.
"Lonesome-Like," 328.
"Long Time Ago, A," 334.
"Long Voyage Home, The," 33, 97, 321, 335.
Lonsdale, Frederick, 261.
Lopokova, Lydia, 291.
Lorber, Martha, 258.
Lord, Pauline, 59, 145, 301, 307, 311.
Los Angeles, Little Theatre, 163.
"Lost Leader, The," 305.
Louisiana Purchase Exposition, 238.
"Love," 98, 338.
"Love Child, The," 261.
"Love for Three Oranges, The," 231.
"Love of One's Neighbor," 323.
"Lover's Luck," 326.
Loving, Pierre, 339.
"Lower Depths, The," 217, 274, 314.
"Loyalties," 261, 313.
"Lucky One, The," 261, 331, 368.
Lucy Stone Club, 229.

INDEX

Lunt, Alfred, 147.
Lusitania, 232.

"MACBETH," 59, 157, 179, 193, 209–213, 308, 366.
McClellan, C. M. S., 18.
McClintic, Guthrie, 63, 311.
McComas, Carroll, 145, 308.
McCutcheon, George Barr, 15.
MacDonald, Anna S., 341.
McFadden, Elizabeth, 318.
McGovern, Terence, 49.
Macgowan, Kenneth, ix, 9, 127, 173, 184, 259.
Mackay-Cantell, Lilia, 297, 340.
MacKaye, Hazel, 300.
MacKaye, Percy, 2, 4, 20, 134, 208, 232, 234, 236–239, 241–242, 288, 291, 295–296, 300, 324, 365.
MacKaye, Steele, 195, 237.
MacNichol, Kenneth, 334.
McQuinn, Robert, 167, 296.
"Madame Sand," 18, 302.
"Madras House, The," 342.
Maeterlinck, Maurice, 78, 80, 133, 264, 289–290, 297, 323–326.
"Magical City, The," 21, 79, 160, 299, 325, 367.
"Main Street," 20.
Major, Clare Tree, 79.
"Major Barbara," 299.
"Maker of Dreams, The," 340.
"Makers of Light, The," 343.
Makhno, the Giant, 2.
Malleson, Miles, 328, 341.
"Malvaloca," 261.
"*Ma Mère l'Oye,*" 342.
"Mama's Affair," 305, 319.
"Man from Home, The," 48.
"Man Who Married a Dumb Wife, The," 154, 297, 365.

Mannering, Mary, 289, 292.
"Man's World, A," 20, 289.
Mansfield, Richard, 49, 81, 84.
Mantle, Burns, 183.
Mapes, Victor, 298.
"March Hares," 24.
"Marco Polo," 40, 322.
"Marie-Odile," 16, 297.
Marion, George, 142, 311.
Marionettes, 110, 168.
Marlowe, Julia, 141.
Marquis, Don, 24, 227.
"Marriage Proposal, A," 340.
"Married Woman, The," 341.
Martin, Helen R., 299.
"Martinique," 367.
"Mary Broome," 342.
"Mary the Third," 20.
Masefield, John, 329.
Mask, The, 9, 158.
Masks, 214, 227.
"Masks and Demons," ix.
"Masque of Cincinnati, The," 241.
"Masque of Labor, A," 238.
Masques, 208, 237, 245.
"Massa's in de Cold, Cold Ground," 227.
Massey, Edward, 79–80, 326–327.
"Matinata," 328.
Matthews, Brander, 3, 127.
Matthison, Edith Wynne, 289, 300.
Maude, Cyril, 261.
Maugham, W. Somerset, 261, 310, 313.
Maxwell, William B., 299.
Mayo, Margaret, 18.
Meader, Clarence I., 326.
"Mecca," 274.
Megrue, Roi Cooper, 14.
Meinhard, Carl, 261.

Meiningen Company, 196.
"Melting Pot, The," 288.
Mencken, Helen, 145.
Mencken, Henry L., 3.
"Merchant of Venice, The," 54, 192, 314.
Merrill, Fenimore, 327.
"Merry Death, The," 326.
"Merry Wives of Windsor, The," 290.
"Merton of the Movies," 23–24.
Metcalf, James, 183.
Metropolitan Opera Company, 299, 369.
Metropolitan Opera House. See NEW YORK METROPOLITAN OPERA HOUSE.
Meyer, Josephine A., 78, 81, 325.
Meyerhold, Vsevolod Emilyevitch, 11, 45, 203, 222, 231, 272.
"Mid-Channel," 289.
"Midsummer Night's Dream, A," 297.
Middleton, George, 23.
"Midweek Interludes, The," 342.
"Milestones," 16, 293.
Millay, Edna St. Vincent, 20–21, 81, 91, 98, 336–337.
Miller, Gilbert, 63.
Miller, Henry, 50, 63, 142, 290, 302, 304–305.
Miller, Marilyn, 308.
Miller and Lyles, 309.
Milne, A. A., 83–84, 261, 308, 311–312, 330–331.
Milton, Robert, 5, 65, 75, 310, 315, 368.
"'Mind-the-Paint' Girl, The," 144, 293.
"Miracle, The," 167, 176.

"Miracle of St. Anthony, The," 323–324, 367.
"*Misanthrope, Le,*" 287.
"Miss Lulu Bett," 145, 308, 316.
"Mr. Faust," 339.
"Mr. Pim Passes By," 83, 308, 330, 367–368.
"Mrs. Bumpstead-Leigh," 291.
"Mrs. Warren's Profession," 328.
"Mrs. Wiggs of the Cabbage Patch," 48.
"Missouri One Hundred Years Ago," 244.
Mitchell, Grant, 147.
Mitchell, Langdon, 15, 298.
"Mixed Marriage," 307.
"Mob, The," 102, 109–110, 307, 342.
"Modern Art and the Theatre," 208.
Moderwell, Hiram K., 9, 185.
Moeller, Philip, 18, 77, 79, 81–82, 87, 302, 304, 308, 313, 315, 323–326, 328, 367–368.
"Molière," 304.
Mollère, Jean Baptiste Poquelin, 287, 303, 326.
Molnar, Franz, 3, 83–84, 161, 262, 287, 295–296, 309, 330.
"Money," 337.
Monkhouse, Allan, 342.
"Monte Cristo," 28–29.
Montgomery, David, 251, 296.
Moody, Dwight L., 229.
Moody, William Vaughn, 301.
"Moon of the Caribbees, The," 31–32, 98, 321, 336, 338.
"Moondown," 323.
Moore, Florence, 251.
Morales, Gustavo, 342.
Mordkin, Mihail Mihailovitch, 9, 256, 289.

INDEX 387

"More Sinned Against than Usual," 56
Moreau, Emile, 309.
Morgan, Agnes, 75, 105–106, 312, 368.
Morosco, Oliver, 50, 129, 299, 305, 319.
Morris, McKay, 147.
Moscow, Kamerny Theatre, 11, 203;
  Moscow Art Theatre, 8–9, 11, 54, 70, 82, 92, 112, 123, 137, 139, 193, 196, 203–204, 262, 267, 271–272, 274, 314;
  Moscow Art Theatre Studios, 123, 188;
  Small State Theatre, 196.
Mosher, John, 334.
"Mountain Man, The," 366.
"Movie Man, The," 321.
Moving scenery, 214–215.
Mower, Margaret, 80.
"Much Ado About Nothing," 141.
Mudgett, David, 132.
Munsey, Frank, 183.
Murray, Gilbert, 116.
"Music Box Revue, The, 1921," 255, 310.
Musical Comedy, 252.
"My Lady's Honor," 323.
Myers, Henry, 25.
Mygatt, Tracy, 342.
Mysteries, 169.

Nash, Mary, 146.
National Theatre (idea), 73, 103, 112.
National Theatre (organization), 5, 72.
Nathan, George Jean, 185, 227.
Nation, The, 184.
"Nave, La," 369.

Nazimova, Alla, 290, 303.
"Neighbors," 327.
"Nellie, the Beautiful Cloak Model," 2.
"Nemesis," 14.
Nemirovitch-Dantchenke, Vladimir Ivanovitch, 274, 314.
"Nevertheless," 301.
"New Criticism, The," 178.
New Republic, The, x, 185.
New York, Algonquin's Vicious Circle, 184;
  Ambassador Theatre, 310;
  American Academy of Dramatic Arts, 124;
  American *Commedia dell'Arte,* 207;
  Apollo Theatre, 8, 170, 308;
  Astor Theatre, 291, 295, 299, 303, 309, 316;
  Bandbox Theatre, 75, 78–79, 160, 297, 299, 302, 322–325;
  Belasco Theatre, 169, 287–288, 292, 294, 297–298, 308, 311, 314;
  Belmont Theatre, 308–309, 311–312, 315–316, 319, 330;
  Bijou Theatre, 307, 311, 313;
  Booth Theatre, 62, 170, 297, 301, 303, 312;
  Bramhall Playhouse, 307;
  Broadhurst Theatre, 311;
  Café Martin, 249;
  Candler Theatre, 296, 299;
  Casino Theatre, 292;
  Century Roof Theatre, 166, 312;
  Century Theatre, 170–171, 176, 288–290, 292, 299–300, 309;
  Cohan's Theatre, 293;
  Comedy Theatre, 75, 79, 288–289, 293, 301, 306, 325–328, 330;

INDEX

Cort Theatre, 305, 311;
Criterion Theatre, 302, 305;
Daly's Theatre, 287, 291–292;
Drama League, 117, 190;
Drama Society, 300;
Earl Carroll Theatre, 63, 170;
Eltinge Theatre, 293;
Empire Theatre, 287, 289, 295, 301, 304–305;
Equity Theatre, 5, 64, 71–72, 134, 167, 190, 273, 314;
Forty-Eighth Street Theatre, 298, 314;
Forty-Ninth Street Theatre, 312;
Frazee Theatre, 330;
Fulton Theatre, 293–294, 319, 329–330;
Gaiety Theatre, 288, 299, 303, 312;
Garden Theatre, 299, 302;
Garrick Theatre, 77, 81–82, 160, 169, 290–291, 302, 304, 306–310, 312–313, 315, 329–331;
George M. Cohan Theatre, 311;
Greenwich Village, 28, 77, 89, 94;
Greenwich Village Theatre, 100, 293, 296, 305–308, 311;
Hackett Theatre, 287;
Harris Theatre (now Frazee), 299;
Henry Miller's Theatre, 170, 305, 310, 315, 330;
Herald Square Theatre, 49;
Hippodrome, 254;
Hudson Theatre, 291, 294, 295, 297, 304;
Jewish Art Theatre, 65, 110, 268. *See also* NEW YORK YIDDISH ART THEATRE;

Jolson's Fifty-Ninth Street Theatre, 310, 313–314;
Knickerbocker Theatre, 291–292, 303;
Liberal Club, 95;
Liberty Theatre, 293, 295, 304;
Little Theatre, 8, 61–62, 169, 293, 295–296, 304–305, 307, 316;
Longacre Theatre, 309;
Lyceum Theatre, 288–291, 293, 295, 301;
Lyric Theatre, 289;
Manhattan Opera House, 302;
Maxine Elliott Theatre, 292, 294, 306, 313;
Metropolitan Opera House, 89, 166, 289;
Miner's Theatre, 49;
Modern Stage Society, 299;
Morosco Theatre, 305;
Music Box, 8, 170, 255, 310;
Nazimova's Theatre, 290;
Neighborhood Playhouse, 5, 55, 68, 72, 84, 102–112, 114, 127, 168, 170, 190, 215–216, 297–298, 300–302, 305–307, 312, 322, 340–343, 365;
New Amsterdam Theatre, 296, 307;
New Theatre, 2, 4, 5, 61–62, 71–72, 170, 288–290;
New York National Theatre, 310, 314.
Palais Royal, 249;
Park Theatre, 308;
Players' Club, 369;
Playhouse, 294, 297–299;
Plymouth Theatre, 169, 302–306, 309;
Polo Grounds, 269;
Portmanteau Theatre, 301;

INDEX

Princess Theatre, 252, 294, 298, 313;
Provincetown Playhouse, 5 32, 55, 68, 71–74, 84, 89–101, 108, 110, 114, 168, 190, 297, 301, 303, 307–309, 312, 320–322, 332–339, 366;
Republic Theatre, 287, 300;
Sam H. Harris Theatre, 296, 299, 314–315, 317;
Samovar, 95;
Selwyn Theatre, 8, 170, 310;
Shubert Theatre, 303, 331;
Sixty-Third Street Theatre, 309;
Stadium of the College of the City of New York, 239, 300;
Stage Society, 96, 154;
Stuyvesant Theatre, 288;
Symphony Society, 89;
Theatre Guild, 5, 18, 55, 64–65, 68, 71–72, 75–77, 81–89, 94, 101, 110, 114, 146, 159–161, 163, 169, 175, 193, 247, 263, 273, 304, 306–310, 312–313, 315, 329–331, 367, 368;
Thirty-Ninth Street Theatre, 290, 298, 299, 301, 318;
Vanderbilt Theatre, 294, 311, 317;
Victoria Theatre, 2;
Wallack's Theatre, 291, 297–298;
Washington Square Bookshop, 78;
Washington Square Players, 32, 55, 75–81, 84, 86, 94–95, 101, 103, 110, 119, 126, 159, 298–299, 301, 321, 323–328, 367;
Weber's Theatre, 288;
Winter Garden, 255, 291;

Yiddish Art Theatre, 60. *See also* NEW YORK JEWISH ART THEATRE;
Yiddish Theatres, 268, 276.
New York American, 182.
New York City Shakespeare Tercentenary Celebration Committee, 300.
New York Daily News, 183.
New York Evening Mail, 183.
New York Evening Post, 183.
New York Evening Telegram, 183.
New York Evening World, 183.
New York Globe, 184.
New York Herald, 183.
"New York Idea, The" 15, 298.
New York Sun and Globe, 183.
New York Times, 65, 182–183.
New York Tribune, 38, 182.
New York World, 182.
"Nice People," 20.
"Nigger, The," 288.
"Nigger of the *Narcissus*, The," 29.
"Night," 335, 337.
"Night at an Inn, A," 300, 341.
"Night Lodging," 305.
"Night of Snow," 324.
Nikko Producing Company, Inc., 309.
Nizhinsky, Vaslaff, 365.
"Nju," 166, 302, 369.
"Nobody Home," 252, 298.
"Nobody Knows the Trouble I Has," 227.
"Nobody's Widow," 16, 291.
"Noose, The," 342.
Nordfeldt, Bror, 330.
North American Review, The, x.
Northampton Municipal Theatre, 72.

Norton, Frederick, 302.
Norwegian Drama, 262.
"Not Smart," 332, 336-337.
Novel, Dramatized, 8.
"Now I Ask You," 321.
Nugent, Elliott, 24.
Nugent, J. C., 24.

OBEY, ANDRÉ, 330.
"Obituary, The," 334.
Objectivity, 195.
"Oh, Boy!" 252.
"Oh, Lady, Lady!" 252.
"Oh, My Dear," 252.
"Old Soak, The," 24.
"On Trial," 25, 296.
"On the Art of the Theatre," 9.
One-Act-Play, 78, 80, 98-99.
O'Neill, Eugene, 2-4, 12, 14-15, 20, 27-43, 49, 55, 59, 62, 64, 81, 83, 87, 91-93, 95, 97-101, 109, 127, 130, 142, 151, 178, 188, 191, 196-197, 200, 202, 212, 300, 305, 307-308, 311-312, 316-317, 320-322, 327-328, 332-339, 342.
O'Neill, James, 28, 48.
O'Neill, Maire, 310.
Oppenheim, James, 335.
Ordynski, Richard, 292, 300, 302.
Oriental Theatre, 174.
Orpheum Circuit, 56.
Osborne, Hubert, 134.
Ostrovsky, Alexander Nikolaievitch, 287.
"Outside, The," 97, 335.
"Overtones," 79, 324, 367.

PAGE, RUTH, 227, 258.
Pageant, 237, 242, 245.

"Pageant of Saint Louis, The," 296.
"Pageant of Virginia, The," 244.
"Paid in Full," 2.
Painter, Eleanor, 288.
"Pair of Silk Stockings, A," 62, 296.
Palmer, Albert M., 47, 67, 195.
"Pan," 334.
"Papa," 21, 166, 304, 369.
Pape, Eric, 288.
"Pariah," 327.
Paris, *Comédie Française,* 123, 196, 261, 268;
  Conservatoire, 123;
  Opéra, 279;
  Théâtre des Champs-Élysées, 279;
  Théâtre du Vieux Colombier, 302.
Parker, H. T., 9, 181, 184.
Parker, Louis N., 244, 291.
Parker, Robert, 336.
Parker, Robert Allerton, 185.
Parkhurst, Winthrop, 337.
"Passing Shows," 255.
"Pasteur," 142, 261.
Paulton, Harry, 308.
Pavlova, Anna P., 9, 256, 289.
Payne, B. Iden, 64, 134.
"Peace That Passeth Understanding, The," 336.
Pearn, Violet, 340, 342.
Peck, Esther, 105, 110-111, 168, 312.
"Peer Gynt," 69, 146, 160, 191, 262, 331, 368.
Pelham, Laura Dainty, 127.
"Pelléas and Mélisande," 166.
Pemberton, Brock, 4, 55, 63, 261, 306, 308, 310, 313, 317, 366.
Pemberton, Murdock, 323.
Pennington, William, 78.

INDEX 391

"People, The," 334, 341.
Perkins, Dagmar, 106.
"Personal Equation, The," 321.
Peters, Rollo, 80-81, 130, 143, 147, 167, 303-304, 307, 309, 315.
"Petrushka," 340.
Pevear, Munroe, 245.
"Phantom Rival, The," 296.
Phelps, Professor William Lyon, 126, 317.
Philadelphia, Little Theatre, 117.
"Philanderer, The," 62, 295.
"Philosopher of Butterbiggens, The," 337.
Picard, André, 311.
Pichel, Irving, 126, 173, 239, 300.
"Pie," 338.
"Pierre of the Plains," 49
"Pierre Patelin," 160, 325, 367.
"Pigeon, The," 62, 293.
"Pilgrim Spirit, The," 243-245, 309.
"Pillars of Society," 289.
Pimentel, L. Garcia, 327.
"Pine Tree, The," 80.
Pinero, Arthur Wing, 144, 261, 267, 289-290, 293.
Pinski, David, 330, 334.
"Pippa Passes," 341.
Pirandello, Luigi, 63, 261, 313.
Platt, George Foster, 289, 295.
Platt, Livingston, 168, 306.
Play, Novelized, 8.
Play, Publication, 3, 8.
Play-Book, The, 126.
"Playboy of the Western World, The," 292.
Playfair, Nigel, 308, 313.
Playhouse, 3, 6, 8, 83, 162, 166, 169-176, 278.
"Plays of the Natural and the Supernatural," 18, 208.

Playwright, American, 2-4, 10-26, 75, 78-80, 94, 124, 148, 150, 162, 260.
"Plot Thickens, The," 261.
"Plots and Playwrights," 80, 326-327.
Plymouth, Massachusetts, Pageant, 243-245, 309.
Poël, William, 134.
"Poetaster, The," 134.
Pogany, Willy, 167.
"Pokey," 328.
Pollock, Allan, 311.
Pollock, Arthur, 183.
Pollock, Channing, 14-15.
"Polly Preferred," 23.
"Polly with a Past," 23.
"Poor Fool, The," 326.
"Poor Little Rich Girl, The," 56-57, 294.
Porter, Gene Stratton, 15.
Portmanteau Theatre, 65, 301.
Potter, Grace, 336.
Pound, Ezra, 341.
Povah, Phyllis, 146.
"Power of Darkness, The," 160, 276, 329, 367.
Powers, Tom, 147.
Presentation, 195, 207.
Press agent, 191-192, 276.
"Price of Coal, The," 341.
"Princess Marries the Page, The," 336.
Princeton University, 29.
"Private Account, A," 326.
"Prodigal Son, The," 334.
Producers, 2, 4-5, 10, 44-68, 71, 73-75, 90, 121, 124, 138, 148, 164.
Producing Managers' Association, 44, 72, 148, 189, 276, 283-285.
"Product of the Mill, The," 318.

INDEX

Prokofieff, Sergei Sergeievitch, 231.
Provincetown, Wharf Theatre, 95, 97, 298, 332–333.
Provincetown Players. *See* NEW YORK PROVINCETOWN PLAYHOUSE.
"Prunella, or Love in a Garden," 61–62, 295.
Published Plays, 3.
Pulitzer Drama Prize Award, 4, 13, 127, 316–317.
"Pygmalion," 296.

"QUEEN'S ENEMIES, THE," 301, 341.
Quintero, Joaquim, 261, 341.
Quintero, Serafin Alvarez, 261, 341.

"R. U. R.," 83, 262–263, 313, 331, 368.
Rachilde, Mme., 341.
Radcliffe College, 127–129.
"Rain," 145, 313.
Rambeau, Marjorie, 146, 310.
Randolph, Clemence, 313.
Rath Brothers, 227.
Rathbun, Stephen, 183.
Rauh, Ida, 78.
Ravel, Maurice, 342.
Real Estate, 277–278.
Realism, 16, 19, 24, 34–36, 194–206, 208, 221, 245, 272.
Realism, Revolt Against, 19, 24–25, 36–38, 205–258.
Reamer, Lawrence, 185.
"Recklessness," 320.
"Red Cloak, The," 325.
Red Cross Pageant, 134.
"Redemption," 59, 303, 366.
Reed, John, 96, 323, 332–333, 336.

Reicher, Emanuel, 65, 75, 298–299, 306, 367–368.
Reicher, Frank, 5, 65, 75, 291, 309, 312–313, 315, 368.
Reichert, H., 310.
Reinhardt, Professor Max, 4, 6, 9, 45, 65, 70, 74, 87, 118, 130, 146, 152, 154, 163, 167, 176, 203, 208, 218, 222, 231, 274, 292.
Reizenstein, Elmer. *See* RICE, ELMER.
Réjane, Gabrielle, 3, 48, 273.
Rélonde, Maurice, 325.
Remisoff, Nikolai, 312.
Renaissance, 259.
Repertory System, 10, 54, 66, 76, 139, 188, 273, 280, 284.
Representation, 195, 207–208.
"Rescue, The," 336.
"Return of Peter Grimm, The," 52–53, 198–199, 217, 292.
Revue, 4, 64, 222, 228, 246–258.
Reynolds, James, 167, 249, 257, 306–307.
"Rib-Person, The," 335.
Rice, Elmer, 25, 191, 212, 296, 328, 331.
"Richard III," 59, 157, 306, 366.
Richman, Arthur, 20, 83, 200–201, 310, 330.
Rickard, Tex, Arena, 269.
"Rider of Dreams, The," 302, 365.
Rinehart, Mary Roberts, 14.
"Rise of Silas Lapham, The," 329, 367.
"Rivals, The," 369.
Road, Theatre on the, 188, 189, 248.
"Roadhouse in Arden, The," 79, 324.
Robertson, Donald, 134.

INDEX

Robinson, Lennox, 305, 310.
Robinson, Thomas P., 319.
Roeder, Ralph, 78, 297, 323–324.
Roerich, Nikolai, 154.
"Roger Bloomer," 25, 212.
Rogers, Will, 6, 228–229, 251, 254.
Roland, Ida, 140.
Rolfe, William J., 125.
"Rolling Stones," 49.
Roman Theatre, 229.
"Romance," 4, 21, 142, 294.
"Romantic Age, The," 261.
Romberg, Sigmund, 310.
"Romeo and Juliet," 6, 50, 141–143, 156, 192, 277, 315, 366.
"Rope, The," 33, 97, 321, 328, 336–337.
Rose, F. H., 342.
"Rose Bernd," 141, 261, 366.
"Rosmersholm," 177.
Rosse, Herman, 6, 167, 173, 214, 227.
Rossini, Gioachimo Antonio, 306, 342.
Rostand, Edmond, 7, 291.
Rostetter, Alice L., 336.
"Royal Box, The," 48.
"Royal Fandango, The," 342.
Ruben, José, 80.
"Rubicon, The," 283.
Rubinstein, Anton, 162.
Ruhl, Arthur, 185.
Russell, Henry, 153.
Russian Ballet, 9, 256, 289, 291.
Russian Drama, 262, 267.
Russian Theatre, 11, 122, 229.
"Russian Theatre, The," ix, 45.

SAINT-GAUDENS, HOMER, 305.
Saint-Gaudens Masque-Prolog, 2, 237.

St. Louis, Municipal Opera, 241.
"Saint Louis, A Civic Masque," 4, 134, 238, 296.
"Saint Louis Pageant, The," 134.
"*Saison Russe*," 274, 291.
Sale, Chic, 251.
"Sally," 307.
"Salome," 328.
"*Salut au Monde*," 110–111, 312, 343.
"Salvation Nell," 2–3, 21, 287.
Salzburg, 176.
"Samson and Delilah," 307, 366.
"Sanctuary," 238, 295.
"Sandbar Queen, The," 328.
Sandow, 252.
Sankey, Ira D., 229.
Sarg, Tony, 110, 167.
Saturday Evening Post, 84.
"Sauce for the Emperor," 334.
"Saviors," 324.
Savoy, Bert, 251.
"Scandals," George White's, 256.
Scandinavian Theatre, 11.
Scarborough, Beechwood, Theatre, 170.
"Scarecrow, The," 20, 291.
Schildkraut, Joseph, 6, 69, 146, 309.
Schildkraut, Rudolf, 146.
Schnitzler, Arthur, 116, 166, 293, 324, 325, 338.
"School for Scandal, The," 289, 369.
School of the Theatre, 79, 109–123.
Schubert, Franz, 310.
Scott, Evelyn, 91, 98, 338.
Scott, Fred Newton, 326.
"Sea-Gull, The," 34, 82, 325.

INDEX

Seldes, Gilbert, 185.
Selver, Paul, 313.
Selwyn, Archie, 4, 156, 185.
Selwyn, Edgar, 4, 14, 49–50, 156, 185, 293.
Selwyn and Company, 64, 293, 297, 303, 310, 316.
"Servant in the House, The," 207.
"Servitude," 320.
Seven Arts, The, 80.
"Seven Keys to Baldpate," 4, 22, 28, 42, 49, 295.
Severn, Margaret, 214, 227, 258, 307.
"Sganarelle," 326.
Shadowland, x.
Shakespeare, William, 125–126, 134, 141, 165, 191–192, 212, 238, 261, 265, 289–290, 297, 300, 306, 308, 314–315.
Shakespearean Stage, 290.
"Shanewis," 166.
Shannon, Effie, 144, 294, 297, 305, 309.
Sharpe, Cecil, 300.
Shaw, George Bernard, 12, 82, 84–85, 110, 116, 261, 293, 295–296, 299, 301, 307, 312, 315, 328, 330–331, 340–341.
Shaw, Mary, 327.
Sheffield, Justus, 81.
Sheldon, Edward, 2–4, 20–21, 128, 287–288, 291, 294, 304.
"Shell-Shock," 321.
"Shepherd in the Distance, The," 323–324.
Sheridan, Richard Brinsley, 289.
"Sherlock Holmes," 81.
Sherman, Lowell, 147.
Sherwin, Louis, 185.
Shinn, Everett, 56.
Shipman, Louis Evan, 14.

Shipman, Samuel, 14–15.
Short, Hassard, 4, 64–65, 255, 310.
"Show Booth, The," 207.
"Show Shop, The," 297.
Shubert, J. J., 4–5, 64, 105, 167, 183, 189, 255, 277–278, 288–290, 293–294, 309–310.
Shubert, Lee, 5, 64, 105, 167, 183, 189, 277–278, 288–290, 293–294, 309–310.
"Shuffle Along," 229, 309.
Sidney, George, 297.
"Silver Box, The," 103.
"Simon the Cyrenian," 302, 365.
Simone, Mme., 292.
Simonson, Lee, 3, 6, 51, 55, 69, 81–82, 84, 110, 119, 153, 159–163, 173–174, 227, 263, 276, 280, 306–309, 312–313, 315, 367–368.
Sinclair, Arthur, 310.
"Sister Beatrice," 289.
"Sisters of Susanna," 326.
Six Brown Brothers, 227.
"Six Characters in Search of an Author," 63, 261, 313.
"Six Who Pass While the Lentils Boil," 18, 301.
"Skin Game, The," 307.
Skinner, Otis, 140, 292.
"Slave with Two Faces, The," 335.
Sloane, A. Baldwin, 306.
Smart Set, The, 185.
Smith, George Jay, 324.
Smith, Harry B., 296.
Smith, Harry James, 291.
Smith, Joseph Lindon, 239, 295–296.
Smith, Rita, 336.
Smith, Winchell, 14, 65, 288, 298, 303, 307.

INDEX

Smith College, 126.
" Sniper, The," 320, 334.
Solidarity, 38.
Sophocles, 125.
Sorel, Cécile, 261.
Sothern, E. H., 140.
Spanish Drama, 261, 267.
Spectatorium, 237.
Spingarn, Joel, 178.
" Spring, The," 98, 338.
" Square Peg, A," 20.
" Squealer, The," 336.
Stage Designers, 3, 6, 12, 55, 90, 99, 121, 124, 148–168.
Stage Lighting, 157–158, 198, 215–216, 245.
Stage Mechanism, 160, 162, 172, 216, 280.
Stanhope, Frederick, 300.
Stanislavsky, Constantin Sergeievitch, 45, 87, 130, 202, 217, 262, 271–272, 274, 314.
Starr, Frances, 142, 288, 297.
" S. S. *Tenacity*," 64, 265, 311, 366.
Steele, Wilbur Daniel, 95, 332–333, 335–337.
Stein, Gertrude, 179.
Stephens, Wallace, 91, 338.
Stevens, Ashton, 184, 274.
Stevens, Emily, 145, 291, 299.
Stevens, Thomas Wood, 6, 64, 131–132, 236, 238, 240, 242, 244, 281, 296.
" Stick-Up, The," 339.
Stokes, Rose Pastor, 324.
Stone, Fred, 227, 229, 251, 296.
Storer, Edward, 313.
Stratford-upon-Avon Players, 298.
Straus, Oscar, 289.
Stravinsky, Igor, 340.

" Straw, The," 31, 34–35, 311, 322.
" Strife," 288.
Strindberg, August, 53, 116, 327, 329.
" String of Samisen, The," 336.
" Strongheart," 49.
Stylization, 157.
" Subjection of Kezia, The," 340.
Subscription, 190, 193.
" Successful Calamity, A," 18, 59, 301, 365.
Sudermann, Hermann, 11, 287.
Sudeykin, Sergei Y., 312.
" Sugar House, The," 325.
Sumbatoff, Prince Alexander Ivanovitch, 140, 196.
" Sumurûn," 9, 292.
Sunday, Billy, 222, 229.
" Sunday," 49.
" Sunny Morning, A," 341.
" Suppressed Desires," 18, 94–95, 118, 298, 328, 332–334.
Suratt, Valeska, 154.
Sutro, Alfred, 261.
" Sweet and Twenty," 335, 338.
" Swing low, Sweet Chariot," 227.
" Switchboard, The," 294.
" Swords," 21, 310, 366.
Symbolism, 195, 245.
Syndicate, 183, 277–278.
Synge, John Millington, 11, 40, 292.

TAIROFF, ALEXANDER YAKOVLEVITCH, 11, 45, 272.
Talmud, Blanche, 106.
" Tamura," 341.
Tanner, Virginia, 300.
Tarkington, Booth, 16, 304.
Taylor, Laurette, 142, 188.

Tchehoff, Anton Pavlovitch, 11, 53, 82, 92, 227, 262, 265, 267, 274, 314, 324-325, 340.
Teixeira, Alexander de Mattos, 264-265.
Tempest, Marie, 290.
"Tempest, The," 300.
"Tendresse, La," 261.
"Tenor, The," 324.
"Tethered Sheep," 340.
"Texas Nightingale, The," 22.
"That Day," 16.
"That Pretty Sister of José," 49.
Theatre advertising, 191.
Theatre architecture. *See* PLAYHOUSE.
Theatre Arts Magazine, x, 9, 184.
Theatre Audience, 60, 121, 159, 181, 187-193, 223-224, 226, 235.
Theatre Guild. *See* NEW YORK, THEATRE GUILD.
Theatre in the College, 2, 5-6, 55, 64, 117, 123-135.
Theatre of "Let's pretend!" 208, 209, 220-232.
Theatre of the Five Thousand, 208, 237.
"Theatre of Tomorrow, The," ix.
Theatrical Press Representatives of America, 276.
Theories of the Theatre, 3, 8, 13, 19, 194-235.
"Thief, The," 292.
Thimig, Hugo, 140.
"Third Degree, The," 63, 202.
"Thirst," 32, 36, 96, 320, 333.
"Thirst and Other Plays," 29.
Thomas, A. E., 16, 290.

Thomas, Augustus, 14, 303, 316.
Thompson, J. Woodman, 134, 167.
"Three from the Earth," 337.
Three Legrohs, 227.
"Three of Us, The," 20.
"Three Sisters, The," 314.
"Three Travelers Watch a Sunrise," 338.
Throckmorton, Cleon, 39, 93, 99, 168, 307-309, 312, 366.
"Thunderbird," 163.
"Thunderbolt, The," 290.
Ticket speculators, 281-283.
"Tickless Time," 336-337.
"Tidings Brought to Mary, The," 261, 331, 368.
"Till Eulenspiegel," 365.
"Till We Meet," 321.
Tinney, Frank, 229, 251, 296.
"To Love," 193, 261, 313.
"To the Ladies," 23.
Tobin, Genevieve, 146.
"Toddles," 3.
Toller, Ernst, 191.
Tolstoy, Count Alexei Nekolaievitch, 262, 314.
Tolstoy, Count Lyoff Nekolaievitch, 303, 329.
"Torchbearers, The," 24.
Torrence, Ridgeley, 302.
"Towards a New Theatre," 9, 271.
Towse, J. Ranken, 183.
Translations for the Theatre, 262-266.
"Treasure, The," 330, 368.
Trevor, Norman, 313.
"Trial of Joan of Arc, The," 167, 309.
Tridon, André, 324.
"Trifles," 25, 79, 96, 326, 333, 339.

INDEX

"Trojan Women, The," 116, 294.
"Trumpet, The," 322.
"Truth about Blayds, The," 312, 369.
"Tsar Fyodor Ivanovitch," 274, 314.
Tucker, Benjamin, 29.
Tucker, Dudley G. 78.
Tully, Richard Walton, 18.
Turgenieff, Ivan Sergeievitch, 262, 314.
"Tweedles," 16.
"Twin Beds," 50.
"Two Blind Beggars and One Less Blind," 323.
"Two Fellows and a Girl," 4.
"Two Sons, The," 334.
Tyler, George C., 4, 48, 84, 153, 288, 292, 304, 308, 311, 322, 369.

Ulric, Lenore, 145, 311.
"Unchastened Woman, The," 16, 299.
"Uncle Tom's Cabin," 48.
"Under the Gas Light," 48.
Underhill, John Garrett, 304, 327.
University of California, 126.
University of Wisconsin, 126.
Urban, Joseph, 6, 9, 49, 152–153, 167, 239, 249, 253–254, 300, 302, 308, 365.

Vail, Lawrence, 328.
Van de Velde, Henry, 172.
Van Vechten, Carl, 268.
Van Volkenburg, Ellen, 339.
Vanderbilt Producing Company, 294.
Varesi, Gilda, 18, 145, 306.

Variety, 64, 222, 227, 246–247, 249, 251.
"Varying Shore, The," 22.
Vaudeville, 228, 247, 251.
Veiller, Bayard, 18, 293.
"Verge, The," 25, 339.
Verhaeren, Emil, 330.
"Very Good Eddie," 252.
"Very Good Young Man, A," 23, 303.
Vienna, Carl Theatre, 279; Josephstadt Theatre, 45, 218, 279.
Vildrac, Charles, 64, 265, 311.
Vogue, 185.
Volinin, Alexander, 291.
"Voltaire," 366.
von Hofmannsthal, Hugo, 41.
von Schiller, Friedrich, 288.
Vonnegut, Marjorie, 80.
"Vote the New Moon," 328.

Wagenhals, Lincoln A., 50.
Wagner, Charles, 366.
"Waldies, The," 340.
Walker, Stuart, 18, 65, 301.
Walkley, Arthur Bingham, 178, 205.
Wall Street Journal, 183.
Wallace, Chester, 130.
Wallace, Edgar, 294.
Wallacks, The, 47.
Walter, Eugene, 2, 9, 15, 53, 196–198, 202, 288.
Ward, Solly, 249.
Warfield, David, 140, 292, 314.
Warner, H. B., 315.
"Warnings" 320.
Warwick, Robert, 313.
Washburn-Freund, Frank E., 303.
Washburn-Freund, Mrs. Frank E., 326.

398 INDEX

Washington Square Players. *See* NEW YORK, WASHINGTON SQUARE PLAYERS.
"Watch Your Step," 167, 229, 254, 296.
Watson, Lucille, 144, 315.
Weaver, John V. A., 25.
"Weavers, The," 299.
"Web, The," 320.
Weber, Joseph M., 288.
Wedekind, Frank, 80, 265, 267, 324.
Weinberger, Harry, 100.
"Welcome to Our City," 128.
"Welded," 28, 31, 35, 38, 322.
Wellman, Rita, 18, 91, 334–336.
Welsh, Robert Gilbert, 183, 340.
Wenger, John, 168.
Wertheim, Maurice, 82.
Westley, Helen, 77, 80–82, 146.
"What d'You Want?" 328.
"What Every Woman Knows," 287.
"What the Public Wants," 331.
"What's in a Name?" 306.
"Where Ignorance is Bliss," 295.
"Where the Cross Is Made," 33, 36, 321, 336, 338.
"Whims," 324.
"Whispering Well, The," 342.
White, George, 256.
White, Hervey, 324.
"White Sister, The," 28.
"White-Headed Boy, The," 310.
Whiteside, Walker, 288.
Whitman, Walt, 110–111, 312, 343.
Whitney, F. C., 289, 304.
"Why Marry?" 24, 303, 316.
"Why Not?" 24, 314.
"Widow's Veil, The," 336–337.
"Wife for Life, A," 320.
"Wife With a Smile, The," 330.
"Wild Birds," 340.
"Wild Duck, The," 303, 365.
Wilde, Oscar, 116, 267, 328.
Wilfred, Thomas, 110, 215–216, 342.
"Will of Song, The," 232.
Williams, Bert, 254.
Williams, Jesse Lynch, 24, 303, 314, 316–317.
Williams, John D., 33, 55, 62–63, 300, 303, 305–306, 313, 316, 321–322.
Willner, A. M., 310.
"Will Shakespeare," 314, 369.
Wilson, Francis, 308.
"Winter's Night," 332, 334.
"Winter's Tale, A," 289.
Winwood, Estelle, 145, 304.
Wisconsin Players, 126.
"With the Current," 340.
"Within the Law," 18, 50, 293.
Wolfe, Thomas Clayton, 128.
Wolheim, Louis, 312.
"Woman, The," 18.
"Woman's Honor," 97, 336–337.
"Woman's Way, A," 18.
"Womenkind," 340.
Woods, Al H., 50.
Woods, Alice, 335.
Woollcott, Alexander, 25, 130, 183.
Woolley Thomas Mott, 126.
"World We Live In, The," 50–51, 160, 193, 262, 313, 368.
Wright, Grace Latimer, 327.
Wright, Harold Bell, 15.
Wycherly, Margaret, 145, 306.
Wynn, Ed, 229.

YALE BOWL, 269.
Yale University, 21, 124, 126.

INDEX

Yale University Dramatic Association, 126.
"Year of the Tiger, The," 318.
"Years of Discretion," 294.
Yeats, William Butler, 11, 116, 166.
"Yellow Jacket, The," 4, 15, 17, 28, 293.
Yermolova, M. M., 140.
"Yes, We Have No Bananas," 249.
Yevreynoff, Nikolai Nikolaievitch, 11, 326.
"You and I," 21, 315, 319.

Young, Roland, 80, 146.
Young, Stark, 185, 268.
"Youth," 328.
Youzhin, Alexander Ivanovitch, 140.
"Yum Chapab," 327.

ZANGWILL, ISRAEL, 288.
"Zaza," 81.
Ziegfeld, Florenz, Jr., 4, 64, 153, 252, 254–255, 308.
Ziegfeld "Follies," 3, 153, 177, 247, 252–253.
Zilboorg, Gregory, 264.